S0-BYG-181

Ageless Nation

The Quest for Superlongevity and Physical Perfection

Ageless Nation

The Quest for Superlongevity and Physical Perfection

By
Michael G. Zey, Ph.D.

New Horizon Press
Far Hills, NJ

Author's Note

All matters regarding personal health require medical supervision. A medical doctor or other health care professional is an essential member of the support network for anyone who seeks to challenge the issues of aging. The ideas, suggestions and procedures contained in this book are not intended as a substitute for professional medical assistance.

The names, circumstances and other noted identifying characteristics of some individuals, couples and families who have been mentioned in this book have been changed to protect their privacy.

Dedication

To My Mother Angela and My Sister Mary Ann. May They
Live Forever.

Copyright © 2007 by Michael G. Zey, Ph.D.

All rights reserved. No portion of this book may be reproduced or transmitted in any form whatsoever, including electronic, mechanical or any information storage or retrieval system, except as may be expressly permitted in the 1976 Copyright Act or in writing from the publisher. Requests for permission should be addressed to:

New Horizon Press
P.O. Box 669
Far Hills, NJ 07931

Michael G. Zey, Ph.D.
Ageless Nation
The Quest for Superlongevity and Physical Perfection

Cover Design: Wendy Bass
Interior Design: Susan Sanderson
Illustration: Aaron Farash

Library of Congress Control Number: #2006923974

ISBN 13: 978-0-88282-276-1
ISBN 10: 0-88282-276-4
New Horizon Press

Manufactured in the U.S.A.

2009   2008   2007   2006   2005 / 5   4   3   2   1

Acknowledgments

In order to complete a project such as this one that covers a universe of topics and a number of years, I have by necessity accumulated a wealth of emotional and intellectual debts. While I can never truly repay such debts, I can at least acknowledge my creditors.

First, let me express my warmest gratitude to Cindy Zey. Her emotional and intellectual support throughout the writing of this book can never be repaid. I can only utter a very simple "Thank you."

Berta Ozromano, my primary researcher on the *Ageless Nation* project, deserves a special note of thanks. Her labors as a researcher, as well as the enthusiasm she brought to this project, were invaluable. I treasure the many conversations and intellectual discussions we shared throughout the writing process.

This book would not have seen the light of day without the efforts of my publisher, Dr. Joan Dunphy, the head of New Horizon Press. Dr. Dunphy and her publishing house have helped me immeasurably in bringing this project to fruition. I would also like to thank Susan Whitten, my editor, for her valuable assistance in making this book a reality. Thank you also to my agent, Jillian Manus, principal of Manus and Manus & Associates Literary Agency in Palo Alto, California.

I must also thank the people and organizations that have added to my knowledge of the scientific and medical bases of the Superlongevity Revolution, as well as the issues and debates that are sure to emerge over the next decade. Included here are: Dr. Donald Louria, chairman emeritus of the Department of Preventative Medicine and Community Health at UMDNJ-New Jersey Medical School in Newark, NJ; and friends and colleagues I have met through the World Future Society, who continue to provide invaluable information on scientific developments.

I also have appreciated the input from various colleagues at Montclair State University. I especially want to thank colleague, scholar and friend, Professor Carl Rodrigues, for the many insights he provides me.

Finally, let me extend the warmest "thanks" to friends and family members who encouraged me throughout this project. I would also like to offer my gratitude to my closest of friends, Michael, Carol and Katie Aloisi, for their support through the years. And of course, I can never thank enough Zooey Zey, an inspiration to myself and all who know her.

Table of Contents

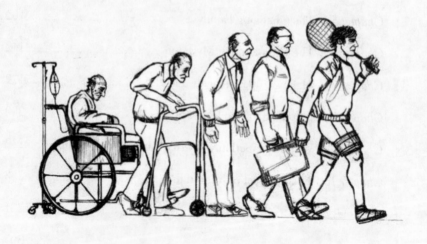

"Ageless Evolution", illustration by Aaron Farash

Introduction

The human species has been haunted by the thought and image of its own mortality. Birth and death, with a limited number of years in between, have defined our sense of reality, our perception of our lives and our concept of our role in the overall scheme of things. The idea of death has been the source of our nightmares and the slayer of our dreams.

We are now at the threshold of the Superlongevity Revolution, the radical extension of the human lifespan that will shake society to its very foundation. Its impact will be felt by every person, institution and organization.

We are replacing our mortality with the opportunity to live to ages our species cannot imagine. How long do you want to live? Do you want to live to the age of seventy-five? Eighty-five? How about extending your time on Earth to one hundred or 110 years? How about 125? Does 150 seem impossible? If given the choice to live forever, would you take it?

During the twentieth century, human beings made tremendous gains in life expectancy. A plethora of medical breakthroughs and scientific achievements —vaccines, antibiotics and a broad range of public health measures, among others—extended the human life span to ages considered hitherto unattainable.

However, in the coming decades, the gains in life span will dwarf even those of the last century. With the help of a plethora of medical breakthroughs including genetic engineering, cloning, nanotechnology, bionics and a host of new drugs to combat cancer and other diseases, we will soon push life expectancy into the one hundred-125 year range. By 2100, as we learn to manipulate our body's cells and control the behavior of atoms themselves, we can expect to live to ages of 300-400 years and possibly indefinitely.

And here's even better news— these same scientific wonders will enable us to remain physically young, healthy and vibrant throughout our lives.

Until recently, average life expectancy in most societies ranged from twenty to thirty years. The journal *Science* notes that not until 1800 did life expectancy in Europe reach forty. By the mid-nineteenth century, the longest life expectancy anywhere was among Swedish women, a scant forty-five years. By 1900 life expectancy slowly increased to the point that in advanced countries like the United States people were living on average to forty-seven years old.

It is at this point that the Superlongevity Revolution begins. Between 1900 and 2000, most industrialized countries posted significant gains in average life expectancy. For instance, the average life span of U.S. males rose from forty-seven to its current seventy-eight years for men and eight for American women. By 2001, Japanese women were living on average eight-five years. Moreover, although Western Europe and the United States were the first to enjoy such gains, many developing countries quickly followed suit with some experiencing average life span increases of over 50 percent in only a few decades. Such gains were largely the result of the introduction of vaccines and antibiotics as well as improvements in the area of public health. Lately we have expanded life expectancy by winning a series of battles against heart disease, some cancers, diabetes and stroke.

Average life expectancy is rapidly increasing each year, in some countries going up by three months every year! Japan now has over 14,000 people one hundred years of age or older. *Science* contends that the average American girl born today will live to see one hundred. [i]

The UK's Government Actuary's Department projected that the country's current population of centenarians could soar from around 10,000 now to 1.2 million by 2074. Around one million people, or one out of eight, who are currently in their thirties could live to be one hundred years old. Thousands of British could live to the ripe old age of 110 or older. [ii]

This rapid expansion of the life span will have a profound effect on every living person—children, young adults, as well as Boomers and more senior groups. Superlongevity will transform all stages of the life cycle and even create a few new ones. It will enhance every aspect of our lives—from our careers and our marriages, to our health and leisure activities.

Explore with me an exciting trend which is almost as dramatic as the radical extension of the life span. The Ultra-human Phenomenon, the ardent and passionate search for physical and mental perfection, will have a fundamental impact on the way we experience all those extra years. Citizens of the *Ageless Nation* do not wish to just live extremely lengthy lives. They wish to live through those extra decades in bodies that are as youthful and healthy as possible.

The book will also offer strategies you can adopt right now to capitalize on the opportunities created by the Superlongevity Revolution. It will serve as a helpful guide to the future for parents, employees, business leaders and managers, educators and government planners.

Come with me on a mind-expanding journey to a rapidly approaching future when the human species will be knocking on the door of immortality.

Superlongevity is being discussed in the media with increasing frequency—*USA Today, Time* and *60 Minutes* feature stories on the social and economic impact of enhanced longevity. The *Wall Street Journal* and *Business Week* are highlighting new "cures" and remedies for old age and advice to readers on how to use such information to both get rich and stay young. A memorable *Time* cover, with the inscription, "How To Live to 100 (And Not Regret It)," featured a young woman's face with a photographic double silhouette of her as a middle aged woman and also as a post-one hundred year old human. In early 2006, *Time* devoted an entire issue to "Medicine From A to Z." The August 2006 issue of AARP's magazine featured a special report entitled "Adding 10 Healthy Years To Your Life."

The interest in superlongevity is always hyped when a celebrity touts the newest medical and pharmaceutical anti-aging breakthroughs. In 2007, actress and entrepreneur Suzanne Somers rode to the top of best-seller lists with her book *Ageless: The Naked Truth About Bioidentical Hormones*. In her book, Somers popularized the idea that bioidentical hormones specifically derived from plants such as wild yams or soy products can reverse the aging process by keeping people physically vibrant, mentally sharp and sexually active. Somers has actively promoted the cause of superlongevity for years in over sixteen books, including *The Sexy Years: Discover the Hormone Connection*, which discusses ways to fight the ravages of age in both men and women, and her *Somersize* series which offers advice on nutrition and exercise to keep young.

Ms. Somers' experience since the publication of *Ageless* also demonstrates the fact that controversy is sure to greet almost any drug or treatment touted to extend our lives or enhance our health. The medical and pharmaceutical establishment has charged that her book exaggerates the anti-aging benefits of bioidentical hormones; some doctors even wrote letters of complaint to the book's publisher questioning the book's accuracy. The American College of Obstetricians and Gynecologists weighed in on the debate, asserting that there's no scientific proof that bioidenticals are either safe or effective. Somers' book drew the ire of the American Medical Association (AMA), which is now calling for more Food and Drug Administration (FDA) regulation of these compounds. The AMA is demanding that the FDA assess the purity of these bioidenticals' ingredients and evaluate their effectiveness and safety. Somers is active in confronting her critics, participating in a highly contentious debate in 2006 on *Larry King Live* over her book's theories with doctors from a variety of fields.[iii]

Possibly to satisfy the needs of large numbers of early baby boomers entering their "golden years", major publishers brought out a plethora of books in 2007 advising readers how to stay physically and mentally young. Popular titles included *Yotox: Anti-Aging Yoga for the Face*, *The Anti-Aging Handbook: Practical Steps to Staying Youthful* and *Resetting the Clock: Five Anti-Aging Hormones That Improve and Extend Life*.[iv]

In 2005 and 2006, such magazines as *Popular Science* and *Technology Review* ran feature and cover articles on the possibility of achieving immortality in humans. Over the last several years, films including Steven Spielberg's *AI* (Artificial Intelligence), *Gattica* and *Bicentennial Man* and even television sitcoms such as the animated *Futurama* have examined moral and ethical issues related to our tinkering with life and the human life span. The hit X-Men films are popularizing the notion that genetic mutation could serve as a pathway to the "Ultra-Human."

One recent *Popular Science* magazine issue explored the possibility that humans might soon become "Superhuman"—one of their illustrations showed a human being with artificial muscles electronically enhanced intelligence, vision, hearing and tensile strength. In 2006 the major weeklies were still churning out new information on life extension. *The Wall Street Journal*, anticipating the financial implications of extended life, regularly has special insets on retirement, alternatives to retirement and financial planning for the long-haul. *National Geographic* published an issue devoted to discerning why small pockets of humanity living in such places as Okinawa and Sardinia are able to routinely live to one hundred years or better. AARP's *Modern Maturity* magazine has made superlongevity a prevailing theme for decades.

In a fortuitous coincidence, the aging of the baby boomer generation has helped elevate society's awareness of the Superlongevity Revolution. The baby boomers have been on the media's radar screen since their appearance in the 1950s. Now the oldest baby boomers are reaching retirement age, and suddenly the media is awash in stories of what impact the boomers' possible withdrawal from the workplace en masse will have on the economy, the employment situation, social security and the health care system.

Our society as a whole will have to address such matters regardless of the actions of this particular generation. However, the sheer number of baby boomers makes the necessity of our dealing with superlongevity and its impact that more urgent.

Watching the boomers closely, we will gain insight into how the species will handle the radically increasing life span. Innovative boomers have little desire to live their golden years as past generations have. They will challenge traditional concepts of "old age" and endeavor to invent a historically novel, and perhaps "revolutionary," senior life stage. Members of this generation are already re-inventing themselves through a combination of "early retirement" and "re-careering." This group will also goad the scientific establishment to rapidly devise new anti-aging products and technologies to help them live longer and remain physically young.

I began writing about superlongevity and the possibility of near-immortality in the early 1990s. My book, *Seizing the Future*, was primarily concerned with the emergence of new technologies in fields such as space exploration, food science, computers, artificial intelligence and biotechnology and the impact that they would have on the human condition. One emerging trend that intrigued me as both a futurist and a sociologist was superlongevity. It was obvious that we were on the verge of breakthroughs that would radically extend the human life span. While everyone else was talking up our entrance into a so-called "Age of Information" (remember the "dot-com bubble?), I began thinking and talking about a revolution in a more tangible area, the extension of the human life span.

My next book, *The Future Factor*, dealt with the broad issue of human destiny and how we would achieve it. The destiny of the human species, I asserted, is to develop, enhance and perfect our planet first and ultimately the universe. I also named certain forces or processes that will help us achieve that destiny. I labeled one of those dominant processes "biogenesis," the human species commandeering the forces of nature in order to radically extend the human life span. One reason that I gravitated to superlongevity was my continuing belief that the longer humans lived, the better the chances that the human race could achieve its destiny.

Throughout the early part of this decade, much of my time and efforts have been spent studying and lecturing on superlongevity. I have given talks at many corporations, universities and some religious organizations on how the increase in the human life span will impact our society and economy.

During this period, breakthroughs in a number of areas were bringing superlongevity closer to reality. We successfully cloned several classes of animals (including 1997's famous sheep Dolly), the human genome was decoded and stem cells were successfully used to treat some diseases in several experiments. Some breakthroughs were qualitatively changing the timeline for achieving superlongevity.

The interest in superlongevity by the public, business leaders, policy planners and educators, as indicated earlier, was being heightened by the aging of the seventy-six million boomers and the impact of this demographic on our economy and health care system.

My own lectures have confirmed the growing level of interest in the subject of superlongevity. I always ask my audiences how long they want to live, and what they think the quality of their lives will be like at those ages.

In 2003 I was delivering a lecture on the subject at the San Francisco meeting of the World Future Society, and was approached by Reuters to do an interview on life extension. In the article I commented that, "Mankind is on the threshold of immortality." This comment became a banner headline carried by hundreds of newspapers across the globe. America Online placed my words on their "Welcome Window" which greets its millions of subscribers. More television, newspaper and radio interviews on the subject followed.

My work permitted me to gauge the public reaction to the possibility of radically extended life span when I was contacted by a number of people from various backgrounds via email, phone and letter. Those on the technological vanguard threw their support behind these views. Financial planners trying to learn how to prosper from this trend had their own set of questions. Human resource professionals were concerned about the impact of an "aging work-force." And parents wanted to know how superlongevity would impact their children.

In early 2004, Dr. Donald B. Louria, chairman emeritus of the Department of Preventative Medicine and Community Health at UMDNJ-New Jersey Medical School in Newark, NJ, who had also spoken at the 2003 World Future Society conference, told me that he was organizing an April conference called "Creating Very Old People: Individual Blessing or Societal Disaster." This conclave was the first to bring together many of the leading internationally-recognized scientists from widely disparate fields working on ways to extend the human life span. Attended by one thousand health care professionals and academics, this historic conference brought to the public's attention the fact that scientists in a host of fields—including nanotechnology, genetic engineering, caloric restriction and stem cell science—were all working on ways to quickly boost the human life span, in some cases to as much as 150 years old. More importantly, it clued these scientists, each locked into his own particular science, that others were working on the same problem from radically different perspectives.

In his opening remarks to the conference attendees, Dr. Louria stated, "If this conference were being held a year ago (2003), this would have been considered a fringe conference. And now it is a vanguard conference, but it is no fringe." He reminded everyone that the United Nations' very conservative population division, for the first time, now took the official position that there is no known upper limit to longevity. He also noted that actuaries have changed their upper limit to take into account ages of 120 years. I will talk more about this conference in the next chapter.

Other organizations have sprung up to deal with various aspects of the Superlongevity Revolution. In October 2002 the first Anti-Aging Drug Discovery & Development Summit was held in San Francisco, California. The World Congress on Anti-Aging Medicine held annual meetings in different cities, growing to the point that by 2005, its conferences would attract upwards of 10,000 medical researchers and biotechnology investors. Besides serving as a site for researchers to discuss scientific aspects of the aging process and assess the efficacy of anti-aging therapies, these meeting bring together the scientific community and venture capitalists. The hope is that seed money can find its way to deserving scientists so they can possibly launch companies to capitalize on their discoveries.

Dr. Louria also stated that it is sometimes difficult to determine whether claims from various scientists, nutritionists and other health care practitioners are valid or not. This question haunts books and conference sessions that deal with superlongevity. Unfortunately, one is often left to wonder what is speculation and what is reality. Louria claimed that this "Creating Old People" conference was "meant to be an antidote to the hucksters," especially authors that made outlandish claims in their books about how to achieve superlongevity. As an example, he used a just-published book, "The Anti-Aging Pill," which said that a substance found in wine was "good for anything that ails you." His comments were well received. Except the scientist who gave the very next talk had mentioned his research indicated that there might be some validity to the book's claim.

The challenge to a futurist and sociologist like myself is to try and realistically examine the claims about the life-extending possibilities of the various medical technologies coming on board. One thing is clear: regardless of individual claims concerning one scientific breakthrough or another, we know that progress is being made in diagnosing and eliminating diseases, and that radical extension of the human life span is inevitable. What we must do now is begin to speculate about the impact of the Superlongevity Revolution and plan for its arrival.

Each year, interest in this subject becomes deeper and wider. In late 2005, my article on the impact of superlongevity appeared as the front cover article of *The Futurist* magazine, the main publication of the World Future Society distributed to policy planners, educators, libraries and futurists of various stripes. In early 2006, the World Economic Forum invited me to contribute to their publication, *Global Agenda Magazine*, an article on the global effects of the Superlongevity Revolution. The WEF is made up of 33,000 high-level government policy planners, corporate CEOs, Nobel Prize winners and other opinion shapers and major players. The publication was distributed at their January 2006 annual meeting in Davos, Switzerland and at their regional meetings throughout the year. The world's power elite is taking very seriously the global impact of superlongevity.

Very divergent groups are interested in the topic of superlongevity. One is what I labeled the policy group, which includes policy planners, actuaries from insurance companies, heads of educational, business and government institutions, and the vast majority of the public. These people are concerned with the immediate issues surrounding the rapid extension of the human lifespan—how long life will affect marriages, pension plans, social security, retirement benefits and pensions, etc. These are valid concerns, and this book deals at length with them.

Others are concerned with more long term issues related to the extended lifespan. A global community of loosely affiliated individuals and organizations are concerned with such issues as the achievement of near-immortality, the merging of man and computer technology, nanotechnology and other arcane subjects. In this group are writers and inventors such as Ray Kurzweil, Hans Moravic and Aubrey de Grey, as well as organizations such as the Better Human Foundation. In contrast to the policy wonks, members of this group are much more focused on the science and technology underpinning the achievement of superlongevity.

Another group is developing the science and technology that will enable us to achieve superlongevity. The are presenting their research findings at conferences including the "Creating Very Old People" meeting. Another group, the financiers, co-mingle with the scientists at such venues as the World Congress on Anti-Aging Medicine.

The "cross-pollination" of ideas between these disparate groups is spotty at best. Techno-futurists and policy types do not often communicate or appear on the same conference programs. Most actuaries are not concerned with whether superlongevity is eventually achieved by genetic manipulation, nanotechnology, or just good personal health habits. And techno-futurists do not spend a great deal of time writing about the health insurance issues related to superlongevity or how much all of this is going to cost.

Sociologists and futurists like myself are forced to bridge these many worlds to make sense of this demographic phenomenon and consider both its transcendent and mundane aspects. One has to understand the possibilities and limits of various life-extending technologies, and then speculate about how they will impact our present and future. We must even consider the implications, however surreal, of near-immortality. And at the same time, you must do this with an eye on the economic limitations of any scientific revolution—can the average person, or the society as a whole, afford to universally distribute all these blessings to its citizens?

Notes

[i] Joel Garreau. "Forever Young: Suppose You Soon Can Live to Well Over 100, As Vibrant and Energetic as You Are Now. What Will You Do With Your Life?," *Washington Post*, Sunday, October 13, 2002, sec. F p. 01.

[ii] Paul Lewis. "1.2 Million People Will Reach 100th Birthday by 2074, says study." *The Guardian* February 8, 2006.

[iii] Carol Azizian. "Debate Rages On Whether Bioidentical Hormones Are A Risky Business." *The Flint Journal First Edition*, January 08, 2007.
"Suzanne Somers Debates Doctors." *Larry King Live*, CNN, November 16, 2006. http://edition.cnn.com/TRANSCRIPTS/0611/15/lkl.01.html

[iv] Annelise Hagen. *Yotox: Anti-Aging Yoga for the Face*. New York: Avery, 2007.
Geraldine Mitton. *Anti-Aging Handbook: Practical Steps to Staying Youthful*. New Holland, 2007.
Elmer Cranton. *Resetting the Clock: Five Anti-Aging Hormones That Improve and Extend Life*. New York: Evans and Co., 2007.

chapter one

The Three Stages of the Superlongevity Revolution

Society has had little time to adjust to the recent rapid increase in human life expectancy. It is hard to believe how low average life expectancy in most societies has been up to now. According to Ramez Naam in his book *More Than Human*, the average human life span hovered between eighteen and twenty-five for most of recorded human history. For citizens of the Roman Empire, which kept meticulous demographic records, average life expectancy at birth was a brief twenty-two years. By the Middle Ages it had risen to about thirty-three years in England.

But the rise in life expectancy throughout most of human history has been slow. In his book *Rising Life Expectancy: A Global History*, Indiana University history professor James Riley claims that life expectancy at birth "probably stayed in the range of the upper twenties to the forties from the 1500s until the late 1700s.

That is not to say that specific individuals did not exceed the averages. Even during these periods, some very famous people lived to fairly old ages. St. Augustine, who lived in the fifth century, died at seventy-five. Genghis Khan, who lived in the twelfth century, survived to age sixty-three. Marco Polo lived to seventy and Michelangelo died at age eighty-eight. Thomas Jefferson and John Adams, both of whom died on July 4, 1826, lived to ages eighty-three and ninety respectively.

According to age researcher Jay Olshansky, the long lives of certain key individuals throughout history do not indicate that extended longevity was

1

common in the periods in which they lived. People who lived into their seventies and eighties were statistical oddities. In fact, he says, we know about people such as Jefferson and Adams because they were famous. However, Olshansky says, their fame depended on their achievements, and their achievements became possible because they lived so long that they could be more productive than someone living to, say, thirty-three years of age. Ben Franklin, in spite of his other scientific accomplishments, is best known today for his role in helping to bring the United States of America into existence. Franklin was already seventy years old when Jefferson wrote the Declaration of Independence. Fifth century BC Roman great senator, Appius Claudius, the power behind construction of the Appian Way and the Claudian Aqueduct, major Roman road and water systems, lived into his sixties.

Then in the 1800s, an upsurge in average life spans occurred in Denmark and spread into the rest of Scandinavia and Britain. Contributing factors included the greater amounts of food available to the general population and Edward Jenner's development of the smallpox vaccine, as well as rising wealth and education. However, historian James Riley states that nothing had a bigger effect than improvements in public sanitation, especially filtered water, indoor toilets and the introduction of common sense personal hygiene habits such as washing the hands and face once a day and taking a bath periodically. Such personal hygiene methods enabled Japan, for instance, to experience a large increase in average life spans during this same period.[5]

The Superlongevity Revolution Begins

By 1900, life expectancy slowly increased to the point that advanced countries like the United States could boast of an average life expectancy of forty-seven years. It is at this point that the Superlongevity Revolution begins in earnest.

Chart 1 shows that the Superlongevity Revolution can be divided into three distinct stages.

Stage I, which I label Life Extension, unfolded roughly between 1900 and 2000. Many of those gains were described in this book's intro. These gains resulted from the appearance of vaccines and antibiotics and improvements in public and personal hygiene.

"Today," Jay Olshansky states, "people are living far longer with things that used to kill us at much younger ages." Not only have treatments for the two big killers—heart disease and cancer—extended patients' lives, but he said, "people today can go to a local hospital and have an appendix removed in a matter of forty-five minutes, which can be a lifesaving procedure that adds decades to your life and which was not a very easy thing to do years ago."

Medical and health conditions improved throughout the last century. Like many baby boomers, my starting point, my point of reference, is the middle of the twentieth century. I have come to realize how dramatically our health conditions have changed even as recently as the 1950s and early 1960s, the time in which most boomers grew up.

From a medical standpoint, these were radically different times.

Looking back at photos, home movies and newsreels from those times, people appear older, facially and bodily. Was their less youthful appearance in some way due to the fact that most adults and seniors living during that period had come through much different medical and health experiences?

It was quite common for families in that era to have recent histories of mothers who bore five, six, seven or more children. Many of the offspring died in childbirth. High fertility ensured the continuance of the family and the species. The mother of one family I studied had seven children. One died in childbirth, two others were claimed early in life by tuberculosis, a then incurable disease. One died in mid-life of a brain tumor. The family debated years later whether he would have survived the disease (as well as the operation to eliminate the tumor) if the diagnostic tools such as the CAT scan and the MRI were available at the time. The remaining three survived into their eighties and nineties—they lived long enough to benefit from the late-twentieth century medical miracles, including antibiotics and heart surgery, as well as blood pressure medication and blood thinners.

Infant mortality was a problem as recently as the fifties. At that time the neo-natal infant mortality rate in the United States was over three times higher than it is today. Outside industrialized countries infant mortality rates were even higher, and today in many regions of Africa and elsewhere they continue to be unacceptably high.

In the 1950s, most American families had knowledge of an epidemic that ravaged the United States and most of the globe—the Spanish influenza. In 1918, the epidemic hit the United States and spread through North America, Europe, Asia and South America. We're still not sure of its origins—it's appearance during World War I made some suspicious that it was an offshoot of some biological warfare tool used by the Germans against the Allies or a result of the various mustard gases used by both sides in trench warfare. As a result the average life span in the United States was depressed by ten years. And this influenza targeted not the old but primarily those between the ages of fifteen and thirty-four. People contracted this flu and died within hours—patients "died struggling to clear their airways of a blood-tinged froth that sometimes gushed from their nose and mouth." And the medicine of 1918 was powerless to overcome this plague, which claimed millions worldwide.

Several other medical events mark the 1950s. The polio epidemic was in full swing. Most people knew some family whose young child had been infected with this debilitating contagious disease. Polio became one of the great plagues of the first half of the twentieth century. In 1952 alone, nearly 60,000 polio-related cases and 3,000 deaths were reported in the U.S. Paralytic polio, the worst form of the disease, causes muscle paralysis and can result in death. Limbs, lungs and other parts of the body would be paralyzed. The first vaccine successful in treatment of polio, the famous Salk vaccine, did not become widely available until 1955. Polio was completely eliminated in the U.S. by 1979.

Antibiotics had been in widespread use for only a few years. Although drugs such as penicillin were developed in the labs as early as 1928, anything like mass production of the drug had to wait until World War II to become a reality. So most people living in the 1950s remembered a recent past in which folks died of simple staph infections that they would have easily survived if they had access to antibiotics. They also remembered the terror of infectious diseases such as rheumatic fever, syphilis, pneumonia and tuberculosis, even though those diseases had within a few years become easily treatable and their disappearance seemed predestined. With antibiotics on hand surgeons could risk more dangerous operations and not worry that infections resulting from the surgery would kill the patients. Patients who had once turned to many kinds of alternative medicine, or refused treatment, now entrusted themselves to antibiotics.

The "health craze" as we know it today had not yet started. True, the popular Jack LaLanne, one of the first physical fitness gurus, preached his philosophy of regular exercise daily and weekly on local channels and syndication. However, there was no nationwide aerobics movement, no constant warnings from health czars and leading health authorities. People who tried to convince you to eat or cook organically were gently dismissed as "health nuts."

The average diet was a cholesterol nightmare. The idea of controlling your health through proper diet was just beginning to be noticed by the public. A cultural watershed event in the late 1950s was the publication and popularity of *Folk Medicine*, written by Dr. Jarvis, a kindly seventy-something year old Vermont doctor. After spending years practicing medicine in the Green Mountains of Vermont, Dr. Jarvis concluded that the hearty and vigorous local families owe their health and longevity to the use of honey, kelp and apple cider vinegar for a variety of healing purposes. He theorized that proper diet, even without the use of drugs, could help anyone burn body fat, reduce high blood pressure and overcome chronic fatigue.

And at mid-century, a heavy number of people smoked! Everywhere you went—parties, college classrooms, homes, theatres, sports arenas, all social and political events—you were surrounded by smokers. The relationship of smoking to cancer and emphysema was poorly researched and not well publicized. People really thought that by smoking filtered cigarettes they were protecting their health. (It wasn't until 1964 that the United States Surgeon General issued the warning that "smoking may be hazardous to your health," and forced cigarette companies to place warnings on their cigarettes.) Smoking ads were everywhere—on billboards, TV, in magazines. The habit was so ubiquitous that it was considered rude to request that someone refrain from smoking.

Even this Stage I extension of lives into the eighties is presenting society with a series of conundrums and challenges that have never been encountered before. We have not even settled on a name for these later years of the Stage I life span. Among those tried are the "young old," senior citizen and other such descriptive phrases.

One thing we can say for sure about living in the Superlongevity Era is that the longer you live, the better your chances of being around for the next medical miracle that can cure what ails you. In other words, the longer you live, the longer you will live.

Early evidence indicates that we are already entering Stage II. In this book, we will look at the emerging impact of the radical extension of human life that we are beginning to experience. We now know that medical and scientific advances across a broad spectrum of fields will dwarf the health-bestowing power of earlier Stage I medical marvels. Genetic engineering alone promises to eradicate a host of debilitating diseases such as Alzheimer's and may eventually do the same for many of the deadliest cancers. By eliminating the diseases that weaken the body or lead directly to death, we increase the likelihood that our species will drastically increase our life span. Nutritional science, especially caloric restriction, will play a role here as well—the *Wall Street Journal* recently reported that studies reveal that radical adjustments in diet and food intake could extend human life to 150 years or more.

CHART 1— SUPERLONGEVITY REVOLUTION

While such a scenario may seem incredible, scientists and futurists

STAGE	NAME	TIME PERIOD	IMPACT ON LIFESPAN	KEY DRIVERS
I	LIFE EXTENSION	1900-2000	Rapid extension of life span from forties to eighties. Primarily adding years to life	• Antibiotics • Improvements in public health • Enhanced nutrition • Heart by-pass surgery
II	LIFE EXPANSION	2000-2100	Pushing past one hundred to 125. People at every age are healthier, more vibrant and physically "younger" than those in previous eras.	Eliminating causes of most fatal diseases through: • Genetic Engineering • Therapeutic Cloning • Stem Cell Technology Enhancement of human outer shell via technologies such as tissue regeneration.
III	INFINITY	2100 and beyond	Near-immortality, capability of living 300-400 years.	Elimination of cell aging, production of fresh body parts. Mastery of basic laws and behavior of cells and atoms through developments in: • Nanotechnology • "Immortality cell" science

have discovered that even their most fanciful prognostications are routinely trumped by events out of today's newspaper. For instance, it was commonly assumed that it would take us years to master the science necessary to genetically design offspring with specific qualities and characteristics. Then, in late June 2003, the world was stunned to learn that the first "designer child" was born to a British couple, Jason and Michelle Whitaker.

The Whitaker's four-year-old son, Charlie, was seriously ill with a rare blood disease, Diamond Blackfan Anemia. Unless he received a bone marrow transplant from someone who was his exact tissue match, he would not survive. The couple turned to the Reproductive Genetics Institute in Chicago to help them conceive a child that would be Charlie's exact genetic match to serve as a blood and marrow donor for Charlie. While several embryos were created using in vitro fertilization techniques, only the few embryos that exactly matched Charlie's tissue type were implanted in the mother's womb. Now their new son Jamie, whose genetic make-up was determined in the lab, will be able to contribute the life-saving blood and marrow to his older brother Charlie.[6]

In 2001, the Human Genome Project researchers mapped the genetic structure of the human body, ten years ahead of schedule! Such unexpected progress accelerated the timetable for uncovering the link between particular genes and diseases such as Alzheimer's, Parkinson's, macular degeneration and many other maladies. Before long, we will perfect the genetic engineering techniques to disarm and neutralize such diseases by placing beneficial genes into the cells of patients suffering from these maladies. Doctors using such techniques already had considerable success combating pernicious maladies such as the "Bubble-boy Syndrome" and Cystic Fibrosis. As we eliminate disease from the equation of human mortality, we will extend human life.

In another unanticipated development, a few years later, researchers were using adult stem cells, those readily available in sources such as bone marrow, umbilical cord blood, the pancreas and brain to successfully treat patients with Parkinson's disease, multiple sclerosis, heart damage and spinal cord injuries. Scientists claim that soon such non-embryonic stem cells will be used to cure a host of diseases and disabilities, including breast cancer, leukemia and sickle cell anemia.

Other recent extraordinary breakthroughs document that we are entering the second stage of the Superlongevity Revolution.

For instance, our war on cancer is being aided tremendously by a new generation of cancer fighting drugs that attack only cancerous growths, not non-cancerous cells. In 2004, the FDA approved Avastin, from Genentech, and Erbitux, from ImClone Systems, drugs to treat colon cancer—the second most common cause of United States cancer deaths. Such drugs are in the vanguard of what is being labeled "precision therapy." According to American Cancer Society President Ralph Vance, a professor of medicine at the University Of Mississippi School Of Medicine, "This is the most exciting time that I have known in the field of medical oncology." The drugs are antibodies engineered in the lab and are the first pharmaceuticals to reduce tumor growth from colon cancer that has spread to other parts of the body.

Around the same time, the FDA also approved two other "precision drugs" designated for treating two rare cancers. Eli Lilly's Alimta targets malignant pleural mesothelioma, a cancer often associated with asbestos exposure, and was also approved for forms of lung cancer. Phamion's Vidazawas was approved for myelodysplastic syndromes, a bone marrow disorder.

According to Solomon Hamburg, a clinical professor of medicine at the UCLA School of Medicine and CEO of Tower Cancer Research Foundation in Beverly Hills, "Targeted therapies are a conceptual breakthrough and have opened up a huge area of investigation into how we fight cancer."[7]

Later we will discuss more fully the role of genetics in combating disease and improving chances of living long and healthy lives. Now that we have successfully discovered the genetic code of the human genome, science is progressing to the next step, determining which genes are affecting which disease or bodily function. The recent discoveries are daunting.

Geneticist Rita Cantor and her UCLA research team found a group of mutations in the middle of chromosome 17, which they claim are a genetic link to autism. Evidence of such a linkage was discovered in a separate study by Vanderbilt University Medical Center researchers.

Around the same time, researchers found some genetic clues in the ongoing mystery of baldness. Markus Nöthen of the Life and Brain Centre of the Bonn University Clinic and Roland Kruse of the Skin Clinic of Düsseldorf University discovered unusual genetic variations on the X chromosome in families with a tendency toward male balding.

Perhaps even more exciting is the discovery of the genetic roots of ovarian cancer. Johns Hopkins University Cancer geneticist Tian-Li Wang and pathologist Le-Ming Shih located the gene that purportedly sparks the most aggressive kind of growth in ovarian cancer. They hope that their research will lead to the discovery of a drug that inhibits this destructive gene.

Researchers are also trying to find the genetic roots of human behavior tendencies, such as alcoholism and drug addiction. James Olson, a pediatric oncologist at the Fred Hutchinson Cancer Research Center in Seattle, inadvertently discovered the possible location of "fearlessness" or plain old reckless behavior when he was probing a gene called neuroD2, which can turn carcinoma cells into neurons. He discovered that the mice missing the genes spent most of their time fighting with each other and seemed oblivious to danger. The researchers think that more information about this gene, neuroD2, might lead to a better understanding of both thrill-seeking behavior and psychiatric disorders in humans.

In early 2006, Columbia University scientists found a genetic key to psychotic thinking. Scientists, who included Nobel Prize winner Eric Kandel, claim that their studies, performed with mice, prove that cognitive problems suffered by schizophrenics are caused by subtle genetic changes that affect their brains during early development. They hope that drugs can be created to treat people early who have the detected genetic defects. Schizophrenia reportedly affects 3.2 million Americans.[8]

In Stage II of the Superlongevity Revolution, we are not just devising ways to extend human life—we are also looking at methods to enhance the human shell, to simply make ourselves look better, to create what I label the "ultrahuman." Many of these techniques were originally devised not to achieve physical perfection, but to improve the appearance of those disfigured by injuries of various types. In one striking instance in September, 2005, University Hospital in Lausanne, Switzerland doctors perfected a technique of growing skin from fetal tissues, and without resorting to surgery painlessly attached this fetal skin to the burned areas. They applied these grafts to eight burn-victim children, one of whose burns covered as much as 82 square inches of his back.

In all cases, most residual evidence of the burns suffered by the children all but disappeared. None of the children required skin grafts. The researchers think that they may be able to apply this technique to applications other than burns. According to biologist Lee Ann Laurent-Applegate, "We have also worked on large physical wounds in some children as well as chronic wounds, primarily venous ulcers in adults, with equally encouraging results."[9]

I predict that it is only a matter of time before members of the public who suffer from no greater malady other than common facial blemishes or acne see this new technique as a way to improve their looks.

The next medical breakthroughs will take place all around the world. One exciting discovery occurred in July 2005 at Brigham and Women's Hospital in Boston. Researchers announced that they had discovered a drug combination that could impede the devastating course of Alzheimer's. The researchers theorized that Alzheimer's progresses because of sticky clumps of a certain protein named beta-amyloid proteins that form and build up between neurons. These proteins eventually kill off these neurons, leading to all of the behavioral problems we associate with this dreaded disease, including memory loss.

This drug combination is delivered to the brain through a nasal spray. The problem researchers found had nothing to do with the effectiveness of the drugs to clear out the clumps of beta-amyloid. Rather, the brain's immune system starts to react against the drug, causing dangerous brain inflammation. The new "drug cocktail" seems to provoke a less strong reaction of the immune system while still clearing out the Alzheimer's-inducing proteins.

While it might seem fanciful that a disease, which is wracking millions of aging seniors and destroying their lives, could be eradicated by something as simple as a nasal spray, spray is only the delivery system. Years of research went into the creation of a drug that is injected into the patient. More trials are scheduled before commercial release.[10]

The fight against cancer is a key element in this second stage of the Superlongevity Revolution. Each year cervical cancer kills about 250,000 women around the world, most of them in developing regions without basic health care. In the 1980s, scientists discovered that human papillomavirus plays a role in nearly all cases of cervical cancer. In 2005, pharmaceutical giant Merck announced that it had successfully tested a new vaccine, Gardasil, which it claims will protect against two strains responsible for 70 percent of all cervical cancer cases and another two that cause non-cancerous genital warts. GlaxoSmithKline has developed a similar vaccine that protects against the two cancer-provoking strains.

The vaccine is preventative—it doesn't protect the 75 percent of sexually active adults who are already infected with the virus. The idea is to vaccinate young boys and girls before they become infected. With proper vaccination polices, in the long run we will eradicate cervical cancer.[11]

Beyond the medical breakthroughs that we have discussed, there are a number of common-sense solutions to disease, such as prevention and early detection, that have led to the lengthening of life. In February 2006, the National Center for Health Statistics announced that for the first time in more than seventy years, the number of cancer deaths dropped, down from 557,271 to 556,902 in 2003. American Cancer Society officials who analyzed the federal death data claimed that the death rates had fallen for breast, prostate, lung and colorectal cancer, the four most common cancers that account for 51 percent of all United States cancer deaths. What makes these raw numbers so encouraging is the fact that every year the population in the later age groups, those people most prone to developing and dying from these cancers, grows. So these raw mortality numbers reflect a tremendous decrease in the percentage of people in the later ages that are dying of cancer. The American Cancer Society has pointed out that the mortality rates due to cancer have been falling for years, but this was the first time the raw number itself actually dropped.

"The prevention, detection and treatment of cancer are all improving our survival," reports Dr. Michael Thun, head of epidemiological research for the American Cancer Society. Another key is the sharp decrease in smoking—lung cancer has taken a precipitous dive since many Americans stopped smoking.[12]

At Stage III, I believe we will discover how to extend life, perhaps indefinitely. A significant body of theoretic and empirical findings suggests that there are few physical limits to the human life span. However, to achieve this Holy Grail of human existence, we must first master the laws of physics and biology sufficiently to control the behavior of cells and atoms.

Later in this book, we will look at some of the many schemes that are being devised to achieve what would be the crowning triumph of all human endeavor, the conquering of mortality itself. We will also look at the psychological and cultural impact of such a momentous event.

GUIDELINES FOR THE SUPERLONGEVITY REVOLUTION
Before we begin our great adventure into the near and distant future, here are some guidelines which I have found to be useful when examining the superlongevity phenomenon.

#1 The Radical Extension Of The Human Life Span Will Ultimately Benefit Humankind.

One would think that everyone would embrace the possibility of living for a very long time in excellent health. However, superlongevity is not welcomed in all quarters. We regularly hear predictions that having a large population of very old people would drain public resources, bankrupt social security safety nets and pension funds and run up the costs of health care. Social commentator Francis Fukuyama warned that by "capriciously" extending human life we would create an "end-of-life society" that would resemble "a giant nursing home."

Critics simply do not share the positive vision of superlongevity presented in this book and in the works of other futurists. Let us remember that nanotechnology, cell regeneration techniques and genetic engineering will enable citizens of the *Ageless Nation* to rejuvenate their bodies and stay forever young.

The fears detractors have voiced about the economic impact of superlongevity are baseless. In my opinion Superlongevity will actually enhance the economic well-being of both the individual and society as a whole. Throughout their long lives such vigorous individuals will contribute their labor and creativity to substantially enlarge, not reduce, the economic pie.

Indeed, people living into their one hundreds as healthy and vibrant individuals will add value to more than just the economy. How different from our own will be the zeitgeist, the mental and moral framework, of a global society whose denizens know with certainty that they will still be alive 300 years from now! I believe People with such a profound stake in the future will feel compelled to create a healthy and prosperous tomorrow. Average citizens will be motivated to become more involved politically as they realize that decisions about long-term issues will impact their own tomorrow and not just that of future generations. People who have succeeded in other fields will have the time and years to devote to public service as "citizen politicians."

In Stage II as well as Stage III, family life and marriage will also be greatly impacted. For the first time in human history, as many as ten generations of a single family might be alive at the same time. Such a development should lead all family members to feel a greater sense of continuity and solidarity with each other. Citizens will also maintain a heightened sense of membership in their nation and/or culture. For instance, one can only imagine how much more interconnected with their nation Americans new and old would feel if the signers of the Declaration of Independence were still alive today.

Furthermore, living longer will only enhance our ability to contribute to the well-being of all. As we live longer, each of us will become smarter, more skilled, and in most cases, wiser. The human species, whose members live longer than they do today, will only contribute more and more to the well-being of the planet and the universe.

#2 The Most Seemingly Unlikely Scientific Predictions About Life Extension Tend To Become Reality.

A few years ago, a newspaper wanted to interview me about all the predictions that had been made about the future that never came true. The interviewer mentioned as examples "flying cars" and household robots as seen in the animated series *The Jetsons*. I told her that in fact the prototype for the "flying car" already existed, and the only obstacles to its introduction to the public were political and economic, not technological. Society is just not ready for it now, but give it ten years, I told her. I added that scientists at MIT, Japanese universities and elsewhere were well on their way to inventing automatons that could do ordinary household chores. (Ironically, the cover of the *Popular Science* February 2006 issue featured a prototype of the flying car under development by a private company.)

However, after we explored the subject for several minutes, I told my interviewer that I would probably have to decline her invitation to contribute to the story, as I feel many predictions which seemed to be remote possibilities have come true. Most technologies we consider commonplace—the airplane (flying machines), radio, television, computers, automobiles and the like—sounded ludicrous, to say the least, when first proposed. Many scientific concepts—Pasteur's germ theory, for instance—took decades to be accepted by the medical community.

Now, we turn on our radios and fly our planes. And tell our children to wash their hands before meals and our surgeons to "scrub down" before entering the operating room.

Today, many of the concepts and technologies helping to usher in the Superlongevity Revolution are similarly regarded. The idea that we will soon be transforming the genetic make-up of individuals, changing the course of family genetic histories and eliminating hosts of diseases with the simple flick of a switch still sounds fanciful if not downright preposterous to most people. But as I have learned, humankind can eventually create anything it imagines—it's only a matter of time before idea becomes reality.

#3 *The Human Life Span Could Be Virtually Limitless.*

I would like to expand upon Dr. Louria's remarks at the "Creating Very Old People" conference I had discussed earlier. Dr. Louria maintained that there is a growing consensus among scientists and policy planners that, "It is no longer a question of whether extraordinary longevity is going to occur, but when." The packet provided to attendees at the conference included a scenario, a prospective timeline for achieving superlongevity. (As with my timeline, he also believes much of these gains will be made during the twenty-first century.)

Many think that such statements are simply a product of the hubris about life extension that has emerged from an era in which we have extended the human life span from the forties into the eighties in a relatively short time. Where's the proof, they ask, that we can continue to make such gains in the coming decades and centuries?

Louria claimed that we will see increases in the United States over sixty-five population from its current thirty-seven million to eighty million by 2040, the over eighty-five population from four million to eighteen million. And that's "without tinkering with the aging process."

The reason Dr. Louria and others make such statements is that this is the only conclusion they can logically make from the available evidence garnered from a host of sciences. Advancements made in such sciences as nanotechnology, caloric reduction, genetic engineering and other fields can easily lead one to that conclusion. Aubrey de Grey has made some fantastical prognostications about human superlongevity, including his famous (or infamous) prediction that he envisions human life spans of up to 5000 years or more. Others, including Ray Kurzweil, use hard science to support their claims about human superlongevity.

You, the reader, must make the final judgment about some of the more sweeping claims about the capacity to extend human life. However, the scientific arguments underlying such claims are convincing enough that major periodicals such as *Nature*, *Popular Science* and *Time* have given accorded them major coverage.

Louria stated, "If we learn how to modify the aging process,..what is the upper limit? Why then do we have to talk only about a 110, 120. Eventually, it could be beyond that." He also maintained that if we are going to extend the life span beyond 120, it is only going to occur by preventing aging, not just eliminating disease.

#4 If The Superlongevity Revolution's Progress Is Ever Hindered, The Likely Culprits Will Be Social, Economic, Religious And Political Factors Rather Than Shortcomings In Medical, Scientific Or Technological Expertise.

Given the breakthroughs in medical and scientific technologies, including exotic technologies such as nanotechnology, it would seem that the extension of the human life span is inevitable. However, the history of technological development makes it clear that the introduction and implementation of technology is often thwarted by a host of factors unrelated to science itself.

Human history is filled with examples of social and other forces dramatically inhibiting technological and scientific development. Many technologies and sciences are not accepted when they first appear. The use of vaccines was attacked by scientists themselves. In the late nineteenth and early twentieth century, towns and villages resisted the use of the automobile on city streets and byways.

Today, nuclear power plants are being built all over the world. But in the United States, no new nuclear plant has been licensed since the 1970s. The reasons are quite clear—anti-nuke environmental groups have been able to erect legal obstacles that make constructing such plants onerous at best.

Companies like Monsanto assumed smooth sailing when it introduced on the European market foods that had been genetically-modified to be more nutritious and have a longer shelf-life. Instead, they found that a well-orchestrated political campaign against what became labeled as "franken-foods" was able to thwart the introduction of GMOs into most European countries.

Later in this book, we will look at how and why the Superlongevity Revolution is already encountering resistance from a number of forces. One group on principle opposes any efforts to significantly extend the human life span. Included here are the anti-growth and anti-technology groups such as environmental and deep-ecology organizations usually quite visible in debates over the environment, new technologies, "urban sprawl" and a host of other battleground issues. Their opposition to superlongevity is rooted in a fairly straightforward zero-growth worldview. From their perspective, superlongevity would lead to an exponential increase in the global population, thereby accelerating the depletion of our severely limited natural, agricultural and energy resources.

Other groups and individuals are not opposed to extended life, but are opposed to certain technologies and scientific methods critical to the achievement of superlongevity. For instance, the opposition of the late Pope John Paul and President George W. Bush to embryonic stem cell research might hinder the development of a life-extending technology. In addition, many religious groups strongly disapprove of science's manipulation of the human genome, another process crucial to the extension of the human life span.

#5 Build It And They Will Come—If You Create Something That People Perceive As Beneficial, They Will Want It, Find It And Use It.

Despite this cautionary statement, I believe all of the resistance I have just described will be ultimately overcome by the desire of the public to embrace the benefits of modern medical science.

There is no instinct stronger, more irrepressible, than the instinct for survival. If people are aware of a therapy, medication, technology or technique that can save their own lives or those of their family, or can ameliorate or eradicate a disease that afflicts those around them, they will do whatever is necessary to locate its source and use it.

Therefore, I believe regardless of the arguments that various cultural and political leaders make against human life extension and enhancement or its enabling technologies, the public will ultimately embrace the concept of superlongevity. Clearly, most members of the public are sympathetic to the pro-longevity ethos. Upwards of 70 percent of those polled by Gallup registered their desire to live past the age of one hundred as long as they remain relatively healthy and physically active. When I have asked audiences whether they want to live to ages of one hundred, 125, even 150, their first response is negative—they envision living endlessly in a state of ever-deteriorating health. But when I pose a scenario in which they would live to those ages in continued good health, their attitude quickly changes. They suddenly see the infinite opportunities presented by living a very long life.

In the long run, government attempts to limit research and implementation of life-enabling technologies and drugs will prove ineffective. Already, in defiance of state edicts and warnings, people are seeking out and utilizing new technologies including gene therapy and therapeutic cloning that they hope will cure their diseases and extend their lives and those of their loved ones.

Why, one might ask, would people defy the powers that be in the case of superlongevity when they have not rallied around nuclear power, genetically-modified foods and other technologies whose implementation has been successfully hindered by political and environmental goods? The answer is that there exists a qualitative difference between people's attitude toward the necessity of these technologies and the medical and scientific products and wonders enabling superlongevity.

People can live without nuclear power, or at least the construction of new nuclear power plants, because at present oil, coal and other sources can meet our need for energy. And if genetically modified foods are kept off the shelves, we will certainly not starve—substitutes abound. However, try depriving people of a technology, drug or scientific technique that they believe can save their lives or the lives of loved ones, and you will see a swift and strong response!

#6 We Are All Ultimately Responsible For Our Own Health.

In this book, you will learn about a virtual scientific revolution that promises to extend your life, as well as the lives of family members and friends. While all of this "good news" about life extension that you will read in this book is inspiring, there is a danger that such information encourages us to become passive consumers of medical expertise and health services—the miracles of science will bestow on us long lives and perfect health.

Nothing could be further from the truth. These medical developments occur around us, outside of the perimeter of our lives. As these breakthroughs cascade upon our society, it will ultimately be the responsibility of each of us to capitalize on their benefits. Even in this so-called "age of information," knowledge of developments in various fields is not evenly distributed throughout the health system. Your family doctor or local medical practitioner might not be as knowledgeable as one would like about the newest medical technologies, pharmaceuticals or medical techniques. They might not have at hand state of the art diagnostic machines, or even know that they exist. The medical field is spread throughout the country and across the globe. Its practitioners might or might not be disseminating the results of their studies of information of newly developed medical applications to other professionals in the field.

A 2006 Time Magazine Story, "Why I Dumped the Baby Doctor," supports much of this idea. The author's subtitle points out, "Pediatricians often treat parents like children. That's why I got a new one." After praising Dr. P for his personal and professional style—he's reassuring, great with children and returns all the mothers' calls—author Michelle Cottle tells us what bothers her about this doctor and other previous pediatricians. She feels she and other moms are routinely treated with arrogance and unresponsiveness.

Doctor knows best is the attitude of these pediatricians. Except, she says, he often does not. For instance, she and her friends were assured by their children's doctors that flu shots never contain thimerosal, which some people suspect is a risk factor for autism. Another friend was told that all flu shots contain thimerosal. After performing some research, Cottle found that for a few extra dollars one can get a less prevalent thimerosal-free version of the shot.

Unlike the situation twenty years ago, any parent, or patient, for that matter, is only a few clicks away on the Internet from even the most obscure research on what they think might ail them. Journals and articles available to only specialists in the field are not ours for the asking. Doctors will eventually have to change their behavior toward patients and accept the fact that the twenty-first century patient is armed with statistics and research on their ailment, which requires a meaningful and constructive dialogue between M.D. and client.[13]

Therefore, radical life extension is going to require full participation in the health process on the part of all of us. In order to become active and wise consumers of medicine, we will have to be diligent researchers of the medical field, reading both popular and, in some cases, more professional journals to gain a full understanding of the potentials and possibilities to cure what ails us. Equally, we must go against the grain of traditional practice and become skeptical patients. Now with the benefit of the Internet and other cyber-based modalities, we can investigate and hopefully validate the information that our doctors impart in the examination room. Since we will all become explorers on the frontiers of time, we will need the proper tools to navigate through this new medical wilderness. With these helpful guidelines, we are ready to begin our adventure into the world of Superlongevity.

chapter two

What Man
Hath Wrought

Let's take another look at the conference of which we spoke earlier, "Creating Very Old People: Individual Blessing or Societal Disaster." It was held on a beautiful late April Spring day and attended by scientists, members of the health field, academics and reporters. Also attending were a number younger people, including a biology class from Marist High School in Bayonne, New Jersey.

Throughout the day we were feted with lectures by some of the more original anti-aging researchers laboring in a wide variety of scientific fields.

Featured at the conference was George Roth, who spoke on the little-known field of Caloric Restriction, or CR, and how it might help substantially increase the human life span. Roth is a scientist with the National Institute of Aging and is also the CEO of Gerotech, Inc., a new biotechnology firm devoted to "anti-aging" strategies. Richard A. Miller, Associate Director of the Geriatrics Center at the University of Michigan, spoke about the possibilities of "immortalizing cells."

Another expert speaker was Woodring Wright, one of the world's experts on telomeres, the structures that cap the ends of chromosomes. He shocked the audience by claiming that by countering what is now considered the inevitable shortening of these structures, we can potentially decelerate aging and reduce the chronic disease and disabilities that we associate with aging. Another speaker, University of Medicine and Dentistry of New Jersey professor Abraham

Aviv, followed by saying that the reason women outlive men by an average of eight years is because their telomeres are longer.

Discussing the promise of stem cell research as a means to rejuvenate the body and prevent disease was Gary Friedman, a Transplant Physician at Saint Barnabas Medical Center of Livingston, NJ. Dr. Christopher Wiley, associate Professor of Anesthesiology at the Dartmouth-Hitchcock Medical Center in Lebanon, New Hampshire, gave an extraordinary presentation on how an arcane new field, nanotechnology, could extend the lifespan indefinitely.[10]

While the press gave the conference some attention, the headlines of the day dealt with the usual pessimistic refrains of war, terrorism and a stagnant economy. Buried deep in the paper was the good news emanating from the conference that mankind was about to take a giant step toward radically expanding the human life span.

But Aren't Some People Already Living Past One Hundred?

Before we examine how genetic engineering and nanotechnology will help extend the life span, let us first take a brief look at what humans already know about keeping ourselves living for a long time.

A study performed by the National Institute of Aging that was featured in a 2005 issue of *National Geographic* magazine uncovered some interesting facts about the ability of certain pockets of humanity to live to very long ages.

Funded in part by the United States National Institute on Aging, scientists explored the superlongevity phenomenon in several regions, including Sardinia, Italy and the islands of Okinawa, Japan. They also examined a group of Seventh-day Adventists living in Loma Linda, California who live to extremely long ages. The Sardinian group is particularly interesting—a significant percentage of the men in this mountain community live to one hundred and more.

What connects these groups is that they all produce a high rate of centenarians, suffer a fraction of the diseases that commonly kill people in other parts of the developed world, and enjoy more healthy years of life.

The study concludes that these populations offer us three sets of best practices to emulate if we want to live a very long life. First of all, all members of these populations eat sparsely. The Adventists ate nuts and beans, and the Okinawans and the Sardinians ate small portions of cheeses and other foods. Later we will discuss the scientific evidence that low caloric intake accompanied by high amounts of the proper nutrients is associated with radical life extension. These groups came to their diet via different means. Economic reasons forced the Okinawans to make do with lower caloric intake. The Adventists follow a diet prescribed by Scripture. All the groups seem to avoid red meat almost totally and have extremely low rates of cancer and coronary problems. Yet the groups do vary somewhat in regard to alcohol. The Sardinians drink red wine in moderation; the Adventists by religious proscription abstain from alcoholic beverages.

There seems to be a number of other factors that enable these populations to live into their nineties and one hundreds with great regularity. All members have a very strong sense of community—the people are all extremely connected with each others' lives and "put family first." "Socially engaged" is the term the researchers used.

Moreover, all of these people remain physically active throughout their lives. Seventh Day Adventist Dr. Ellsworth Wareham at ninety-one still assists with heart surgery. Seventy-five year old Sardinian Tonino Tola's work day would put your average workaholic to shame. By 11 a.m. he has already milked four cows, slaughtered a calf, split half a cord of wood and taken his sheep on a journey through four miles of pasture.

The Okinawans examined in the Okinawa Centenarian Study have a fifth the heart disease, a fourth the breast and prostate cancer and a third less dementia than Americans. Besides a lean diet of Okinawan vegetables, tofu, miso soup, and a little fish or meat coupled with a vigorous lifestyle, they possess a strong sense of purpose that serves as a buffer against stress and stress-related diseases, such as "hypertension."

Also, like the other long-lived groups, the Okinawans have a strong sense of communal connectivity. Okinawans refer to this as *moai*, a mutual support network that provides financial, emotional and social help throughout life. Okinawan seniors are reported to have far fewer heart attacks than their United States counterparts and lower rates of breast and prostate cancer.

It does not seem to matter where that sense of purpose emanates from. The study claims that the Seventh Day Adventists' strong religious bent plays a part in its member's ability to live past one hundred years of age. Another study, of 34,000 California Adventists conducted by the National Institutes of Health from 1976 to 1988, found that diet again played a role in the achievement of superlongevity. The Adventists' consume beans, soy milk, tomatoes and other fruits, thereby lowering their risk of developing certain cancers. By eating whole wheat bread, drinking five glasses of water a day and consuming four servings of nuts a week, the Adventists reduced their risk of heart disease. Their tendency to abstaining completely from red meat was linked to the absence of cancer and heart disease in this population.[11]

In 2005, nutritionists, psychologists, gerontologists and other specialists from throughout Cuba, as well as Mexico, France and Spain interviewed twelve Cuban men and women said to be one hundred years or older. Also at this meeting was Dr. Eugenio Selman, Castro's personal physician. Among the centenarians was Benito Martinez, at 124 possibly the oldest man on the island. That age would also make him the oldest person in the world, though his assertion has evidently never been authenticated. The six common elements they could all agree contributed to their long lives were both physical and more in the social psychological vein. These factors included of course appropriate diet. But these people also mentioned "the motivation to live," medical attention, intense physical activity, cultural activities and a healthy environment.[12]

SELF-HELP, WESTERN STYLE

For a culture who believes that medical doctors and pharmaceutical companies are the primary source from which good health springs, the idea that some fairly isolated and technologically simple communities are outdistancing us in the achievement of superlongevity through a combination of diet, exercise and lifestyle must come as a bit of a shock. Worse, the common factors identified in these cultures – staying active, finding a purpose, keeping friends, having faith, taking time off and celebrating life – seem impractical and even a bit alien for people living in today's world of cell phones, instant messaging and fragmented families. (The only practice linked to longevity that we might emulate is the "primitives'" habit of drinking red wine on a daily basis. That we can do.)

If we are proactive at all in maintaining our own good health, many of us do it via the advice and therapies of public health celebrities and diet and supplement gurus. In 2006, *Newsweek* magazine sought some of these gurus and asked them how they go about living the healthy life. Do they practice what they preach?

They interviewed Professor Bruce Ames, a professor at U.C. Berkeley and well-known anti-aging high-priest. His prescription: "If you want to age faster, a good way to do it is to be short of some vitamin or mineral. I think everyone in the world should take a multivitamin as insurance. I take one daily." He also takes a pill containing acetyl-carnitine and lipoic acid, both of which are used in the cell's energy center known as mitochondria. Ames states that in his studies rats administered both of these substances functioned better and their immune systems improved. His company, Juvenon, which we will discuss later, sells the pill that can deliver these nutrients.

Prof. JoAnn Manson of Harvard Medical School suggests taking calcium, Vitamin D, plus a multivitamin. Best-selling author Dean Ornish suggests fish oil and a multivitamin (an iron-free multivitamin for men and postmenopausal women). Health author Marion Nestle takes an occasional multivitamin, but suggests that people concentrate on eating lots of fruits, vegetables, whole grains, and fatty fish. Irwin Rosenberg, Tufts nutritional scientist, takes vitamin B12 and vitamin D. He mentioned that because the sun provides a major dose of vitamin D, if you live in cold climates where winter life is primarily indoors, you might want to take extra amounts of vitamin D.[13]

But vitamins and minerals are only a small portion of the products being sold by the anti-aging and health industry. In fact, compared to the major number of supplements offered by this industry, vitamins seem surprisingly quaint and vanilla.

A 2006 issue of *Business Week*, which was purportedly attempting to "expose" this new industry, probably gave it a major boost in the arm. The more I read the article, the more I was tempted to try some of the hormones and other concoctions which promise to keep us "forever young."

The magazine story focused on one Dr. Ron Rothenberg of the California Healthspan Institute in Encinitas, which pitches to its patient's regimens of diet, exercise, and hormones that will make them feel younger and live longer. One of his patients, Dr. Howard Benedict, a retired dentist is on a $10,000-a-year regimen of thirty vitamins and supplements. In addition, Benedict takes testosterone gel and injections of human growth hormone.

Among the benefits Benedict claims to receive from these injections and supplements, plus a huge protein smoothie, is a reduction of his arthritis pain, which had curtailed his physical activity considerably. The dentist Benedict states that: "I feel like I'm twenty years old with my wife. It's just amazing."

Anti-aging clinics such as Rothenberg's go well beyond vitamins and minerals. Their therapies have entered into the controversial world of biologic drugs, which includes the now famous human growth hormone (HGH) and other concoctions that promise to turn back the biological clock. The industry purportedly brings in $56 billion a year now, a number projected to increase by 2009 to $79 billion.

The overseeing organization in this new field is the American Academy of Anti-Aging Medicine, better known as A4M. It describes itself on its website as a "medical organization dedicated to the advancement of technology to detect, prevent and treat aging-related disease and to promote research into methods to retard and optimize the human aging process." This organization runs conferences on a variety of anti-aging strategies, and importantly certifies doctors who wish to practice in the field. Since 1996, 1500 doctors have sought board certification in anti-aging medicine. According to founder Dr. Ronald M. Klatz, A4M has grown from twelve physician members to 17,500 in eighty-five countries, and has provided training to 30,000 doctors worldwide in 2006.

The ultimate aim of the anti-aging movement is what they label "rectangularization"—a person lives for years in a healthy state, right up to the point of death, instead of living for years with infirmities and debilitating illness.

For organizations such as A4M, HGH is a basic staple in the fight against aging. Originally approved by the FDA in 1985 to help short children grow, many in the anti-aging industry view HGH as much more: they see this hormone as a magic bullet for boosting immunity, memory and heart function and to increase muscle mass. Its effect on bodily strength is so well-accepted by the public and those in the health fields that athletes like Barry Bond suspected of taking HGH and similar performance enhancers are generally perceived as "cheating," gaining a profound edge over competitors not using the hormone.

A couple whom I count among my closest friends turned to HGH in the mid-1980s to help their young son eventually reach normal height. By age ten it was obvious that their son would be significantly undersized in adulthood if something was not done to alter the situation. He was suffering from a disorder which was stifling his growth. His parents finally found a doctor who prescribed the growth hormone for Bobby, but only after an intense battery of tests were administered to insure that the boy was a legitimate candidate for the hormone. The wonder drug worked—their son filled out to a normal 5'10", well beyond a projected height of 5'4".

Now, HGH is being touted as a drug that can improve health and, if we accept the theories of Rothenberg, who has taken growth hormone himself,

HGH could help you live to the ripe old age of 125. Ironically, federal law prohibits anyone from distributing HGH specifically for anti-aging purposes. In December of 2005, it was announced that a whistleblower suit was filed against a unit of Pfizer Inc. for promoting HGH for anti-aging use. However, the FDA does allow growth hormone to be prescribed for "adult growth hormone deficiency," whose symptoms are depression and increased body fat. It seems to many critics that it is not too difficult for an adult to legitimately fit this "deficiency profile" and legally acquire drugs such as HGH. Since there is no "exact science" diagnosing adult growth hormone deficiency, critics assert, anti-aging physicians can simply claim they are restoring HGH in patients to its appropriate, youthful levels, whatever that is.

Dr. Klatz, when asked whether HGH reverses aging, states that the drug helps to reverse "the physical processes of aging," including bone and muscle loss. He adds that the fears regarding the use of HGH are unfounded. According to Klatz, the doses administered to adults are merely replacing hormones to the normal level of a thirty year old, and are only one-third to one-seventh of the dose that's been shown to be safe in children. He claims that for twenty years HGH has been used clinically in hundreds of thousands of young people and tens of thousands of adults.

This level of good health does not come cheaply. Rothenberg's complete health assessment, which includes a two-day series of meetings with a nutritionist and an exercise physiologist, can run $2,500 or more. Diet supplements and natural hormones can run as high as $250 a month, and HGH can cost $2,000 a month. Rothenberg is said to be a living testimonial to the efficacy of this regimen. At fifty, he was "off his game, tired and mentally burned out." Now, with the help of supplements and testosterone, he is a veritable "ball of fire," running his practice and training other anti-aging physicians.

The anti-aging doctors prescribe testosterone, which comes in the form of skin gels, as well as the hormone DHEA, which can convert to estrogen and testosterone in the body, to enhance heart health, sexual performance and memory in men, and fight menopausal symptoms in women. The hormones estrogen and progesterone are also on the "must have" lists in anti-aging clinics. According to health guru Dr. Klatz, testosterone and estrogen can help maintain the health of cells in your body.

In spite of thousands of testimonials to the efficacy of such drugs, HGH, testosterone and other such substances are immersed in controversy. Are they safe? Can overuse lead to cancer or heart disease? What are the long-term effects of using such drugs? Regulation of the drugs by the FDA is loose, to say the least, and most users want the government to retain its laissez-faire stance for the foreseeable future.

The anti-aging industry is quick to react when criticized. When the *Journal of the American Medical Association* asserted in a 2005 article that 30 percent of the growth hormone prescriptions in the U.S. are written for non-FDA-approved uses, A4M filed a lawsuit against the authors Perls and Olshansky in an Illinois circuit court. Thomas Perls, a geriatrician at Boston University Medical Center who studies centenarians, argues that, "It is pure science fiction to say we can change the rate of aging in an organism as complex as ours." He claims that it is better to focus on diet and exercise.

Despite criticism, the anti-aging component of what I label the "Super-longevity Industry" is growing. Since 2003, Patrick Savage and his identical twin, Dr. Paul Savage, have opened seven branches of BodyLogicMD, as they call their anti-aging centers, and hope to double that number in a few years.

Anti-aging doctors like Savage and Rothenberg view themselves as "the personal family doctor from the Norman Rockwell era," working to keep their patients youthful and happy.[14]

We'll look further at the potential of some of these wonder-hormones in the chapter on the Ultra-human phenomenon.

All of these therapies and pills, diets and exercise programs, can only help us extend our lives. But their impact, as I think you will agree, pales by comparison to the life-extending potential of new sciences being invented in laboratories around the world, including those devoted to stem cell science, gene therapy and eventually the holy grail of the Superlongevity Revolution, nanotechnology.

STEM CELL RESEARCH AND THE PROMISE OF REGENERATIVE MEDICINE

One of the most promising and also controversial areas of eliminating disease and thereby extending human life is stem cell research. Human stem cells are unique cells that can transform into all the parts needed to create a living being. Stem cells are the body's basic engines of growth, the mechanism by which a single fertilized egg is transformed into a human. Embryo stem cells are undifferentiated cells which develop into skin, blood, bone, nerves and eye tissue. Brain stem cells in a human fetus, for example, morph into the neurons and all other cells needed to make a mind.

The progress in applying stem cells to varying diseases has been rapid throughout this decade. The work is largely pointed toward finding cures for Parkinson's disease, Lou Gehrig's disease, and other human afflictions. In 2002 United States doctors used embryonic mouse stem cells to treat Parkinson's disease in a rat. In 2003 Australian doctors edged closer to perfecting a technique by which stem cells could repair damaged brain cells of multiple sclerosis sufferers. In June 2003 surgeons with Ohio Heart Health Center, during coronary artery bypass surgery on a heart failure patient, injected a patient's own muscular stem cells into his damaged heart muscle in an attempt to re-grow new functional heart muscle.

In 2006, Canadian scientists reported that stem cells they harvested from the brains of mice can restore some walking ability in laboratory rats with spinal-cord damage. The researchers injected the cells into rats that could no longer walk after their spines were crushed. The cells migrated to the spinal cord, merged into the injured tissue and developed into cells that produced myelin, the insulating layer around nerve fibers that transmits signals to the brain. Many patients with spinal cord damage have intact nerve fibers at the point of injury but no myelin, causing paralysis.[15]

Eventually, scientists hope to use stem cells to grow new muscle in a patient with a damaged heart, restore a failing liver or repair damaged nerves in spinal injury patients.

Unfortunately, stem cell research has been plagued by ethical and moral controversies. In 2001, President Bush banned the use of embryonic stem cells in federally-funded research projects, restricting financing to about sixty existing strains of stem cells, or lines. Only already existing stem cells could be used in research.

To make matters worse, in 2005, journalists uncovered evidence that a respected and highly-productive researcher in the stem cell field, South Korean researcher Dr. Hwang Woo Suk, had faked some of his findings as well as forged consent forms. In 2003, Suk had shocked the scientific world when he claimed to have cloned the first human embryo stem cells.

I believe that within the next decade or so stem cell research will successfully find cures to a number of diseases. We will most likely use both adult stem cell strains (or lines) and stem cells from embryos either damaged or scheduled to be destroyed. Research is proving that adult stem cells (ASCs) and embryonic stem cells (ESCs) each have their own strengths and weakness.

The debate over whether to use adult or embryonic stem cells might in the long run become moot. Increasingly adult stem cells have proved their worth as hardy combatants in the war against degenerative diseases. In the laboratory, at least, adult stem cells as well as those found in umbilical cord blood have already produced outstanding success and authentic results in the search for the cure for diseases, such as: brain, ovarian, testicular, breast cancers; surface wound healing; stroke and heart damage; Parkinson's disease; spinal cord injury; and rheumatoid and juvenile Arthritis.

In March of 2006 scientists from the University of Louisville reported a second successful experiment in its stem-cell research. They took adult stem cells from a human nose and injected them into a rat with a spinal-cord injury. The nose cells were transformed into nerve cells, and just weeks later the rat was able to move normally.[16]

In the same month, German researchers announced that human testes could be a source of embryonic-like stem cells. If their findings are correct, they have provided science a way to grow tissue to repair the body without having to destroy or create embryos. Dr. Gerd Hasenfuss, of Georg-August University in Gottingen claimed that his team has found that cells from the testes of adult mice that normally turn into sperm have the ability to be transformed into different types of tissue, including heart, liver, skin, muscle, pancreas and nerve cells.

They have now begun studying the cells from testes in men and are optimistic of getting similar results. If they can repeat these findings in people, the cells could produce tissue that would end up being a perfect match for a patient. Hasenfuss said this would avoid "the ethical and immunological problems associated with human embryonic stem cells." Professor Bob Williamson, chairman of the National Committee of Medicine of the Australian Academy of Science, said that the discovery bolstered the growing body of evidence that adult stem cells have the capacity to turn into a number of cell types. "It's in the bag," say stem cell scientists.[17]

The Moraga Biotechnology Corporation, an adult stem cell company based in Los Angeles, California, announced that it had discovered in adult tissues a very primitive stem cell with properties that are similar to embryonic cells. Importantly, the Company's scientists found that these adult stem cells were able to differentiate into most tissues and organs of the body—including spermatogonia. These very early embryonic stem cells appear to be retained in adult tissues as "Blastomere-Like Stem Cells (BLSCs)." Such a discovery would obviate the use of embryonic stem cells altogether.[18]

Another discovery, announced in 2007 in the journal *Nature Biotechnology*, could help our society circumvent the often acrimonious debate over the ethical and medical issues surrounding embryonic stem cells. According to Dr Anthony Atala, the director of Wake Forest University School of Medicine's Institute for Regenerative Medicine in North Carolina as well as senior editor of the report, stem cells found in human amniotic fluid appear to possess many of the beneficial qualities of embryonic stem cells. Amniotic fluid is the liquid that cushions babies in the womb.

These stem cells were harvested from the fluid left over from amniocentesis tests given to pregnant women. The study demonstrated that such cells were able to transform into new blood vessels, fat, bone, nerve and liver tissues as well as heart muscle. The *Nature Biotechnology* article claims a number of advantages of amniotic fluid-derived stem (AFS) cells over other types of stem cells. For one, they are more readily accessible than both embryonic and adult stem cells, Secondly, they can be induced to replicate rapidly in culture. And perhaps most importantly, these amniotic fluid stem cells do not form tumors when implanted in laboratory animals like embryonic cells do. This tendency is often ignored by the mass media in its reports on the stem cell controversy.[19]

One researcher, Dr. Dario Fauza, prompted such cells to grow tissue to repair defective tracheas and diaphragms in sheep. Fauza, coordinator of the surgical research laboratories at Children's Hospital Boston, has asked the FDA for permission to use this cell technology to do the same for children born with herniated diaphragms. If the FDA gives Fauza the go-ahead, this project would become the first human clinical trial involving amniotic fluid stem cells.

In another groundbreaking experiment Swiss scientists Dr. Dorthe Schmidt and Dr. Simon Hoerstrup of University Hospital Zurich have used amniotic fluid stem cells to grow heart valves in sheep.

There is still a question whether stem cells derived from amniotic fluid can give rise to the many different types of cells that embryonic stem cells can produce. According to Dr. Robert Lanza, an embryonic stem cell researcher and the head of scientific development at Advanced Cell Technology in Massachusetts, there might be limits to their flexibility. "They can clearly generate a broad range of important cell types, but they may not do as many tricks as embryonic stem cells," Lanza claims.

The reason embryonic stem cells are more flexible is that they are derived from days-old embryos—all of their development is yet to come. According to Dr. Atala, amniotic fluid stem cells lie somewhere between the two major categories of stem cells, embryonic and adult. An amniotic stem cell is "not as early as a human embryonic stem cell and it's not as late as the adult stem cells," Atala says.

However, amniotic fluid stem cells are powerful tools, and definitely figure to play a critical role in the development of the emerging field of regenerative medicine.

The United States government, which spends over twenty-five billion dollars on various types of scientific studies, seems to believe in this promising new avenue of medical research. The National Institutes of Health are already directing money to those studying therapeutic applications of stem cells derived from such amniotic fluids.[20]

The corporate world is most definitely jumping on the bandwagon of stem cell research. At the 2006 Wharton Health Care Business Conference, the future of stem cell research in the battle against disease and aging was clearly defined: stem cell therapies are a solid hope in curing age-related diseases and rare conditions for which good treatments don't exist.

Robert F. Willenbucher, who leads Johnson & Johnson's newly-formed stem cell internal venture effort, was very enthusiastic about the potential of adult stem cells. While a lot of attention is on embryonic stem cells—primitive cells taken from embryos that have the potential to become various specialized cells, adult stem cells have a great potential in the field of regenerative medicine. His comments were supported by Steven Nichtberger, president and CEO of Tengion, a regenerative medicine company in King of Prussia, Pa. He described his company's quest to grow replacement bladders using a patient's own cells. His company is planning to manufacture these "neo-bladders" at a central manufacturing facility.

Martin McGlynn, president, CEO and director of Palo Alto, California—based StemCells, a biotech company, said his company is targeting human neural stem cells derived from adult brain tissue. The company has FDA approval to begin transplanting the cells into children with Batten disease, a fatal, inherited neurodegenerative disorder. "That will be the number-one agenda item for our company in 2006," he said. Stephen W. Webster, president, CEO and director of Neuronyx, a biopharmaceutical company in Malvern, Pa., said his researchers are working with stem cells from adult human bone marrow to devise treatments for heart disease and other disorders.

William M. Caldwell IV is CEO of Advanced Cell Technology, which has its new headquarters and research facility in Alameda, Calif. His company's research agenda includes developing therapies for macular degeneration, heart disease and skin problems, such as burns. He boldly stated that, "Our company is totally dedicated to embryonic stem cell development ... and potential cures." His company is relying in part on funding from the state of California, where voters in 2004 approved an initiative to provide three billion dollars in state funding for embryonic stem cell research over ten years. "We are one of the benefactors of that," Caldwell said.

Unfortunately, controversies such as the Bush ban on embryonic stem cell research and the Hwang stem cell fraud case has scared many investors. Reni J. Benjamin, senior biotechnology analyst for Rodman and Renshaw noted that he was "one of the few on Wall Street to take a stab" at the stem cell field. While regenerative medicine can take healthcare in a whole new direction, venture capital companies are cautious, he noted. Plus, many venture capitalists simply do not understand the science. He strongly suggested that biotech stem cell companies explain the status of their research and the near-term potentials for stem cell applications to specific diseases.

Tengion's CEO Steven Nichtberger has confidence in stem cell research and discoveries despite the recent fears among some investors. In fact, Nichtberger sees others' trepidation as another opportunity for his company to succeed. As a teenager, he had a poster on his bedroom wall carrying the James A. Baldwin quotation that sums up Nichtberger's philosophy on life and business: "Those who say it can't be done are usually interrupted by others doing it." In the field of stem cell research, Nichtberger's company is the one who is "doing it."

The company's success started with the pioneering work of the aforementioned Dr. Anthony Atala, the Wake Forest Institute for Regenerative Medicine Director who announced that human amniotic fluid houses stem cells. For almost twenty years, Dr. Atala worked on growing a bladder from a patient's own cells and implanting it. The April 2006 issue of the British medical journal *The Lancet* announced that Dr. Atala had successfully grown bladders from patients' own cells and then implanted them in seven children with spina bifida, a birth defect that damages the nervous system and other body parts, including the bladder. The bladders are still functioning capably in the children. Dr. Atala now plans to try his discovery in people with bladder cancer, but this is just the beginning. Dr. Atala has his mind set on growing livers, nerves and heart valves as well.[21]

Tengion's efforts to market the artificial bladder demonstrate the raw power of capital combined with scientific expertise to invent and quickly perfect breakthrough medical technologies. Tengion has poured millions of dollars into Dr. Atala's research at Wake Forest. In 2006, Tengion and Wake Forest entered into an official collaboration that is the very definition of the term "win-win situation." Under the multi-year, multi-million-dollar agreement, Tengion will provide funding to Wake Forest for research to be conducted at its Institute for Regenerative Medicine under the direction of Dr. Atala. Nichtberger stated that this relationship would enable Tengion "to work more closely with some of the leading regenerative medicine researchers in the world and accelerate our efforts to make regenerative medicine products a reality for patients." Wake Forest, of course, now has a conduit to quickly bring its products from the laboratory to the market. In the long run, the major winners will be the patients needing replacement organs such as bladders, livers, and the like.[22]

Under Nichtberger's leadership, Tengion announced in 2007 that it was indeed making progress in getting the neo-bladders to market—the company launched its Phase II clinical trial of this remarkable creation. It is no wonder why the risk-taking Tengion is attracting millions of dollars from investors. Tengion garnered fifty million dollars in second-round funding led by Quaker BioVentures in Philadelphia and Bain Capital in Boston to aid its research activity and develop its product pipeline, which some hope would include artificial kidneys and livers. Over the last few years, other investors have included Oak Investment Partners and Johnson and Johnson Development.[23]

Regardless of the obstacles facing this new science, its potential to drastically extend the human life span is unquestioned. The issue is not if, but when stem cell research meets its destiny to minimize human suffering and expand human potential to live a full and healthy life.[24]

THE QUEST FOR IMMORTALITY GENES

One hope for radically extending the human life span is discovering the so-called "immortality gene." We know there are genes or sets of genes that influence our health, intelligence and susceptibility to certain diseases. Why not, it is reasoned, find the gene or genes that influence the aging process itself.

This quest has intrigued some researchers like Nir Barzilai, MD, director of the Institute for Aging Research at Albert Einstein College of Medicine in New York. He is gathering data for a study aimed at identifying genes that play a role in extreme longevity. He feels that if he can locate these genes and understand their effects, drugs could then be developed that would imitate many of the chemical signals that the genes send to the body.

When would this miracle happen? Dr. Barzilai thinks that we are perhaps ten years from locating such a gene. But he predicts we will make a major discovery quickly enough that it could happen in time to benefit baby boomers."

Barzilai is not the only person looking for the genes which they hope holds the secret to immortality. There are at least half a dozen other scientific groups studying the genetic make-up of centenarians in places such as Okinawa, France and American Amish communities to find these longevity genes.

Barzilai is focusing on the American descendants of the Ashkenazim, which is a branch of the Jewish people that settled in Eastern Europe hundreds of years ago. The members of this group are known for their longevity. This group has been isolated for a long time, and its members have not married outsiders until recently. Hence, the gene pool can be isolated for research purposes. One longevity gene they have found that is present in 24 percent of these centenarians (and only 8 percent among younger people) is thought to stave off cardiovascular disease by enhancing the body's ability to remove cholesterol. This very same gene may protect us from cognitive decline as we get older. Other researchers have discovered a gene in this group linked to breast cancer.

There is a belief now among scientists that centenarians possess special genes that protect them from many of the diseases that can kill others at a much younger age. Barzilai claims that "the centenarians have some kind of genetic armament" that allows them to survive to very old ages. These longevity genes slow down the aging process by making cells better able to withstand the battery of assaults, including bad diet, genetic mutations, inflammation, radiation and toxic chemical by-products we know as free radicals.

How do gene hunters forage for just the right genes? Modern technology, especially the advanced computer, has enabled researchers to examine and analyze the genetic structure of the human being in ways that would have been inconceivable only a few years ago.

First, a machine scans a person's DNA. Based on that scan, a computer then creates an image, or profile, of the person's genetic makeup, or genome. It is important to note that each gene and each code on that gene has its own identity, with its own distinct markings and patterns. This is where the computer is most invaluable—if we are studying a centenarian, the computer can simply run that person's genomic information against that of the genetic data of other centenarians. When the computer finds similarities in the genetic patterns of the centenarians that are not in the genetic patters of a non-centenarian control group, we have a solid clue that the gene specific to the centenarian group is possibly a "longevity" gene.

Since 2003, Barzilai, who is studying nearly 1,500 individuals, has discovered three longevity genes, all of which shield the person against heart disease. In this way, the genes extend life span. Thomas Perls, M.D., director of the New England Centenarian Study at Boston University School of Medicine identified a fourth longevity gene that may play a role in heart disease prevention.

Barzilai has also been studying the behavioral patterns of his subjects. He has found that the subjects are not suffering from debilitation and chronic illness which we associate with old age. These centenarians remain active and healthy until the end of their lives. They don't so much die as "give out." We will re-visit this strange phenomenon, sometimes referred to as "compressed morbidity" when we discuss caloric restriction later in this chapter.

I was fortunate to witness a discussion by University of Michigan gerontologist Richard Miller at the aforementioned "Creating Old People" conference on his research into the genetic foundation of superlongevity. He works with mice in a laboratory, and has studied the impact of genes on making one old or young. In a decade, nine gene mutations have been discovered that let mice live up to 50 percent longer. Dozens more longevity genes have been found in tiny worms and fruit flies. According to Miller, "If we can produce drugs that could slow aging to the same extent we can slow aging in mice or rats, the average person would live to 110 or 115."

Such work is not only performed by researchers connected to hospitals or government. A private company, deCODE, headquartered in Reykjavik, Iceland, has utilized its access to the genetic records of the current inhabitants of Iceland to discover two genes that protect the brain cells of Icelandic 90-year-olds. Current projects include studying the genetic roots of cardiovascular disease, cancer, asthma, pain, and schizophrenia. They want to eventually develop and commercialize drugs that treat common diseases. I will discuss deCODE a bit further when I deal with the Superlongevity Industry.

It is hoped that as companies like deCODE discover the genetic roots of diseases, we will come closer to extending life, perhaps indefinitely. William Heiden, chief executive of Elixir Pharmaceuticals in Cambridge, Mass., sounding a bit like Richard Miller, states that, "If someone is predestined to live to 75, maybe drugs can take him to 90; if he is predestined to live to 90, maybe we can take him to one hundred or 110."

Research on aging has yielded drugs targeting major killers. Many such drugs are in human trials. Studies of free radicals led AstraZeneca to develop a promising stroke drug which could be available by 2008, that soaks up free radicals that spread damage after a stroke.

Pfizer is also trying to develop gene-based drugs that boost good cholesterol. Other companies such as Serono are studying treatments for obesity and diabetes based on genetic roots of such diseases. Biotech firm Geron just began human tests of a cancer therapy that targets enzymes that reset telomeres, tiny molecular clocks that tell cells to die after a certain number of divisions; these clocks malfunction in cancer cells. Geron's drug aims to fix them so the tumors expire on schedule.[25]

SUPERLONGEVITY AND THE STRANGE WORLD OF CALORIC RESTRICTION

Most of the techniques and technologies that will extend our lives decades longer than we ever lived before—stem cell science, cloning, genetic engineering—depend on relatively recent breakthroughs in physics, genetics and medicine. But one of these, in its most basic form, has nothing to do with the high tech world of genetic engineering or biotechnology. In theory, this technique is already accessible to the general population without the help of the scientific establishment.

Marco Polo, as he traveled throughout the kingdom of Genghis Khan towards the end of the thirteenth century, wrote about an intriguing group of individuals he referred to as the Yogi, "a class of people who are indeed properly Brahmins, but they form a religious order devoted to idols." He remarked on their dietary habits—"They eat very little, but what they do eat, is good."

He mentioned one other detail worth noting about the members of this religious caste—every one of these Yogi lived from 150 to 200 years!

We have no way of fact-checking Polo's report, but the idea that these very old Yogi lived on healthy extremely low-calorie diets is an eerie echo of what scientists for almost a century have been discovering in laboratory experiments— by radically reducing the caloric intake of certain animals, while at the same time ensuring that the animals receive a healthy intake of vitamins and minerals, we dramatically increase their life spans by as much as 30 percent to 40 percent.

This technique is called Caloric Reduction or CR for short. It is estimated that such radical adjustments in diet and food intake could extend human life to 150 years or more. The link between caloric restriction and increased life span has been demonstrated in studies on a wide variety of animals, including rats, guppies, spiders and a microscopic water invertebrate called the rotifer.

Scientists have discovered that animals on a strict caloric-restriction diet not only live longer, but they also benefit from another phenomenon mentioned earlier, *compressed morbidity*. This term simply means that those on CR experience few of the maladies associated with old age at the end of their lives.

At the National Institutes of Health, rhesus monkeys fed 30 percent less than their normal food intake avoid age-linked maladies. Animals on such diets are more physically active than control groups on normal diets. They also maintain that activity later in life. Their memory is still sharp in later years and they retain their ability to learn, a benefit that might be explained by the findings of a 2002 University of Florida study that demonstrated that caloric restriction slows the rate of death of brain neurons. These monkeys develop fewer tumors and less heart disease, and they look and act like younger animals throughout their lives. When they finally die they rarely have signs or symptoms of cancers or stiff arteries.

NIH's study on rhesus monkeys is still a work in progress—they are now in about the twentieth year of the study, and monkeys generally live an average of twenty four years in the lab. The researchers still must empirically test the full impact of CR on the longevity of these animals. The next few decades will probably provide some very good news about the impact of CR on higher primates. Dr. Roth mentioned in his speech that one of the monkeys, which died in 2004, had been in captivity since 1968, and was estimated to be already four to eight years of age at the time. He was not put on caloric restriction until 1988, which indicates that we can gain superlongevity benefits from CR even if the regimen is adopted later in life. Already, the CR monkeys are besting control groups on overall death rates and chronic disease rates.

Most of us intrinsically realize that it is better to eat in moderation than to gorge ourselves at every meal—obesity has been linked to any number of diseases, and most definitely shortens lives. The old Confucian saying, "Eat until you feel three-quarters full," indicates that the benefits of eating in moderation have never been a secret. So does the old adage, "Man does not die: he kills himself and he digs his grave with his teeth." But unlike your ordinary diets, caloric restriction involves cutting calorie intake to a drastically low level.

If we could somehow get humans to live on such CR-based diets, they could live for long periods, say 150 years, without all the illnesses and infirmities that plague old people in today's society—cancer, Alzheimer's, crippling arthritis, etc.

Most nutritionists doubt that we can actually convince people to adopt severely reduced diets of 600-700 calories per day for their entire lives, even for the lofty purpose of living for 150 years. We can't even convince people in this sugar and carbohydrate intoxicated culture, where our meals too often consist of 1200-calorie fast-food hamburgers and rich desserts, to live on a healthy intake of 1200-2000 calories per day. There is no conceivable way that modern man is going to live on 600 calories per day from meals that consist of salads.

Many see the solution to this problem in the development of drugs that mimic the net effects of CR-based diets without imposing the severe restrictions of the diets themselves. To do this, though, we must first determine why calorically-restricted diets work in the first place.

Researchers now surmise that animals and other organisms that consume less food experience less damage to the DNA inside their cells. Why? One theory, but by far not the only one, is that a cell that is provided less energy (calories) will also produce fewer free radicals, the waste products that damage it. Another is that food deprivation almost doubles concentrations of melatonin, considered a potent scavenger of free radicals, in the gastrointestinal system.[26]

Armed with such theories, companies that comprise the Immortality Industry are looking to develop drugs that mimic the effects of caloric-restriction. One company, Boston-based Biomarker Pharma, founded by biologist Stephen Spindler, is trying to find the genes that become active in animals placed on the CR diet, and then develop drugs that can target and control these genes. Another such company is GeroTech, founded by Dr. George Roth. In his talk at the Teaneck conference, Roth mentioned a handful of companies that are involved with developing various CR types of mimetics. The aforementioned Juvenon markets its Juvenon Cellular Health Supplement™, a patented combination of natural micro-nutrients, as a product that is particularly effective in protecting tissue from toxic oxidants. The company is led by a team of world-class scientists, most notably University of California at Berkley's Dr. Bruce Ames, Ph.D., winner of the United States National Science Prize and other international honors. Other companies include Irazu Biodiscovery and Lifespan Genetics, which holds a patent on a method for testing genetic changes related to caloric reduction.

These companies have a vast array of natural substances at their disposal to mimic the actions of caloric reduction. Roth mentioned that there are a number of substances that are believed to mimic the CR effect. Resveratrol is found in red wine and grapes and is marketed by many supplement companies. Metformin appears to produce a CR mimetic effect and extended lifespan in mice and is marketed by Biomarker.

Throughout 2006 and 2007, Resveratrol became a major focus in the search for the perfect CR mimetic, due in large part to a series of lab experiments over the last twenty years involving caloric restriction and increased longevity. We can expect that interest to continue well into the future.

In 1989 researchers theorized that one reason caloric restriction increases life span is because CR activates a "starvation response" in the body. The genetic machinery involved in such a response, it is believed, evolved eons ago to enable us to make it through periods of severe food shortages by retarding the rate of aging in the body. In order to free up energy to slow aging, this genetic response blocks growth and reproduction. The energy is redirected to cellular systems that limit damage from harmful "free radical" molecules and other toxins produced as metabolic byproducts in cells.

Researchers deduced that there must be something in the body's genetic structure that first senses when the body is no longer taking in as many calories and then triggers cellular changes that retard aging.

Many scientists are trying to determine what gene or gene family contains the CR off-on switch. After finding the switch, the so-called "holy grail of gerontology," the next step is to find the drug that can turn that switch on in the hope that by doing so we can prevent our bodies from developing a score of degenerative diseases in much the same way CR does in animal lab experiments.

After years of research on CR in animals, two scientists, Dr. Leonard Guarente and Dr. David Sinclair, have concluded that a family of seven genes known as SIRT, or Silent Information Regulator Genes, is that elusive switch.

Which drugs will work best when it comes to mimicking the bodily effects of caloric restriction? Sinclair's work, along with others', has convinced him that resveratrol could be the missing link in the quest for CR mimetics. In 2003 Sinclair discovered that resveratrol boosted yeast cells' life span by 70 percent via a mechanism resembling CR, and later found it boosted the life spans of fruit flies and roundworms. In 2005, Italian scientists reported that resveratrol increased the life span of short-lived fish species by 50 percent. Not only did these fish live longer, they were also more active and achieved faster swimming speeds as they aged than did untreated control fish.[27]

Sinclair went on to co-found a company, *Sirtris Pharmaceuticals*, to research and develop commercial drugs utilizing potent forms of resveratrol. Other co-founders included Richard Pops, Paul Schimmel, Christoph Westphal and Richard Aldrich. The founders have wide experience in both business and medicine. Aldrich is the head of RA Capital Management, LLC, a biotech business advisory and investment firm, and is on the board of directors of several other biotech companies, including Biogen. Additionally, Westphal, Sirtris's CEO, has both Ph.D. and M.D. degrees from Harvard Medical School. Sirtris has developed a modified form of resveratrol, called SRT501, which is now being tested in people for safety. By the beginning of 2007 Sirtris had already raised eighty-two million dollars to fund its research. Dr. Guarante went on to form his own company, Elixir, with celebrated researcher Dr. Cynthia Kenyon, to develop pharmaceutical products based on gene variants that will help to slow the aging process.[28]

Many companies are already exploiting the public's interest in resveratrol. Resveratrol Partners LLC is having a hard time keeping up with demand for its Longevinex, a resveratrol dietary supplement. Other companies marketing resveratrol supplements include Vitacost, Source Naturals Inc., and

Jarrow Formulas Inc., which produces Resveratrol Synergy.

Will resveratrol help to extend life? Newspapers reported that Harry Highkin, a retired biologist in Kailua Kona, Hawaii, credits resveratrol supplements with keeping him alive. In 2000 Highkin was diagnosed with an early form of leukemia, and began taking thirty-six capsules, equaling 1.44 grams, of resveratrol daily. He is now almost ninety years old. Three years ago Sinclair found his own research so persuasive that he began taking a resveratrol supplement.

Interestingly, the FDA has taken a laissez-faire approach to resveratrol. A 1994 law prohibits the FDA from preventing dietary supplements going on the market. The federal agency can only take regulatory action if a product is found to be unsafe.[29]

Caloric restriction not only has its adherents but also a fan club, the Caloric Restriction Society. The group's fourth annual conference was held in Tucson, Arizona, in April 2006. It featured CR researchers and dedicated practitioners, including its president Brian M. Delaney, who wrote *The Longevity Diet*, Aubrey de Grey, who I mentioned has predicted that humans can live for 5000 years, and other doctors and medical experts involved in CR and related biotechnologies.

The advent of such drugs would be a watershed event in human history. We would automatically be pushing the limits of the Superlongevity Revolution. Imagine eating a normal, healthy diet but somehow fooling your genes into thinking you're on a caloric-restriction diet. You would live to 150 years of age or more, stay physically active, remain youthful looking and have a sharp memory without the signs of cancers or stiff arteries associated with old age.

What is most striking about this technique and the benefits that are derived from it is that CR is one of the least experimental of the new breakthroughs believed to foster the next phase of Superlongevity. It works in nature, as we are only trying to mimic what we are able to achieve in the lab without the use of drugs or genetic manipulation.

According to author Ramez Naam in his book *More Than Human*, once we develop such drug therapies, people in their twenties or thirties who use them could extend their life spans by many decades. And most importantly, evidence suggests that people would be living those extra decades as young people. Their bodies would look and feel like that of a thirty year old, their minds would remain agile and flexible, and their memories would remain sharp. Their 130-150 years of life would be full, productive and healthy. David Sinclair states the research surge "promises to extend your healthy years so that a ninety year old could be disease free…" and enable you to physically feel like a much younger person. The science of aging "has split the atom," he adds. The achievement of superlongevity "is no longer an 'if' but a 'when.'"

Dr. Roth proved himself to be a true believer in the CR technology. He stated emphatically at the end of his talk that "Caloric Restriction remains the most robust and reproducible intervention for lifespan extension." He pointed out, however, that a more practical strategy for humans will be CR mimetics. This will extend the quality and quantity of life without reducing the intake of food. As Roth exclaimed, we will truly be able to "have our cake and eat it too."

NANOTECHNOLOGY: A MIRACLE IN THE MAKING

No science is more likely to advance humanity to the very threshold of near-immortality than an arcane science known as nanotechnology, the science of the very small.

Imagine incredibly small machines, computer-based robots called nanobots, traveling inside our bodies and brains, destroying pathogens and cancer cells, destroying toxins and repairing DNA errors. One such device, imagined by Dr. Robert Freitas, is the *microbivore*, a nano-sized robot that is programmed to recognize a particular disease, like the flu, or measles, and could cure that disease in a matter of minutes. Now imagine these nanobots performing functions that reverse the aging processes and radically extend our lives.

If this seems like a fanciful slice of science fiction, read on.

According to the Foresight Institute, the leading clearing house of information about this new science, nanotechnology is "a group of emerging technologies in which the structure of matter is controlled at the nanometer scale, the scale of small numbers of atoms, to produce novel materials and devices that have useful and unique properties." Nanotechnology is based on the theory that any material or object can be constructed from the "bottom up," one atom or molecule at a time.

When perfected, nanotechnology will not only extend human life expectancy but will help usher in the Superlongevity Revolution's Stage III, the "near-immortality" stage.

How small is "nano" scale? Inconceivably small is a good starting point. A meter is about as long as a yard. A *nanometer* is one-billionth of a meter, visually one millionth of a pinhead. A nanoparticle is defined as any object smaller than one hundred nanometers.

The true miracles of nanotechnology are a few decades away. We will have to develop the ability to control the behavior of atoms at the atomic level, something which we cannot do as yet. However, as was made clear by Dr. Wiley in his presentation on the subject at the "Creating Old People" conference, the breakthroughs that will make this possible are occurring at a rate that is dramatically ahead of schedule. Scientists and researchers continue to make progress in this direction. By the early 1990s IBM's research division had already shown that they could manipulate individual atoms. By employing the tip of an atomic force microscope, they were able to construct a copy of IBM's logo out of xenon atoms. We have also been able, at least in the laboratory, to form stable compounds and structures by the precise placement of atoms. Japan has a long-established nanotechnological program operating with the support of its Ministry of International Trade and Industry. Under the George W. Bush administration's prodding, the United States now has its own National Nanotechnology Initiative.[30]

Stanford has been awarded a twenty million dollar grant from the National Cancer Institute to be paid out over the next five years to integrate nanotechnology into cancer research. The goal is to slip nanoscale devices — which can be as small as one ten-thousandth of a cross-section of human hair — into living cancer cells to detect, monitor and treat cancer.[31]

Truth be told, the early interest in nanotechnology centered more on its ability to manufacture goods than nanobots and body parts. It was predicted that nanotechnology would enable engineers to model the desired molecule on a computer screen, and with the help of a nano-assembler equipped with the proper raw materials, produce any product in minutes. Ultimately we could produce larger and more complex products, such as chairs, rocket engines and computer chips out or the atoms soot or refuse. This may sound like something out of *Star Trek*, but most scientists are betting that we will get there in a few decades.

The Foresight Institute has high hopes for the application of nanotechnology to medicine. Once nanomachines are workable we should be able to fix or cure everything.

Spare Parts and Organ Replacement

Nanotechnology will enable us to reconstruct damaged organs—limbs, eyes and bones—quite effortlessly. According to scientist J. Storrs Hall, "virtually any organ will be available in an artificial form, in general with better performance than the original."

More importantly, J. Storrs Hall claims that such nanotechnologically-created organs would function more "organically" than do our mechanical artificial hearts and limbs. These would be molecular devices, not mechanical ones, and thereby work in conjunction with all aspects of the body's normal functioning. He thinks that powered organs like the heart and muscle will operate in a very straightforward way. The liver, which performs chemical functions, and those that do the "physical sorting" at the molecular level, like the kidneys and lungs, will be next in line for replacement. He even thinks that at some point nanotechnology will enable us to replace blood vessels, the nervous system or the skin.

Nanotechnology and Radical Life Extension

Possibly the most exciting applications of nanotechnology will be in the areas of diagnosing and curing diseases and also in extending life by repairing and extending the life of our cells.

The most imaginative concept emerging from the field is the nanorobot, a programmable and controllable microscale robot that is made up of nanoscale parts fabricated to nanometer precision which will allow medical doctors to carry out reconstructive and curative procedures in the human body at the cellular and molecular levels.

According to Hall and others, to attack cancer and reverse aging, nanorobots would go into individual cells and fix genetic errors. These robots will also have to repair the damage caused by free radicals and radiation.

Here's how a nanobot could help fight cancer in a person's body. Your body is equipped with something called a "p53 tumor suppressor system." Half of all cancers are caused by a malfunction of that system, so these nanobots would have to either replace the system entirely or fix what's wrong to prevent a person from developing cancer. The p53 system is only one of many cancer suppressing systems that the nanobots would have to regulate and repair.

But the greatest impact that nanotechnology will have is in extending, perhaps indefinitely, the life of the cells. There are many reasons that our cells break down and eventually cause us to age. These pathologies include cells dying off, cells quitting or turning to fat, mutations in the genes, garbage build-up inside and outside of cells and damage to extracellular structures.

So, over time, damage accumulates in cells. But over our lifetime, our cells continue to divide, regenerating themselves and thereby keeping us alive. In this process, we get rid of damaged cells, replacing them with new ones. Unfortunately, at about the time we reach seventy years of age, the cells stop dividing— what is called the "Hayflick limit" —the cells have a built-in upper limit on the number of times they will divide, a limit that is actually the body's way of protecting against cancer. And then we're left with the damaged cells, which continue to become more dysfunctional over time.

One of the major reasons that we go through the process that we call "aging" is related to this period when all we are left with are these last damaged cells.

Researchers think that we will be able to send these nanobots, these thinking "all-seeing" microscopic computers, into the cells to overcome this problem and thereby extend our lives indefinitely. There might be "census-taking" nanobots that wander around the body, taking a count of which cells are working, which are not, and killing off the bad cells. A nano-machine might extend the cell's p53 system and other such sub-systems whose major job is to repair DNA. Cell repair nano-machines would break down the garbage that has built up inside of cells and even clean up accumulation of toxins around the cells.

All of these processes would counter the negative things that happen in cells that make us age. These actions by the nanobots would thus halt the aging process.

But some theorists are going even further, presenting an application of nanotechnology that would literally set our world on its head. They think that nanotech might enable us to not only halt the aging process, but actually turn back the body's age, literally rejuvenate the body that we possess at any given point in time to an earlier, more youthful, stage.

Dr. Freitas, a leading nanotech proselytizer, claims that nanotechnology might enable us to achieve what he calls "dechronification," literally rolling back the body to a younger physical state. Dechronification will first arrest biological aging, then with three separate kinds of procedures that are performed on each one of the tissue cells in your body, literally reduce your biological age.

As a result, Freitas claims, "If you're physiologically old and don't want to be, then, for you, oldness and aging are a disease, and you deserve to be cured." If you make sure that you go for annual checkups, cellular cleanouts and major cell repair procedures, "your biological age could be restored once a year to the more or less constant physiological age that you select."

It is for this reason that we will look at not only the near-term impact of the Stage II extension of human life to the 125-150 range, but later on try to envision what life would be like if we ever achieve the possibility of living into near-immortality.

When nanotechnology has made this all possible, Freitas encourages us to rollback to the "robust physiology of your early twenties." That would be "easy to maintain and much more fun." According to Freitas, "That would push your Expected Age at Death up to around 700-900 calendar years." Not forever? Freitas cautions that even with the best nanotechnological care, we might still eventually die of accidental causes.[32]

In a 2005 interview with the website www.Nanotech.biz, Dr. Freitas was quite steadfast in his claims. "If we combine the benefits of a human physiology maintained at the level of effectiveness possessed by our bodies when we were children (e.g., dechronification), along with the ability to deal with almost any form of severe trauma (via nanosurgery)," Freitas asserted, "then there are very few diseases or conditions that cannot be cured using nanomedicine."

Is their any disease or malady impervious to the magic of nanotechnology? According to Freitas, nanorobots would have problems handling brain damage in which portions of your brain have been physically destroyed, especially if unique information has been irrevocably lost.[33]

When will this all happen? Nanomedicine will not be possible until nanotechnology makes those theoretic and practical breakthroughs that are at least few decades away. As even Freitas admits, "The development pathway will be lengthy and difficult." Significant progress will have to be made in any number of areas, including the nano-manufacturing process, before nanomedicine as I just described is available.

But when the first nanobot streaks through a patient's body, slaying viruses and rejuvenating cells, and when the first nanotech-manufactured body part is attached to a patient as a living vital organ, you will know that humankind is on the threshold of immortality.

Unlike many theorists dealing with the more "wow" areas of nanotechnology, J. Storrs Hall does not hesitate discussing the nuts and bolts of the economic aspects of new medical technology. He mentions that private and public spending on health ballooned from twenty-seven billion dollars in 1960 to 1.3 trillion dollars in 2000, and is expected to double that by 2010. In the short run, nanotechnology's research and development will be costly. By the end of the twenty-first century, though, the same kind of drastic cost reductions that are projected for manufacturing and other high-tech applications will find their way into medicine. In other words, near-immortality, when it comes, will come relatively cheap. Storr speculates that by the late twenty-first century the "cost reductions will begin to take hold and finally settle down to reasonable maintenance costs for the human machine."

Just Hang on For A Few More Decades

In his book *Nanofuture*, J. Storrs Hall states an idea which is repeated in one way or another by many in the superlongevity community. "If you can hang around for the next few decades, you can probably expect to be here for quite a while longer than that." Ray Kurzweil made nearly the same observation at an address at the World Future Society meeting in 2004. Kurzweil takes 250 supplements each day as well as weekly intravenous therapy, a regimen he claims has helped his body age only two years over the last sixteen years of his life. He is now fifty-six years old.

Our discussion of stem cell research, genetic engineering, caloric restriction and the new wonder drugs indicates that one or more of those fields will discover miracles that will enable us to live possibly indefinite lives. Proponents of each field are sure that their specific field has the final answer. The Foresight Institute claims that regardless of their efficacy in curing illnesses and extending life, they cannot equal the potential of nanotechnology to "unlock the indefinite extension of human health and the expansion of human abilities."

Based on the available information, there is overwhelming evidence that one if not all of these therapies, including caloric restriction, will soon enable all of us to live very long and disease free lives. Therefore, parents, as well as our education institutions, should be preparing those in their teens and twenties for life in Stage II of the Superlongevity Revolution.

chapter three

The Second
Wind

Even if only a few of the breakthroughs in areas such as nanotechnology, caloric restriction, genetic engineering and the other scientific fields actually deliver on their potential, we will be living for decades longer than we are now.

As a society and as individuals, we have done very little preparation for this new era conditioned by superlongevity. In the next several chapters we will consider how the radical extension of the human life span will profoundly impact all aspects of our lives, including the family, marriage, work, leisure and education and what should be done to ready us for this breakthrough.

Most of us devote a large portion of our lives to our careers as well as all the education and training that it takes to prepare for and stay current in our fields. This chapter will look at how superlongevity will literally redefine the very nature of what we mean by the term career.

Until recently, most people have followed fairly conventional and predictable work and career patterns. A person trained for a career for a set period of time (e.g. college, technical training), worked in that career for thirty to forty years and then retired. Many people moved to Florida, Arizona or North Carolina. At any service center on the Garden State Parkway in New Jersey during the day hundreds of seniors, mostly retired, are eating and relaxing. In a continued ritual they stay for a half hour and re-board a bus. Most likely they are going to Atlantic City for an afternoon of gambling, strolling on the boardwalk and dining. Many of these people are in their late sixties and seventies, and are living the type of retirement that has become an accepted, and expected, phase in American life cycles.

However, superlongevity will change many of the old rules. If you retire at fifty-five, you might expect to live thirty or forty more years. The idea of simply pursuing a life of leisure for that length of time is unacceptable to many people. And in the near future, when at age fifty-five we have eighty or one hundred years more ahead of us to be lived as healthy, physically young people, the idea of a complete withdrawal from the world of work and productivity will be unfathomable.

In the future, people anticipating careers spanning nine or ten decades will forge a whole new approach to their work lives. They might start their work lives in the conventional fashion, choosing to get their initial training, acquiring college degrees and then graduate degrees, and then start their careers. But this is where I think the career paradigm shift will emerge. At some point in this initial career, a person might take a job sabbatical to refresh and recharge the mental and psychological batteries or upgrade skills. He or she might then return to current jobs and fields, but all the time envisioning and planning for their next career. Toward the end of this career, at age forty-five or fifty, people might take career hiatuses in which they acquire skills for their next career, as well as pursue personal interests. People might take exotic trips such as a fishing expedition to the Amazon, for example. This hiatus might be followed by full time schooling or retraining, at which point the person will re-career. There are clear indications that many people reaching this stage will choose to try entrepreneurship, a choice which is made ever easier by increasingly user-friendly computer and information technology.

This process will unfold in sequences varying greatly from person to person. However, we can say with reasonable certainty that retirement as we know it today will seem like a relic of a quaint past. (See Chart 2)

Not only the concept of retirement will be changed, superlongevity will affect the career choices of individuals at every stage of the life cycle. Knowing that their "careers" might extend for fifty years or more, younger careerists, even those not yet ready for full-time employment, will be encouraged to experiment with unique career patterns. More young people will opt to not only attend college but also pursue post-graduate education in order to train for the complex jobs required in our advanced society. These younger workers will also realize that superlongevity affords them the luxury of time to pursue advanced education

The Changing Career Landscape

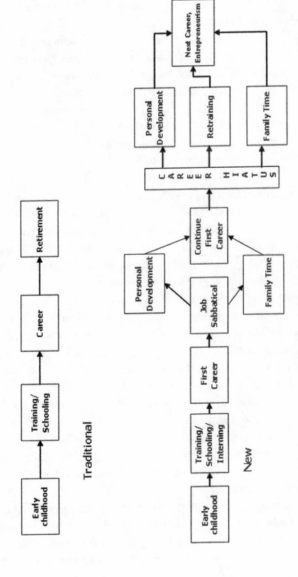

Traditional

New

well into their late twenties. It will become the norm for those in their forties and fifties to withdraw from the labor force, return to school and start a whole new career. This type of strategy makes perfect sense for people expecting to spend another 30 years or more in the work force.

In my research, I have encountered many people whose unique work histories presage the way future generations will structure their careers. One man with whom I spoke, a United States Air Force intelligence expert who had joined the service at age eighteen, comfortably retired from the service as a Master Sergeant at thirty-eight, with a very good retirement income and benefits package. However, he had no desire to discontinue working altogether. While in the Air Force he had gotten seriously involved in stamp collecting, availing himself of service-based travels to amass fairly unique and hard-to-find stamps from around the globe. He began buying and selling these items over the internet as a hobby. After his twenty year stint with the Air Force, he started to pursue this hobby full-time, and realized that this little avocation could not only provide some extra income but, if he wanted to, invest the time, become a very lucrative small business. Even though he took regular jobs for a while, he soon realized that he found the life and rewards of full time entrepreneurship much more exciting, engrossing and rewarding.

This pattern of "non-retirement" consistently emerged in my research. One former executive I spoke to, a CFO (chief financial officer) at Lucent Technologies, turned down lucrative offers to manage and consult. After a lifetime of work at a desk and computer screen, he decided to turn one of his avocations into a new career and set himself up as a personal handyman. Many of his early customers were former colleagues from the communications industry. Another communications industry executive semi-retired, followed his dream of becoming a park ranger on a golf course for a year or so and then returned to the corporate world as a "new business developer." A former Bell Atlantic executive I spoke to, after tiring of the corporate rat race, at age fifty-five decided to pursue an academic career as business professor. Happily, he was eventually granted tenure.

I have also come across numerous people who after they retired found themselves inadvertently lured back into their fields. Roy, an Assistant Principal I know in the New York City school system, retired with full benefits and a generous retirement at age fifty-five after thirty years of service. A year or so later he was contacted by a company to help lead seminars and classes for adults who desired to be certified as school teachers in the very system from which he just retired. He now works in this program on a periodic basis, choosing which days and hours he will work. The NYC school system really wishes that baby boomer teachers and administrators such as Roy would never leave their jobs in the first place—there are simply not enough qualified professionals to fill positions the boomers are vacating. I find it ironic that Roy is now teaching in a program established to train people to replace himself and other boomers who have left the system. The greater irony is that many of the fledgling teachers Roy is mentoring toward their teacher proficiency exams are themselves ex-managers, executives and health care workers nearing retirement and looking to re-career as public school teachers.

Commentators have mentioned that we are creating a new kind of career stage in America and elsewhere: the "not-quite-retirement" phase. More and more people are considering it undesirable to go directly from full-time work to full-time leisure. Thus a new category of employment has arisen, the so-called bridge job, a term economists use to describe part-time or full-time jobs typically held for less than ten years following full-time careers. The Center on Aging and Work at Boston College reported in a 2005 working paper that one-half to two-thirds of workers are now taking such "bridge jobs" before fully retiring, leading them to predict that the number of workers 65 and up is expected to increase 117 percent by 2025. [34]

As people begin to navigate their ways through dramatically extended life spans there will be many attempts to label this unknown territory of ages fifty or sixty onwards. In a sense, the very labels we append to these extra, active years tells us as much about our hopes and impressions of what those years are supposed to be like as they do about any objective description of those years.

Parade Magazine conducted a survey in 2006 that provides a panoply of the conflicting images of this new life phase. *Parade*, along with the Harvard School of Public Health and the MetLife Foundation asked readers to come up with a name for the post-sixty stage of life.

Perhaps a portent of a coming transformation of the later years is the fact that their survey respondents summarily rejected the label "senior citizen." Harvard's Susan Moses explained that "the old language of aging no longer reflects people's active lives."

One label that people seem to agree on is "seasoned citizens." As one fifty-two year old said, "Seasoned because the varying experiences of a lifetime — both sweet and sour—make us what we are."

The respondents to the study not only provided labels for this new stage of life. They also revealed the rich complexity of life activities today among those in their fifties, sixties and beyond. The vast majority reported only good news about their current quality of life, repeatedly proclaiming themselves in the prime years of their lives. Not surprisingly, many of the survey respondents independently chose the term "prime time". for the twenty-year span between sixty and eighty. A seventy-three year-old Berkeley, California Chinese-American who spends his time practicing ballroom dancing and sharpening his speaking skills at his local Toastmasters Club, said he was reveling in the "Age of Dignity." He reminded us that the Chinese culture emphasizes venerating the elderly, a cultural practice we in the West ought to adopt, especially in the face of the demographic changes about to wash over our society. He is doing his part to foment such change, remarking that "I'm hard at work teaching my fellow American septuagenarians to revel in their age of dignity."

Most of the terms readers suggested reflect people's belief that their older years are filled with activity and new opportunities— "Life 102," "The Third Half," "Geri-Actives" and one which I particularly liked, the "Re-Generation." People reported on the activities that made up the personal development of their lives, including skydiving, studying new languages, traveling, gardening, horse training and mastering new skills that once were considered too time-consuming when most of their activities centered around earning a living and raising children. Many of them realize that they are taking part in a great experiment, creating the new lifestyle of the radically expanding life span. As one seasoned citizen remarked, "It's my practice to present an image that encourages younger females to say, 'That's what I want to be when I grow up.'" One 17 year old that responded to the study suggested that people in their sixties - eighties be called the "Re-Invented Generation," because "they are participating in activities I would never even dream of them doing and are reinventing how older people live."

The respondents to the *Parade* survey spoke passionately and with one voice on the issue of public and private attitudes regarding the later stages of the life cycle. The public and media at large, as well as the seasoned citizens, must be re-educated about the benefits of living into advanced ages, especially in our youth-oriented society. A seventy-four year old woman from San Diego, stated that "I ski, swim and stand on my head in yoga, and I'm frustrated by society's attitude of putting the word 'still' in front of these activities."

Several talked about now having the opportunities to "give back," refuting the idea heard too often that the older generation is busy "spending my children's inheritance," as one nasty bumper sticker implies. Terms survey respondents offered, "longevity," which includes the stem of the word "give," and "Legacy Launchers," reflect this sentiment.

All this activity is actually good for you. As one seventy-three year old describes it, "when you give, the years drop away, you beam, and your heart is full to bursting. Isn't that what life is all about?"

We can only hope that as people live to ever-greater ages, their answer to his question is a decisive "yes."

BABY BOOMERS SHOW THE WAY

Even as we debate the terminology and definitions of these new stages in the human life span, society is actively trying to adjust to the social, economic, and cultural impacts of the radically extended life span.

Since the oldest baby boomers have turned sixty years of age in 2006, the point in life which has been considered "retirement age," the media has been filled with stories about whether boomers would choose to retire en masse, and what impact that would have on Social Security, Medicare and society in general.

By coincidence, two critical demographic events are unfolding simultaneously. First, a massive cohort of the United States and Western population, the baby boomers, is moving into the later part of the life cycle. Second, they are doing so at the time when science and technology are dramatically expanding the upward ceiling of the human life cycle. Therefore, a disproportionately large part of the total population is aging just in time to live extraordinarily long lives.

The boomers always seem to find a way to make themselves the center of attention. Born from 1946 to 1964, the seventy-eight million members of the baby boom generation have made their presence felt at every stage of their lives. They crowded the kindergartens and grade schools in the 1950s and 1960s, overwhelmed college dorms and classrooms throughout the 1960s and 1970s and then supplied American businesses with the largest and most educated group of employees in United States history. Often, they caused radical political and cultural upheavals.

The evolving work and retirement patterns of baby boomers, the first generation that will experience superlongevity en masse, should provide many clues to how careers and post-career life will evolve over the next decades. If current boomer behavior is any indication, we are in for some major changes. They already are transforming what we called the "retirement" phase from one whose principle activity is leisure to one which emphasizes the pursuit of new interests, avocations and careers.

In an article that I wrote about baby boomers in business which appeared in the Christian Science Monitor and other United States papers, I brought up the big question that businesses and others are asking: "Will they stay or will they go?" [35]

Businesses, corporations and school systems realize that they are facing a looming manpower problem if a sizeable number of the seventy-eight million baby boomers who are eligible for retirement decide to quit. The replacement group, the Gen-Xers, number only forty-six million. Boomer retirements have been blamed for shortages of skilled contractors, electricians, plumbers, accountants, nurses and engineers. Over the next decade, school districts and universities will need 2.2 million new teachers, administrators and librarians. The Boomers are nearing retirement age just as the thriving United States economy creates a greater, not a lesser, need for this generation's bodies and minds. The United States economy is generating two million or more jobs each year, driving the United States unemployment rate to historic lows.[36]

Looking closer at what this all means, the good news for United States companies is that 76 percent of boomers say they intend to keep on working and earning, according to Merrill Lynch's "The New Retirement Survey." The bad news for their current employers is that the boomers expect to exit from their current job or career at around age sixty-four and then launch into an entirely new job or career. We will look at some of those options later in this chapter and elsewhere. [37]

Jersey Central Power and Light (JCP&L), a major energy supplier in the northeast U.S., had to act quickly in the face of major baby boomer retirements from its ranks. The company was concerned that it would not be able to replace the older electrical utility workers. The workers in these physically demanding jobs face odd hours and dangerous working conditions, such as climbing thirty foot utility poles in nasty weather with safety gear strapped to their bodies.

In order to attract young people into these jobs, JCP&L launched a college training program in 2003. The strategy, pioneered by Public Service Electric & Gas is helping utilities in the state hire qualified workers at a time when young people are turned off by jobs such as lineman and substation technical worker which they view as "blue-collar" occupations low in skill and by implication, low-status. In reality, such jobs require a great deal of intelligence as well as physical acumen, and to succeed in those types of jobs, workers must be trained in math and computer science.

The JCP&L program enrollees spend two and one half days a week at the Phillipsburg training center working on simulated electrical substations, climbing poles, and learning about utility equipment and safety requirements.

PSE&G, New Jersey's biggest gas and electric utility, faced a similar problem in 2002. The company started a program in response to a startling reality—between 2007 and 2012 PSE&G projects it will lose 27 percent of its work force, according to program manager Lina Hollman.

PSE&G runs a college-training program in conjunction with community colleges in Passaic, Middlesex, Mercer and Essex counties. The program has produced 38 graduates of its two-year utility program that were then hired. Both utilities' programs are extremely rigorous and attempt to develop a more well-rounded employee who is technically skilled, computer literate and familiar with math. Graduates of the PSE&G program must serve a fourteen week internship and are paid a minimum of twenty-one dollars per hour—after six months this increases by approximately five dollars an hour. At JCP&L, fourteen people are scheduled to graduate in 2008, and another eight trainees already have been hired by the utility.

While both companies are seeing success from their programs, it is not enough. Due to current and projected boomer retirement rates the companies are so short of trained employees that they will need many more trainee graduates to keep the manpower pipeline stocked.

In order to generate interest in the utility training programs, both companies realized that they would have to begin the recruitment process at the high school level. In the colleges, even at two-year institutions, many students are already committed to a major or career. To attract better-skilled candidates company recruiters worked with high school guidance counselors and vocational schools, trying to identify college-bound students with the potential to master advanced technology and computers.

The companies are not restricting their recruitment to the conventional 18-23 year old male college student. The first female to graduate PSE&G's program was a thirty-five year old Newark, New Jersey mother of three who was attracted to the program because it provided her the opportunity to get on-the-job training while she pursued her college degree.

If these utilities follow a similar format to the New York City schools example I mentioned earlier, the positions of instructor and trainer in the utility training programs may be filled with the Baby Boomers the students are training to replace.[38]

To stem boomer defections, employers must first begin to understand why these people might choose to retire? The most obvious reason is because they can. Social Security benefits and company pensions often accompanied by lifetime health benefits and supplemented by Medicare, as well as the 401(k)s that now total a staggering $1.8 trillion waiting to be claimed and spent are all making it easier for people to retire. Add to this mix the lure of a very attractive post-work lifestyle. This twenty-first century "golden age of retirement" offers seniors fun-filled round-the-world cruises and "active adult communities" featuring year-round golf, tennis and other sports. (In the next chapter we will look at how these activities will morph into other pursuits.)

Plus, boomers are more likely to view retirement as a normal lifestyle choice as they see their friends, siblings, spouses and co-workers deciding to pursue the post-work good life. Exacerbating this situation is the fact that today's "lean and mean" corporate climate has bred a high level of worker dissatisfaction with their jobs and their companies. According to Gallup surveys, worker morale at United States companies has never been so low.

Organizations should use the Boomer retirement dilemma as a practice-run for how to retain employees as a whole new career paradigm. As I mentioned earlier, careers in the Superlongevity Era will take on a whole new look. People will look to "re-career" probably sooner rather than later. Therefore companies hoping to retain older valued employee will be up against not only their workers' wishes to go into retirement but also their desire to re-career by starting their own business.

Organizations will have to be extremely innovative as they endeavor to retain valued employees. For beginners, they should strike the terms "retirement" as well as "early retirement" from corporate vocabulary. Companies should send clear signals to their older workers that they are part of the organizations' future plans. One way is to include older workers in their training programs—surprisingly, recent surveys show that workers fifty-five and over are receiving only one-third the training hours that those forty-five to fifty-four are receiving. Business Week reported that several companies, such as Con Edison and United Technologies, make training and education available to older workers to increase retention. [39]

To persuade as many boomers as possible to remain in the work force, American and other western companies could emulate Japanese companies and encourage older workers to stay by offering them bonuses and flexible time schedules.

Japan has had to be innovative to keep workers form retirement because it is facing worker shortages caused by its rapidly aging population and plummeting birth rates. The proportion of people over sixty-five years old will reach 20 percent in 2006, up from 10 percent just twenty years ago. Japan's sixty-five and over population is projected to be 35 percent as fewer younger Japanese choose to start families. Nevertheless Japan's worker crisis is just slightly ahead of many Western countries in being forced to deal with this demographic issue. Italy will be in the same position in 2006, and Germany will get there by 2009. The United States will not reach that figure until 2036.

We need to plan how we will handle this problem. We can learn from Japan's response to a shrinking and aging work force. For one thing, the Japanese government passed a law in 2005 that requires companies by 2013 to raise their retirement age to sixty-five from sixty or rehire their retired workers. At this point companies violating the law face only "administrative guidance," not penalties. Of course, if companies in general do not comply, lawmakers could add strength to this law. However, trends in workplace hiring suggest that the law might not be necessary to convince companies to hire seniors. Demographics are already pushing Japanese companies, especially in the manufacturing sector, to find innovative ways to retain these valuable workers sixty and over.

One company, Kato Manufacturing Co., facing a dearth of working-age people for its factories, advertised in the local paper for keen people over sixty to apply. To Kato's surprise, over one hundred candidates applied, even though most of the jobs required the applicants to work on weekends. In order to retain older workers, manufacturers like Sanwa Electric Co. introduced various technologies to reduce the physical strain older workers might experience in a manufacturing plant. Akita Kogyo Co., an auto-parts maker near Toyota Motor Corp.'s headquarters in central Japan, decided that at least half the workers needed to work on a new project should be over fifty-five. It rigged its factories with elderly-friendly devices that minimized the amount of heavy lifting required of these "senior" workers. In order to retain their older workers, Kobe Steel Ltd. and other Japanese companies are offering them guaranteed contracts for a year or more.[40]

Japan's efforts to retain older workers have willing partners in its aging employees, whose work ethic envisions labor not as a dreaded obligation but as a road to self-fulfillment. One star engineer, Toshio Kimura of the Mitutoyo Corporation, takes pride in his unique skills in operating precision-instruments machinery. Mr. Kimura proclaims that "no one else can do this anywhere in the world—that's why they let me stay. I want to work till I'm eighty."

The response of the boomers to efforts to retain them will reveal much about how people facing ever-longer lives will navigate their way through their work and careers. As we will see, in this new Superlongevity Era, nothing, not our lives, careers, marriages, or our so-called retirement, will be as it was.

TIME OUT—WORK SABBATICALS AND CAREER HIATUSES

Is it possible to work at one job, company, or career path for a century or more? My guess is that most people would answer no, regardless of how much they like their present jobs or company. In the future, as the Superlongevity Revolution matures and people live, and work longer, citizens of the *Ageless Nation* will routinely take job sabbaticals and career hiatuses.

Sabbaticals are a tradition in academia. Tenured professors are offered the opportunity to take off a semester or two at half or three-quarters salary to pursue research, write books or academic articles.

This feature has been used by non-academic institutions as well as a way to retain and refresh employees. Companies experimented with such sabbaticals during the booming late 1990s, but the idea faded during the subsequent economic downturn. It is returning again, especially at creative companies that rely on their employees to generate ideas. Publishing, high technology, advertising and consulting companies are more sabbatical-friendly than manufacturing or finance firms. For example, Doubleday, Nike and Intel offer this option.

A 2005 *Wall Street Journal* article described a director of publicity for Bertelsmann's Doubleday Broadway Publishing Group who took a six week sabbatical to travel to Mexico and Costa Rica and relax at home with her children. For some time she had been thinking about doing a new, more responsible job at the company. According to this woman the time off cemented her wish for the new job. "The sabbatical gave me confidence. I was also able to let go of the work I was doing. It was a big deal for me." Upon her return she launched a new imprint at Doubleday, where she serves as publisher.

In a recent study of about 390 employers conducted by the Society for Human Resource Management, Alexandria, Va., only 6 percent said they offer paid sabbaticals, while another 17 percent claimed that they offer unpaid sabbaticals. A significant number of these employers are in the government and nonprofit sectors.[41]

But I predict this will change as the life span continues to increase. The reason is simple. When people could look forward to between a thirty-five and forty year career, it made sense that they planned to spend it with a single employer. In fact, many viewed this as desirable option. Companies like AT&T and IBM prided themselves on possessing a cadre of longtime employees who were loyal, understood the company and its business.

However, since work careers may soon extend to eighty or one hundred years, it is more likely that people will start their employment at Company X but will be aware that the chances they will finish their careers at the same company are slim. The company might not even survive that long. The reality of a century-long career will change perceptions about worker's relationship to a particular company. Since the employee will be aware that his relationship to the company is temporary, he might be prone to leave for another employer or even another career, quicker than he might in today's relatively short-lived career environment.

Hence, companies that want to retain experienced and well-trained professionals for as long as possible will have to somehow reduce employees desire to move on. Job sabbaticals are a one way to do so. This sabbatical could be paid time off, with a commitment on the part of the employee to return to work at the company after the down-time period is over.

This would be attractive to older employees who already have worked for many years and grown weary. They may think that retiring or leaving the company is the only way to take a break from the daily and monthly grind.

The company sabbatical can fulfill the person's need for an extended time off. During the sabbatical they can pursue various activities, enjoy their leisure or further their education. Companies are beginning to realize that employees consider time as important a commodity as money.

A sabbatical possibly can be a very good antidote to burnout that occurs on jobs. Canadian psychologist Sharyn Salsberg Ezrin studied fourteen executives who took sabbaticals at various points in their careers. According to Ezrin, all thought their experiences valuable. In fact, they felt that the sabbaticals recharged them for the next leg of their careers. Ezrin says that the experience of change from their work routines, what she labels "sanctioned freedom," enabled them to renew and reinvent themselves. They came back to their jobs more enthusiastic about the job and the company itself.

One subject of her study, a corporate lawyer and former Conservative parliamentarian, used the three months afforded by his firm's mid-career sabbatical program to write a novel of political intrigue. Although the novel did not hit the best sellers list, the fact that he completed and published the novel led to a tremendous feeling of accomplishment. He came back to his practice refreshed, with a sense of renewal. Another corporate lawyer was tempted by the impending sabbatical of his wife, a university professor, to ask his law firm for a few months off to "recharge." He was shocked when a managing partner actually granted his wish. He and his wife went to Paris for few months. He enrolled in an intensive French course offered in Paris by the Alliance Francaise, and also took the time to take numerous photos as a record of his experience of living in another country. Taking those photos, he adds, was an essential part of his being recharged, focusing him on the experience and helping him look at it in a more intense way.

According to Ezrin, often family members were not just willing supporters of the sabbatical experience but also participants in the experience. The job sabbatical became a way for the family to strengthen its bonds. So often employees, especially managers and professionals, see their relationship to their spouse and children suffer because of the amount of hours, and years, they must devote to job and career. Some employees no doubt will choose to leave the company rather than see their family bonds weaken and possibly disappear. The sabbatical seems like such an easy solution to this dilemma—give the employee some time to refresh family ties. A Random House VP spent his four-week sabbatical with his family, returning to his job "with a renewed sense of enthusiasm," he says.

In Canada, companies such as Sun Media and McDonalds Restaurants of Canada Ltd. offer top performing employees corporate sabbaticals. United States companies such as Procter & Gamble, allow employees to take an unpaid sabbatical with full benefits of up to twelve weeks after only one year of employment, and every seven years after that.[42] At Newsweek, a unit of Washington Post Co., reporters and editors are eligible for six months of sabbatical at half-salary after fifteen years. At Random House full-time North American employees who have logged at least ten years of service are eligible for a four week sabbatical, and after twenty years, five weeks. Employees are expected to take their sabbatical during the qualifying year. At Intel Corp. of Santa Clara, Calif., which has offered paid sabbaticals to its United States staff since 1981, employees get eight weeks for every seven years of service.[43]

What also will become commonplace as a result of the Superlongevity Revolution is not just a job sabbatical but something more drastic, a career hiatus. People will literally stop working for a year or more, perhaps at age forty or fifty or even later, not so much to refresh and renew themselves for their current careers or jobs but to begin the process of re-careering, choosing to enter completely new lines of work.

As the life span increases, people will be planning the desired course of their lives in fairly orderly fashions. However, each of these life plans will be subject to change. The way I envision the career hiatus process occurring is: In many cases, people will make conscious decisions to leave their jobs, know how long their hiatus will last, and have good ideas of their next career moves. They will have their educational options pretty well scoped out, and know exactly how long the training for the new career will take. In some cases, a person might imagine they are retiring, and after a period get tired of their "self-development" (which I will deal with at length in the next chapter), and return to work. Or, they might simply be pursuing a personal-development activity, (such as playing in a band), and discover they like this new activity so much that they now want to make it their next career.

I had the opportunity to get a profound insight into how the extended lifespan is already changing the manner in which people approach their careers and their "re-careers," when I visited friends living on Callawassie Island in South Carolina. This beautiful island, located fifteen miles south of Beaufort and eighteen miles north of Hilton Head Island, is a supposed retirement community that brochures claim offers a "pleasant, serene living experience" along with activities that include golf and tennis. Spacious luxury homes ring the island, in the center of which is a spacious golf course.

For many, Callawassie Island embodies the very essence of a retirement paradise. But even here, we see how the Superlongevity Revolution is already reshaping work, careers and retirement.

One of the people with whom I spoke was a former accountant. He retired to the island in his late fifties, absolutely positive that his days would be filled with golf, tennis and other leisure activities. His wife, an investment banker, followed him into retirement on the island a year or so after he moved down there. One of his goals in retirement was to write a novel about the antebellum South. What better place to do this than in this locale. He researched his novel in the various libraries and historical societies ringing the nearby Savannah and Charleston areas. Eventually, he learned so much about the history of Savannah that on a lark, he took a temporary position as a tour guide for the city, shepherding Yankees and other visitors on a whirlwind historical tour of this venerable old city. Over time, he developed his own tour guide business, which will grow as large as he wants. He is still working furiously on his novel, when he can get some time away from his new enterprise.

His wife is involved in community work, serving as an adviser to a local hospital. Many of the newcomers to Callawassie with whom I spoke had similar stories of pursuing one form or another of paid and unpaid community service. One person I met who "retired" there after a highly successful management career in telecommunications became a volunteer in Beaufort's literacy program and spent many hours teaching adult males to read. He also served on Beaufort's town board helping the city prepare for future development of their businesses and tourist industry.

Many of the denizens of the island come from the financial field, so even as they try to transition to retirement they somehow find themselves drawn back to their fields. Or, more precisely, their fields continue to pull them back. The skills and expertise that these people have developed in fields such as accounting, finance, management, communications and marketing are still valued by the business community. While they might have left their jobs and fields, their former employers, contacts, and clients still want to utilize their talents. So the "retirees" are constantly un-retired, at least temporarily, by companies that employ them as consultants and advisers. I found this to be the case with many of the individuals I met there—the world was simply not ready to let them go.

The more talented you are, the less chance you have to "retire" in the sense that we understand that concept today. Yes, you might choose to quit your job, but increasingly, whether you know it or not, you are merely on a career hiatus. Thanks to the Superlongevity Revolution, people at sixty, seventy and beyond will increasingly be physically and mentally "young." And such healthy mentally agile seventy year olds will be drawn back by companies needing their invaluable expertise derived from decades of training and work experience. I knew a nuclear engineer who assumed he had retired when he resigned from his company at sixty-five. He soon was asked back as a consultant on a per diem basis. After a few years of almost non-stop per-diem work, much of which involved fairly extensive travel, he finally informed the company that he was terminating this "temporary" consulting arrangement. Needless to say, the company still periodically inquires into his availability for other assignments.

The media has already detected the early signs of the trend for executives to take a career hiatus. The *Wall Street Journal* quotes Kelvin Thompson, a senior partner at search firm Heidrick & Struggles, who asserts that taking a career break "is no longer considered a showstopper." According to Thompson, "There's still a stigma associated with it in some areas, but I think that stigma is more envy sometimes nowadays." It is becoming more common place and acceptable for executives to essentially quit their jobs and take off a few months or longer, often without knowing where their next job is coming from. They are doing this for a number of reasons, including corporate restructuring and plain old burnout.

The article discusses one executive, Ms. Trudel, who decided to cut loose from the business world for almost a year. She was suffering from burnout and had the money set aside for this job hiatus. Although she did some consulting during those months, she used this time away from her usual career to meet two goals. First, she wanted to pursue personal interests that she had largely ignored during her career. The other goal was to quiz members of her extensive network of former colleagues and recruiters about what kinds of jobs she might find more satisfying.

During her hiatus she visited Belize and Guatemala, took Spanish lessons, went to the theater and the ballet, joined a book club, became involved with her church and started working out regularly. She even became a docent at the Metropolitan Museum of Art.

Realizing how much she missed the arts, she decided to take a temporary position, a public relations assignment at New York's Wallace Foundation, which supports cultural and educational programs. She fell in love with the job and after her three-month assignment ended, she took a permanent position. Granted, positions in this field do not pay as much as those in mainstream corporate America do (she makes about 40 percent less than in her prior job), but she feels the payoff in personal satisfaction more than makes up for the loss in monetary returns. Plus, she works fewer hours and now has more time for other interests.

Some high-profile executives have made changing careers more acceptable. Brenda Barnes voluntarily left PepsiCo Inc. and six years later took a top executive job at Sara Lee Corp. Ann Fudge took a two-year hiatus from Kraft Foods Inc. and then assumed command of advertising firm WPP Group PLC's Young & Rubicam Brands.

The *Wall Street Journal* article also described some people who were dissatisfied with their jobs, but too busy working to take time to decide what they really wanted to do with their lives. A senior vice president of a large nonprofit health plan, frustrated by his company's management hierarchy, quit his job to scope out his next career move without being distracted by the buzz of the workaday world. But he was 59 and worried that he might not get another job. So he hired an executive coach, specifically to help him analyze what he disliked about his old job. He also took time to relax—he started building a pond in his backyard, took pottery classes and studied Tai Chi. Having the opportunity to reflect on the past, he realized that what he disliked most about his former job was his lack of authority and inability to make final decisions. The career coach fortunately had connections inside the health-care industry, and the ex-senior VP landed a job as CEO of a start-up company which was offering a new kind of health plan for those eligible for both Medicare and Medicaid.

At present a career hiatus has an element of risk, especially for those nearing retirement. Even our Sr. VP was asked by the start-up why he was "out of work." His answer—that he quit because he was not satisfied with the organization's culture—was acceptable to the recruiters and the company itself.

Some fields ask few questions about why their applicants are switching jobs and even careers. The real estate industry is one of them. They expect that their sales associates will have been employed in numerous fields unrelated to either sales or real estate. A recent news story described a typical sales staff at Coldwell Banker, one of the oldest real estate companies in the United States. One sales associate was a former doctor, an OB/GYN specialist who claims that the long hours spent in her former career prepared her well for the non-stop activity of buying and selling homes. The company boasts that on their sales teams you can find people who used to be lawyers, doctors, business owners, teachers, accountants, or recent college grads. [44]

In the future in an environment in which people work a century or more, it will be normal for people to pursue careers, take job hiatuses, re-career, train, retrain, etc. So there is less likelihood that any hiring agent would ever ask an applicant who has already succeeded in two previous careers and/or positions "why did you quit your last position." Multiple career patterns will be the norm for everyone coming through that agent's door. [45]

AGELESS NATION AND OUR ENTREPRENEURIAL FUTURE

When we speak of careering and re-careering, I am not necessarily referring to working for a series of major corporations. Rather, I am speaking of a new mixture of old style employment along with the brave new world of entrepreneurship.

My first experience with eBay occurred in the late 1990s; at that time that tickets for the NY Yankees baseball club started to become very scarce. Many of the tickets to games were held by season ticket holders and unavailable to those just wanting to see a single game. I heard that ticket holders were auctioning tickets on the eBay website. I registered for free and bid what I thought was a fair price for the tickets. I eventually won the tickets at a bid considerably above the tickets' list price, sent the owner a check, received the tickets, and voila, I was at a Yankee game. What a wonderful system, I thought, for moving goods. And what an easy way for the owner of those tickets to make money!

Since then, eBay has mushroomed into an industry. In fact, in many ways eBay is an important component of the economy. Once a mere auction site, it is now a place for millions of people to become entrepreneurs, selling goods and services in specialized "stores" which exist for the most part in cyberspace.

One of the strengths of eBay is that it enables the citizens of *Ageless Nation* to establish and operate businesses with almost no investment, no particular inventory and even very little business skill. What he or she must learn is how to navigate through and utilize the eBay system, a skill which any person can acquire either through books such as *eBay for Dummies* or one day courses eBay runs throughout the United States.

While people of all ages are using eBay and other online marketplace sites, this has been a special boon for people age fifty-five and older. Some are using eBay to supplement their pensions and savings. But for many, it has become a creative outlet—after they discover their innate entrepreneurial talents, they are hooked. However, eBay is more than a sales tool—it is a way for folks to develop new friendships around the products they sell. For instance, if you are trafficking in baseball memorabilia, you certainly want to follow up a sale with an e-mail or chat discussing baseball history, even your old memories of the game.

This new entrepreneurship is an early indication of the shape and tenor of what work life will be like in the Superlongevity Era. Work will be valued both for its monetary value and for its intrinsic value. In her *Wall Street Journal* article "And the Opening Bid Is... The eBay auction site is giving the fifty-five-plus crowd a chance to flex its entrepreneurial muscles," Mylene Mangalindan described a man who retired in December 1999 from his rare-coin company. At first he did what many think will be their main retirement activity, playing golf. Just for fun he began trading his leftover coins on eBay. After depleting his coin supply he started selling other collectibles. By that time he was hooked, and started buying fresh merchandise to sell. This entrepreneur, who lives in Marina del Rey, now says that he would rather load images on eBay than play golf, the activity he thought would be his main avocation after "retiring." He sounds fulfilled when he states that "I'm doing what I want to do."

A 2006 internal eBay study found that one out of five United States eBay users is fifty-five or older. An AC Nielsen survey revealed that more than 250,000 United States eBay sellers claim they retired early specifically to become eBay-based merchants.

Many people literally stumbled into this new entrepreneurial opportunity. A boyfriend of one of my students awhile back had bought for the princely sum of five dollars a box of records at a church-run garage sale. He wanted only a few of the vinyl relics he purchased, and decided to try to sell the rest. Someone suggested he use E-bay as a selling tool. He quickly taught himself how to take photos of the records and post the items on eBay for auction. Imagine his surprise, no, his absolute shock, when anonymous bidders started a global bidding war for some of his records that boosted their "value" into the hundreds of dollars.

Of course, trading on eBay and other such sites requires technological savvy—becoming part nerd will help in the competitive world of online business.

Certainly, one has to master the Internet as well as eBay's internal cybernetic mechanics. According to recent reports, buyers and sellers are using the Internet and other new communication modalities to best their competitors. These days, eBayers now go to garage sales and flea markets, the favorite haunt for online sellers searching for fresh merchandise, armed with cell phones. When they see a product they like, they phone their spouses at home and tell them to compare its price on eBay. The eBayer might even have a handheld internet device to check the price on the spot. To ensure that they can hit as many as thirty to fifty garage sales in a day, they use their car's global positioning device to direct them from place to place.[46]

And for those seniors in countries which are not particularly friendly to entrepreneurial activity, eBay can be a lifesaver. *Business Week* reported that thousands of Europeans are using eBay to do an end run around decades of state-imposed regulations and anti-entrepreneurial thinking. The magazine profiled a company that was started by a family that started buying and selling ski equipment on eBay just as a way to make extra cash. Eventually they found themselves selling ski equipment all over the world and now find themselves having to expand their warehouse capacity. AC Nielsen International Research reports that 64,000 Germans will earn at least 25 percent of their income from selling collectibles, furniture, electronics and more on line. Germans also make good customers, buying $6 billion in merchandise on eBay in 2004.[47]

Certainly, eBay and other such online auction and selling sites will transform the so-called post-career phase in peoples' lives. It will more than likely tempt many to leave their corporate, education, and government jobs long before standard retirement age--—employers beware.

Even non-eBay merchants sometimes stumble into quite successful small business ventures. I knew of one woman who retired and moved into an active adult community. Although she had spent most of her career in a variety of banking jobs, she also was a fairly skilled self-taught seamstress-designer. At first, she would occasionally perform some minor clothing repairs exclusively for family members that lived nearby. However, as word quickly spread throughout her community that a bona-fide "tailor" resided there, residents started to request her tailoring services. Of course, our retiree charged them for her services. Her business began to grow, to the point where her base clientele numbers over 200 people.

As you can imagine, she is very busy, although she insists that no customers, under any circumstances, call on Sunday. That's the day she has allocated for relaxation and spending time with her great-grandchildren. After all, an eighty-five year old woman needs some time for herself.

EDUCATION FOR LIFE

In the *Ageless Nation*, our increasingly complex jobs and careers will oblige us to be smarter, more intellectually agile and more mentally flexible than our current work environment requires. In this new world, the vast majority of people will have to pursue education, training and re-training throughout their lifetimes. Up till now, most of us complete our schooling and learning before we enter our career in earnest. Now, training and further education will become an omnipresent and ongoing part of everyone's life.

Superlongevity will require that every citizen become a lifetime learner for a variety of reasons. First, as we've discussed, most people will naturally desire to change careers, jobs and companies some time down the line. Armies of fifty and sixty year olds will be expected to re-enter universities to acquire the certification and/or degrees their new chosen professions demand. Interestingly, companies desiring to retain these experienced workers itching to change careers will sponsor these employees' further education just to keep them in the corporate fold. Second, the changes wrought by technology and other factors will make some careers obsolete, while simultaneously creating new ones. Individuals in those declining fields will need to take additional courses or pursue other ways to earn credentials in order to qualify for a new job in a new area of expertise. Third, workers' chosen fields will periodically require upgraded skills, so even employees deciding to spend decades in one field will be challenged to acquire new skills to continue to perform at levels of excellence.

Fortunately, there is a veritable arsenal of educational breakthroughs and new pedagogical technologies that will enable the citizens of the *Ageless Nation* to pursue lifetimes of learning.

The Online Education Revolution

To meet the educational needs of the citizens of the *Ageless Nation*, universities and other training institutions will be expected to offer their services beyond the physical confines of their campuses. A plethora of new electronic technologies already exists to enable colleges and corporations to meet the lifetime training needs of the national and international public. Such distance learning will incorporate the full gamut of new technologies, including the Internet, digital TV-on-demand, webcams and the like. Virtual reality technologies will enable students all over the world to sit in a "virtual classroom" and learn from their "cyber-professor," without ever leaving their homes or offices.

A woman I know started her higher education, directly out of high school, at Baruch College in New York City. With one semester remaining, she met a man who would shortly become her husband. He was serving in the Air Force, and was stationed at the time in Okinawa. She left college without finishing her degree, assuming that she could finish those credits anytime. After she married this career officer, she discovered that finishing an education was no easy task. The Air Force relocated them to Hawaii, Massachusetts, England, Texas and other spots. How can you finish a degree when you live in one area for two years at the most?

When they were stationed in the Yorkshire area of northern England, she learned of a college program operated throughout Europe by the University of Maryland. She would not have to physically attend many classes, taking the lion's share of courses online. She enrolled in a psychology program, transferred her earned credits from Baruch, and proceeded to attend school. She received the class lectures via the Internet, communicated with her professors and fellow students via e-mail, and spoke on the phone with all involved when necessary. Even attending part time, she earned her degree in less than two years. She and her family attended an elaborate weekend-long graduation at the program's headquarters in Heidelberg, Germany, highlighted by a boat trip on the Neckar River. It was on that little jaunt that she finally met in the flesh her professors and classmates that she had worked with over the months.

The "virtual" online trend in education is already making lifetime learning a reality. According to the United States Department of Education online computer teaching is the fastest-growing segment of higher education. According to their statistics, since 1997, enrollment in distance education courses nationally has more than doubled to about three million students. Others, however, place this figure much higher. Michael P. Lambert, is executive director of the Washington D.C.-based Distance Education and Training Council (DETC), the body that sets the standards and offers accreditation for distance education institutions. He claims that the growth rate of online learning and distance learning is increasing 20 percent per year during the first decade of the twenty-first century. "My best estimate is that there are 5 to 6 million people taking distance courses in the United States each year," Lambert said.[48]

Online degrees are available from fully-accredited institutions such as the University of Phoenix, Devry University, Capella University, Kaplan University and Walden University. The biggest of the online schools is University of Phoenix, with more than 100,000 online students. It offers certificate, undergraduate and graduate degree programs. According to most reports the areas most attractive to online students are finance and health care, two extremely hot occupational fields.

Walden University, based in Minnesota, started in 1969 as a distance-learning school long before the word Internet entered the public's vocabulary. The university used telephones and the United States mail to deliver its courses. Now, Walden has more than 11,000 online students. According to the school's president, Paula Peinovich, the university focuses on the needs and interests of mid-adult learners. She states that the school wanted to give an opportunity to adults who had started doctoral studies and had not been able to complete them. Now, the for-profit university, accredited since 1989, has schools of education, psychology, business management, health and human services. While predominantly graduate in its offerings, the school has a small undergraduate program. Although traditional universities are just now adding a cyber-degree format, Walden feels it is fifteen years ahead of them, mainly because it has pioneered and mastered the technological and institutional challenges inherent in online education.

In addition, many traditional universities are now offering online courses. Drexel University's School of Business announced plans to make 10 percent of its current courses available online. The University of Texas offers an MBA degree through its almost completely electronic TeleCampus. Many students in such programs have at their command an extensive cyberlibrary more comprehensive than the average bricks-and-mortar university library. Any university distance learning program without its own cyberlibrary can purchase either an entire digital library or just the specific resources it needs to augment its current library capabilities from the online Jones International University.

One of the more impressive of these traditional university offerings is NYU Online. This program brings the resources of one of the nation's largest private universities, New York University (NYU), to the desktop of adult students who want to go back to college and earn their degrees. Their outstanding faculty, many of whom are experts in their fields, create online classroom environments that they claim are "flexible and sensitive to the needs of working adults."

Importantly, programs such as NYU-Online let the user manage their own schedule, and learn at their own pace. The selling point is that the student can combine education and career without sacrificing quality in and commitment to either aspect of their lives.[49]

Institutions that embark on the road to cyber-education should be aware of just how much of a draw this type of program can become. The University of Louisville enrolled fifty students in its first online classes in the fall of 2000. By 2004 about 3,500 students are enrolled online. At its start, the university offered online only one degree program in special education. Now, the university features eight degree programs, including five master's degree programs in areas such as justice administration and communication. Kentucky Virtual University acts as the state clearinghouse for online courses. Students go through the virtual university to take online classes at the institution of their choice. A little over 200 students were taking courses through the virtual university in the fall of 1999. By the fall of 2002, about 9,800 students were taking classes, and this jumped to 21,765 students in fall 2003. KVU is seeing about a 3,000 average student increase per semester.

These classes are broadening access for students who otherwise might not be able to attend college because of a job, family situation or disability. Surveys found that students accessing virtual programs in Kentucky tend to be female and over the age of twenty-five, in contrast to the more prevalent student age range of eighteen to twenty-four, based on data from the National Center for Education Statistics.

Kentucky higher-ed officials claim that students choose online classes for schedule reasons, for geographical reasons, or personal reasons such as job, career, or domestic responsibilities.[50]

Online education is the perfect modality for those whose career might now span sixty, seventy or eighty years. It will enable our time pioneers to prepare for a new career without having to lose income or risk their current job security. Studying from the convenience of home, on their schedule, has opened up whole new worlds for these aspiring career-changers, without disrupting their current lives.

Corporate-University Partnerships
As we've discussed, the extended life span generated by the Superlongevity Revolution will require all of us to engage in ongoing training and retraining.

To ensure that their employees living in the *Ageless Nation* continuously upgrade their skills, corporations have entered a new era of cooperation with educational institutions.

Numerous universities and corporations are teaming up to help employees improve their abilities. Fairleigh Dickinson University offers to New Jersey's major drug and chemical companies a pharmaceutical/chemical MBA program which it delivers at on-site corporate facilities. Seton Hall University has entered a collaborative partnership with companies such as CE Technologies to bring its e-learning program to corporate and media websites.

One of the more impressive and elaborate of these corporate programs is the Boston University Corporate Education Center (BUCEC). The center offers award-winning programs in business, project management, information technology training, and professional education. Interestingly, BUCEC is totally geared to the needs of the individual corporation, providing customized corporate training, instructor-led classes, as well as online training programs.

The Center has industry experts teach the courses, which are geared to both large and small groups of students. And BUCEC provides participating corporations private consulting, training, and mentoring to best meet their organizational development needs. And following a very desirable practice, BUCEC will run the program at the company's facility if necessary, as well as at a BUCEC facility or online. BUCEC's programs are also available globally through Boston University's Affiliate Network of worldwide training partners. One of their programs, offered through the Center's sister organization Boston University Center for Professional Education (BUCPE), would be particularly useful to citizens of our nascent *Ageless Nation*. This center focuses on non-credit short and "to-the-point" programs meeting professional education and certification needs of such industries as biotechnology, financial services, real estate, facilities management and law.

If a person at age fifty or sixty wanted to stay in his or her field, but perhaps move on to another organization, a certification program would be a very good life solution.

Life Planning and Training as a New Educational Goal

But is all of this—online degree programs, corporate-university partnerships, and certificate programs—sufficient to educate citizens of the *Ageless Nation* for the long journey into the uncharted distances of time? Is there another type of education that they require, one that shows them what they really must know about living the full and very extended life?

As we progress through the first decade of the twenty-first century, a whole new form of education is emerging, commonly labeled "life planning." The promulgators of this new pedagogical program are aiming their services at people moving through what they consider a new stage of life beyond middle age, a stage they have labeled "the next chapter."

Interestingly, community colleges seem to be the institution of choice to serve as a vehicle to create, organize and deliver this training to the population. Throughout their history, the two year community and county colleges have always been resourceful and adaptive to new educational opportunities. Who better than these institutions to provide guidance for older citizens of the *Ageless Nation* as they enter these bonus years?

Recent opinion surveys conducted by Civic Ventures show that post midlife adults do not plan to pursue the traditional model: formal retirement followed by the pursuit of a full-time leisure lifestyle. They want meaningful engagement opportunities that offer them continued growth and learning. They are more likely to seek a mix of activities including project-driven civic engagement. This shift will result in a blurring of the boundaries between unpaid service and compensated work. This will require community colleges to radically rethink their seniors programs if they wish to reach out to and serve aging baby boomers.

Traditional volunteer opportunities offered to seniors represent one example of this change in approach.

The programs that are evolving at this time provide a glimpse into the nature and function of "life planning" education. Many of these programs are receiving guidance from Civic Ventures, a national nonprofit organization that works to expand the contributions of older Americans to society. In 2001 Civic Ventures started a project called "Life Options," which has recently been renamed The Next Chapter.

At that time the Civic Ventures' initiative asked community organizations to develop a new set of approaches that enable adults in their "post-midlife" life stage to become involved in civic programs. However, even at this early stage this original mandate seems to have morphed into a multi-goaled set of programs. The core components of these programs include life planning assistance, meaningful engagement opportunities through employment and service, continued learning for new directions and peer and community connections.

Cuyahoga Community College (CCC) has developed a program to help boomers in areas such as self-assessment and life planning. In the CCC program, each participant is required to "write your own definition of retirement, determine what you need to make it happen, and link up with organizations that can utilize your unique talents, skills and experience."

Mesa Community College (MCC), with the assistance of the Maricopa Community College's Center for Civic Participation, is offering civic engagement opportunities to boomers. MCC runs discussion sessions on life planning, and also try to get "post-mid-lifers" involved in community service activities. Arizona's Maricopa County Commission on Productive Aging was formed to raise awareness of the aging demographics and inherent opportunities. The commission's recommendations challenged libraries, colleges and other community partners to think creatively about how to serve the needs of aging boomers. [51]

In the future, the concept of "life planning" and "life training" will evolve into something much more elaborate than programs such as those proposed by Civic Ventures.

Later in this book, I will present a vision for a form of "life planning" education aimed not just at aging boomers or the wise elders of any society. This type of education, which I label Superlongevity Training®, would serve the population at all stages of the life cycle. In fact, I am suggesting that this training start at fairly young ages. Early schooling will play a key role in preparing citizens for the demands of the *Ageless Nation*. Besides teaching students the traditional subjects, schools now will familiarize even very young students on how to navigate their way through a life that will last much more than a century.

Education and training experiments will abound. For instance, the long-lived citizens of this brave new era will themselves become active education producers. Entrepreneurs will establish what I label "wisdom companies," consulting and training organizations through which they will not only transfer skill-based knowledge but also impart their "perspective" and outlook. Such companies might serve as a complement for the more classroom-based "life planning courses" currently proposed, offering their clients a program tailored to their individual needs.

We will all welcome the wisdom and sense of perspective of such "wise elders" in a world in which people will not only survive but live to healthy, strong ages.

chapter four

The Emerging World of Personal Development

We are only now beginning to discover and appreciate the benefits of the very long life spans generated by the Superlongevity Revolution's many scientific and medical breakthroughs. While the 150 years or so of life that perhaps are ahead of you will provide you ample time to succeed fabulously in several careers, they will also provide you a great deal of non-career time, perhaps periods lasting a few years or more. The good news is that a veritable new world of self-development opportunities is emerging that will enable you to spend and enjoy your non-work hours, months and years in ways that until recently were not available to most people.

Superlongevity will change how we use our so-called free time, both while we are actively engaged in careers and during hiatus periods. In the *Ageless Nation*, longer life span will unleash a craving for novel experiences and personal enhancement. We will use this free time not only for entertainment activities but increasingly as opportunities for "self-development." Through the process of re-creation we will refresh, rethink and ultimately re-create and re-position ourselves for our next life adventure. In this new era, we will consider our free time periods as "time-out," not merely time off.

Next, we will explore this emerging world of personal development activities that people will engage in while on job sabbaticals or career hiatuses, and even during their non-work moments while fully employed. These activities are not specific to any particular stage of the lifespan—I believe that as we radically extend the lifespan, people will take hiatuses at earlier and earlier stages of their lives. It is not inconceivable that the "time out" concept will become popular even for younger people upon graduation from college.

Recent surveys certainly indicate that we are ready for this new life phase. As the 2002 Allstate Financial Retirement Reality Check revealed, retirees today say they feel seventeen years younger than their physical ages and want to keep learning new skills and/or academic subjects, travel, have sex and maintain a full and active life. Baby boomers in the survey stated that they feel the so-called older years will be the best years of their lives, and will be more fun, active and rewarding than their parents' experience in the later years of their life spans. The Boomers indicated they plan to immerse themselves in vacations (taking at least four trips per year), family activities, gardening, fishing, golfing, volunteering, reading, exercising and home improvement. They say the extra years for time out will provide opportunities for fun and personal development. Some will use their "early retirement" package as golden opportunities to take career hiatuses to pursue adventures such as climbing Mt. Everest, learning how to cook Cantonese, speak Mandarin, or repair a Harley. Organized adult and senior team sports, including soccer and softball leagues, will explode.

We will look at how these extra years will be a time for giving. A major life goal of the *Ageless Nation* citizens will be to develop perspective and acquire wisdom. The wise elder, a role that has virtually disappeared from modern society, will make an unexpected return. People will do volunteer work at a local mental-health center or the Junior League, or offer their knowledge and wisdom to people living in developing nations through programs like Volunteers for Overseas Cooperative Assistance. Some will become mentors to school-age children. Some will contribute to family life—as we will see in the next chapter, increasingly people will be part of a fully functioning multigenerational extended family.

Also, we will get a glimpse at the ultimate form of self-improvement, the development of a perennially vibrant brain and active mind. New findings suggest that the brain possesses a quality known as *neuroplasticity*, the ability to rewire and revitalize itself. The individual pursuing re-creation and self-development in any form receives an unexpected bonus—research shows that by challenging the brain with new experiences and ideas we keep our brains more efficient and dexterous as we grow older. In addition, we will view the other ways science has devised to not only maintain our mental capacities but perhaps even to raise IQ.

THE WONDERS OF A VERY LONG LIFE

More people than ever are living to ages of a hundred and more. The United States 2000 census counted approximately 50,000 centenarians and demographers expect that number to soar to 800,000 by 2050.[52] This is a conservative estimate—that figure is sure to increase dramatically if any of the scientific wonders we examined so far come to pass. There is such a profusion of centenarians that it became hard to get a televised one hundredth birthday greeting from news reporter Willard Scott—he mentions twelve centenarians every week on the "Today" show, but omits the other ninety people reaching the century mark that week.[53]

Living a very long life—to one hundred or 150 years of age—in relatively good health and as a physically vibrant individual, benefits the person involved and society itself. Living for a long time enables the person to develop an enormous amount of physical, mental, financial, and social capital. These people become smarter, and develop wisdom and perspective. As we extend ourselves through time, we expand our social networks, extend our influence and grow our families.

Literary works and media reports regularly inform us how people have utilized their long lives to create great inventions and works of art, and how they realized goals that would have been unachievable without the gift of those extra years.

From Dawn to Decadence, a fascinating book by noted historian and social commentator Jacques Barzun, is an intellectual tour-de-force. It is a veritable history, social commentary and analysis of the evolution of Western culture. Barzun demonstrates clarity of vision and an encyclopedic knowledge of science, culture, politics, religion and technology. One review exclaimed, "Jacques Barzun doesn't know everything—it just seems that way."

I knew of Barzun's writings for several years, and assumed from the quality and scope of his book that he was a thinker at the peak of his intellectual powers. I placed him somewhere in his fifties or sixties, a professor actively teaching. Then I read an interview in which the interviewer complimented Barzun on the breadth of knowledge and profundity of thought he exhibited in the book. The author graciously and professorially responded that he could not have composed this classic when he was in his fifties.

No, he composed this tome a bit later—the book was published when the author was ninety-two. He felt as a young man of fifty or fifty-five he did not yet possess the perspective, knowledge and wisdom a book of such historical and intellectual breadth. He needed those extra four decades to get it right.

The Superlongevity Revolution will endow the human species with the years necessary to develop wisdom and sense of perspective, invaluable qualities, which should only increase in strength and depth the longer you live. The dictionary defines wisdom as "the sum of learning through the ages" and "wise teachings of the ancient sages." I define perspective as the ability to realistically assess the present within the context of events of the past. Imagine if you happened to be fortunate enough to have lived over a span of a century and a half in which tremendous historical, economic, or technological changes have taken place. While any history book can describe the way conditions used to be, only someone who has literally lived through the changes can have a true sense of what it was really like to watch society undergo such a transition. Speak to anyone who fought in World War II or lived through the Depression, and you will gain insights into what life was really like during the 1930s and 1940s that history books and newsreels can simply not deliver.

Some fear that people living to a century and a half might mimic the behavior of some older folks that they have encountered today. Do we not risk weighing society down with a preponderance of centenarians who cling to their memories of the "good old days" and reflexively reject new ideas and trends? The answer is categorically "no." In the new era seasoned citizens, thanks to science and technology, will be healthy enough to be full participants in the present, fulfilling their roles as workers, managers, teachers and artists. And with as many years stretching ahead of them as behind, these "elders" will have little time or need for sentiment about the past. They will be too busy building futures for themselves and their families.

Jacque Barzun's life story imparts a simple lesson: living to great ages opens the possibility of achieving great accomplishments. This aphorism will be even more correct when humankind uses the breakthroughs in nanotechnology, genetic engineering and pharmacology to eliminate the various mental and physical infirmities many of our species still experience in our later ages that obstruct our ability to continue to achieve. Imagine having the wisdom and knowledge that comes with age and applying those gifts with the healthy body of a young adult.

I believe that in the future, as we start to live to ages that our species has never reached before, the very nature and meaning of life will change dramatically. The very long life that we the citizens of the *Ageless Nation* will experience will not only enable us to reach that potential, but will allow us to reinvent and enlarge that potential as well. Those extra years will bequeath to us a second, third and fourth chance to realize our dreams.

There are a host of activities that people will have at their disposal to develop their minds and enhance their lives, and put them in position to exploit the opportunities Superlongevity will place before them.

HOBBIES, AVOCATIONS AND JOBS

As we add years to our lives, we are increasingly blurring the lines between hobby, vocation, and job. In *Ageless Nation* many of our leisure activities will transform themselves into new careers. While we might not consider these activities our new career, we might pursue them with such vigor that they at least take on the flavor of an avocation.

One dictionary defines the concept avocation as "an activity taken up in addition to one's regular work or profession, usually for enjoyment; a hobby. " Other definitions include "an auxiliary activity" or a "distraction or diversion." Suggested synonyms are "sideline" and "spare-time activity." However, the very same dictionary defines avocation as "one's regular work or profession."

Citizens of the *Ageless Nation* will be quite comfortable with what seems to be a semantic confusion, because this ambiguity will joyously haunt free time activities. An example should help add to this pleasurable uncertainty.

Many towns and cities in the United States celebrate New Years Eve with an event known as *First Night*, an evening long entertainment extravaganza in which revelers can sample a wide variety of musical and theatrical acts—rock bands, comedy groups, classical orchestras, light opera companies—at venues interspersed throughout the city or town environs.

A few years ago, I attended one such *First Night* in Morristown, NJ, not realizing that my experience that night would afford me a glimpse into the future of the human life cycle.

One of the acts I saw was one of the best "cover bands" I ever had the pleasure to experience. They played rock and pop music numbers of the last several decades—the Eagles, Beatles, Rolling Stones, and America, as well as more current music, including country and even hip-hop favorites.

As their website professes, "The collective passion for classic rock, pop, soul and blues...and just 'plain old making great music' has been a driving force...even a 'mantra' in assembling 'The Kootz' band." Yes, they chose for the band a name which played on a derogatory term for older people—the Kootz. Later I discovered that this band is in fact a "franchise operation." The group, which is more like a musical organization, has anywhere from twelve to sixteen members in their fifties and beyond that rotate through the various club appearances booked by the company's manager Glenn Taylor. While the band is made up of interchangeable parts, so to speak, the level of musical proficiency of each member is uniformly excellent. Various versions of the Kootz appear at rock clubs, civic events, resorts, private parties, biker bars, bistros and coffee houses in and around the New Jersey and New York area several times each week, both as a full electric band and an acoustic 'unplugged' version. The Kootz are becoming a regional institution.

While their public appearances focus on cover versions of other artists' music, the Kootz band members are also creating. Their first CD contained only 5 cover songs, the other cuts being highly tuneful and creative original pieces written by some of the band members themselves. The Kootz members are expanding their musical as well as their professional horizons.

As they also disclose on their website, the fact that most of the band's members were in other occupational situations musical and otherwise that were keeping them from playing the music that they really loved was a huge motivating force for them to all band together. Those occupations include construction company owner, medical doctor, electrician, prep-school teacher, part-time funeral director and weekend organist at Yankee Stadium. However, throughout their work lives they all hankered to do the only thing that could provide them the ultimate "self-actualization," playing the music they loved.

The members of this thriving musical organization illustrate perfectly how the longer life span is expanding human potential into areas that were hitherto unknown. In the past, most of us put away forever our toys and dreams we had as youths by our twenties, and did what we must to make a living and prosper. Now thanks to the Superlongevity Revolution you can revisit, re-cultivate, and re-energize our dreams, assuming we have the retirement income and health to do so.[54]

The example of the Kootz is only one of many in which people are literally changing the very nature of the lifecycle. One sixty-four year old photographer is quickly becoming one of the hottest figures in his field. In 2003 American Photo magazine named him one of the nation's master photographers. His two critically acclaimed books *Iron: Erecting the Walt Disney Concert Hall* and *Frozen Music* have been praised for their evocation of the "poetry of

architecture." His 2006 book, *Dance in Cuba*, which deals with the folk dancing and flamenco of Cuba's dance heritage, has received international acclaim.
In an interview on *CBS Sunday Morning*, the photographer says he is
only at the early stages of his new career. And he is correct, in the sense that
he has only been in this more artistic field for five years. His real challenge is
not mastering the skills of his trade—it has already been established that he
can take memorable pictures. His one remaining obstacle is the image the
wider American and international public have of him. We already have
placed him in a niche and how can we help it. He is the quintessential crime
fighter and public prosecutor Gil Garcetti.

Gil became a household name as the Los Angeles District Attorney super-
vising a number of sensationalized trials, including the Menendez Brothers case
as well as what might be the most publicized trial of the last century, the prose-
cution of supercelebrity O.J. Simpson. At age fifty-nine, shortly after he lost his
re-election bid for DA, he decided to re-focus his energy and try his hand at turning his lifelong hobby, photography, into a profession. Now, at sixty-four,
Garcetti is doing much to become Gil the professional photographer.

As Gil Garcetti revealed to CBS correspondent Bill Whitaker, he considers himself the poster boy for career change.[55]

The Superlongevity Revolution bestows on all of us the ability to try new
experiences. Again, many of these activities will defy rigid definition—is it a
leisure pursuit, hobby, avocation, job or all of the above. In an interview I did
for Cox Communications, I mentioned that people now have the time to get
involved with activities that they might have experienced at younger ages but
lost the opportunity to pursue as they grew older.

One of those activities is team sports. I described a surge in senior slow-
pitch softball leagues filled with, as the newspaper described them, graying
boys who started out in Little Leagues more than half a century ago. These
leagues provide those fifty and over the opportunity to play a sport they love in
organized leagues with twenty or thirty game spring and summer schedules.
Most of us played this sport as youths, but either lost the time, or the ability, to
play this game at the high school and college level. Playing team sports at a
later age is a special and unexpected recreational treat. It also provides something that is usually absent as one gets older, the opportunity to develop not
only new friends but a whole new peer group. To the extent that remaining

socially connected has been found to be a critical component of living a long and healthy life, you might say that senior baseball and other such team-based sports "covers all the bases" when it comes to superlongevity.

I have noticed a very subtle dynamic at play in these organized, competitive senior softball leagues, what I refer to as "enforced health"—players stay on the same team year after year and play mostly the same cast of characters. You are expected to start the season in shape and in good health. So these players work out all winter, or might even play in a winter basketball league to keep themselves "game sharp." Everyone on the team and in the league notices immediately if someone's performance—their running, hitting and fielding—is dropping off. When he gets a single, the last thing he wants to hear his team or worse his opponents say is, "Five years ago you would have gotten to second on that hit." Therefore, the players strive to maintain themselves physically and improve their playing skills any way they can.

Not long ago, I was asked how people will spend the extra years now or soon at their disposal. I responded that "It will spur the creation of a leisure industry that we haven't seen yet." I mentioned that as the average lifespan increases, marketers are going to have to adjust to the tastes and pursuits of a more age-diverse public, especially since in the United States alone the sixty-five or older segment will balloon from its current 13 percent of the population to 20 percent by 2030. I indicated that Hollywood might finally be aiming for audiences who appreciate "mature themes" rather than focusing only on "the eighteen to thirty-four year old daters," citing the release of films like *Capote* and *Good Night, and Good Luck*.[56]

TRAVELING THE PATH TO PERSONAL DEVELOPMENT

As the Superlongevity Revolution extends the human life span to ages never seen in history, we can expect every institution and practice to be impacted. Hobbies will become avocations, which then will become jobs. Education will become a form of mental expansion instead of mere training for a better job. In that vein, travel will increasingly change from a strictly leisure activity to an enjoyable learning experience.

The key to this change is that as a result of the Superlongevity Revolution we will not just live longer; we will do so as young and physically healthy individuals. This is a major reason why, as we saw earlier, we will not retire in the traditional sense—we will go on hiatuses. And since we are in effect fully engaged in the world around us, routine activities such as traveling will evolve into something more than just an opportunity to "veg out" on a beach or at a resort pool, or spend our days and months golfing or playing the slots at a casino. That is not to say that we will avoid such pleasures completely. Rather, we will just seek more "engaging" experiences in our so-called leisure activities.

Mark Searle, a professor in the department of recreation and tourism management at Arizona State University, sees clear indications that people will desire to be more connected to the places they travel. Instead of skimming the surface of another culture while staying in an American chain hotel, people suddenly want to sink more deeply into it. Tim Mack, president of the World Future Society, calls it "immersion travel."[57]

Emblematic of this trend are the travel tours created by Elderhostel, which seek to get the tour participant as close to the subject matter as humanly possible. Want to learn about Italian culture and history? Elderhostel's trips will have you spend seven days in Padua and another week in Venice. In Venice participants study the unique Venetian culture, painting, and architecture by visiting these important churches, monuments, and museums, including St. Mark's, the Frari, the Ducal Palace and the Accademia di Belle Arti, where we view the city's most famous works. There you also take motorboat cruises to the picturesque outer islands of Torcello and Burano. In Padua, whose university hosted Galileo, participants listen to lectures on the painter Giotto, visit the Basilica of St. Anthony and visit the medieval center with its colorful fruit and vegetable markets.

Such innovative travel packages also are beginning to blur the lines between personal development and "leisure travel." Even "fun" experiences are expected to in some way contribute to knowledge, skills and overall personal growth.

One of Elderhostel's tours enables the participants to learn a language at the same time they are seeing the sights. This package, entitled "Immersion in Spanish Language and Mexican Culture," makes sure that the only language you will hear, and use while you see Mexico is conversational Spanish. While you are perusing Cuernavaca's flower markets, garden nurseries and quaint villages, and taking trips to the murals of Diego Rivera, the Palace of Cortez, and spectacular pre-Columbian ruins, you are also learning how to speak Spanish. Beginners learn functional phrases and vocabulary useful in travel, while advanced students review the basics and move on to more complex grammatical expressions. The tour treats the language instruction seriously, with classes of five taught by a native instructor, in a relaxed atmosphere, of course. As the promo reads, "we experience local events and truly 'live' the language and culture of Mexico."

While the lifelong learning institutes do a wonderful job exploring the issues and influencing policy decisions, Elderhostel goes one step further. In their package participants meet the people involved in such decisions. They travel to Jamestown in upstate New York, where over a series of days they are taken through a series of policy case studies by actual experts and practitioners in the field. The seminars, which are run by ambassadors and other veteran Foreign Service experts, examine the challenges facing U.S. diplomacy, such as peace in the Middle East, security in Europe and obstacles to global stability posed by Third World population growth, poverty and nuclear proliferation. The Chautauqua Institution offers this program with the American Foreign Service Association, the professional association of the Foreign Service.

More intense tours, which combine learning and traditional "sightseeing" are often run by groups who themselves have a particular political or ideological focus. The Rockford Institute, a conservative organization known for its seminars and its magazine *Chronicles*, host annual trips to places which have cultural and historical significance. The Institute's "Winter School" trip entitled "Lions and Christians: Christian in a Pagan Empire," explored such sites as the tomb of Saint Peter under St. Peter's Basilica and Roman Patrician houses that were turned into churches, as well as the Christian Catacombs along the Appian Way. Lectures and instruction tours are included. And this group will have nothing to do with your local Hilton—the group lodged at the Centro Diffusione Spiritualita, a quiet and well-kept convent in Trastevere, which is evidently convenient to the Vatican and Rome's Centro Storico.[58]

The Future Foundation's survey, "The World of Travel in 2020," reflects many ideas we have introduced here. According to the report, the new type of traveler, whom they label the "third age" traveler, is looking for new experiences which broaden outlook and perspective. It suggests these "third-age" travelers will collect experiences instead of cars or watches and fill out "life calendars" of places they want to visit and things they want to do.

The report also suggests that the final frontier for tourism is space itself.

In my earlier works, I predicted that "space tourism" would emerge as a hot industry in the early twenty-first century. If you become one of the early passengers to go "out there," you will certainly have something to brag about to your Earth-bound friends. The industry has already sent its first tourists to the space station. Twenty million dollars is what it cost Americans Gregory Olson, Mark Shuttleworth and Dennis Tito to spend time on the International Space Station. In 2005 British billionaire Richard Branson claimed that his Virgin Galactic could within two or three years carry passengers to the edge of space. Already 38,000 people have made deposits for flights on Virgin Galactic that will cost $200,000 per seat. Members of the public that have not yet reached billionaire status can still experience some aspects of space travel. Since 2004, Zero Gravity Corp. has sold $3,750 weightlessness flights on G-Force One, a modified Boeing plane.

Entrepreneurs are brimming with new ideas for this new frontier of travel. Honolulu architecture firm Wimberly, Allison, Tong & Goo has a concept for an orbiting Space Resort with an artificial Earth gravity (so the toilets flush and travelers can take showers). Could the next travel destination be the Moon, an asteroid or a planet?[59]

In the world of career hiatuses and job sabbaticals, travel will become an integral part of the personal development modality. Some people, possibly a bit more affluent than the average person, might use those extra years to not just travel to foreign locations but rent homes in a variety of locations during the year giving themselves the opportunity to soak up the local culture. There has emerged what are known as "destination clubs" such as Distinctive Retreats and Exclusive Resorts, which provide a network of plush homes in such locations as England, Hawaii, Italy, Mexico, and around the United States.[60]

Or you might opt to travel all year round. Instead of taking a cruise, some folks are living on cruise ships for the entire year. At this point, more seniors are living on cruise ships than those of younger ages. Ironically, according to a study published in the *Journal of the American Geriatrics Society*, living on a cruise ship provides a better quality of life and is cost effective for elderly people who need help to live independently. Cruise ships have better health facilities than most nursing homes for elderly people and they provide a more varied lifestyle.

Much younger people on a job sabbatical or a career hiatus might choose to live on a cruise ship for a year or more. With their good health facilities, single room apartments having a private bathroom, showers with easy access, cable television, security services, entertainment and all the food you can eat on a daily basis, cruise ships provide luxury living accommodations. And most importantly, you will get to meet a host of new and interesting people and also have the opportunity to see the world. Many of these cruises offer classes and lectures on a host of subjects. One estimate priced a year on a cruise ship at $33,000 and higher. [61]

In the Superlongevity Era, travel will most certainly be a path for self-discovery and personal development.

EDUCATION FOR SELF-ENHANCEMENT

In the last chapter, we discussed how education would become a lifelong pursuit for job advancement, career growth and change. There is another aspect of education that we will tap into as we discover the many facets of the radically extended lifespan – we will use our free time in the Superlongevity Era not just for entertainment activities but also as a way to improve and enhance our general knowledge base.

Remember when you attended college how you noticed courses in the college catalogue which you would love to take, but alas you had so little room in your tight schedule for those "free electives." After all, the college required you to take so many general education courses, and then your major required you to take another thirty or forty credits. Late in your senior year, you were left wondering why you never had space in your class schedule for courses you wanted to take in subjects like Independent Film, Roman Civilization or Renaissance Art.

Well, one of the benefits of living to 150 is that you finally have the time, via hiatuses or semi-retirement, to indulge your curiosity and explore knowledge. And in most cases, you will not have to worry about being graded.

The concept of lifelong learning has been going strong in Europe and elsewhere. The Universities of the Third Age (U3As) which provide lifelong learning opportunities for older adults largely free of work and family responsibilities are pioneers in personal development education. Started in France in 1972, the program offered retired persons a program of lectures, concerts, guided tours and other cultural activities. The program mushroomed from that first modest experiment, and became the model for the U3As that flourish in China (which has more than 20,000 U3A's), Japan, Spain, Poland, Italy, Siberia, Malta, and Australia.

The "Third Age" in the title refers to a phase of life that comes after we traverse through the first age of dependent childhood and the second age of independent adulthood in work and home-making. The U3A movement is based around the supposition that a third age is one of active retirement. Obviously this book takes issue with that idea, but at least the "third age" concept introduced a novel concept, that our older ages are not a time of dependence and senility but of robust physical and mental activity and personal growth. One of the major aims of U3As is the encouragement of that mental activity in a creative learning environment.

A perusal of courses offered at U3As around the world reveals the program's eclectic approach to personal development education. One can find a course for every learning need and interest, including courses entitled "Creative Writing," "the Operas of Verdi," "Jane Austen," "The Living Bible," "Italian Cooking Demonstrations," "Classical Greek," "Contemporary Fiction," "Aspects of the Biology of Growing Older," "Appreciating Wine," and one which statement than title, "Philately – More Than Just Stamp Collecting." The U3A branch in Johannesburg, South Africa offers a course in Basic Zulu.

New School University in NYC is a pioneer in late adult education in the United States. In 1962 a group of 151 retired New York City schoolteachers, unhappy with the educational opportunities available, formed the Institute for Retired Professionals (IRP) at what was then called the New School for Social Research (now New School University.) The IRP developed a unique concept: students would not be students in the conventional sense, but rather would be what IRP labeled "peer-learners." Every participant shares in the responsibility for the classes. The students would define the area of study, and then become simultaneously curriculum creators, learning leaders, and students. The IRP peer-learners, who range in age from fifty-four to ninety-two, develop and participate in challenging study groups. These non-credit group classes meet weekly, with no exams, and of course no grades. All that is required is active student participation. As the catalogue says, "participation in study groups is an essential element in our continuing vitality."

The list of just one semester's courses is intriguing and covers a wide spectrum of knowledge: "Violence: Theories and Consequences," "Understanding Contemporary China," "Defining America: The Supreme Court Shapes Our

Everyday Life," "Sociology Explains It All" and "Art in Current Museum Exhibitions." For the music lover, the program offers study groups in "The Genius of Gilbert and Sullivan" and "The Beethoven Quartets: Bridge to the Modern." Courses give you the opportunity to improve your French or develop your skills in collage creation and acting.

One two-semester course that I found fascinating was entitled "An Interdisciplinary Look at the Concept of Time," which examined time from philosophical, scientific, and humanistic standpoints. The reading list includes Plato, Aristotle, Augustine, Kant and a host of other notables. The course focuses on time in science and the arts—they review the classic physics of Newton, Einstein's relativity and entropy, and examine time in art, the cinema, literature, music, drama and poetry. The class format varies among lecture, reading and discussion and weekly reading assignments average 35 pages. And the course requires little or no scientific background. Interestingly, the course coordinator is not a scientist herself but a former financial analyst and trader. Other invited speakers might have a more scientific background.

Perusing the program's catalogue, I noticed that many of the courses used professionals from other fields as facilitators. A course entitled "How Societies Choose to Fail or Succeed," which explored the ideas of historian Jared Diamond, was led by a former pediatric radiologist. Leading a study group on James Joyce's Ulysses was a retired psychiatrist.

Not surprisingly, the innovative model for personal development education pioneered by the New School IRP has been adopted by more than 400 colleges around the United States and has become the catalyst for the phenomenon known as the Institute for Lifelong Learning movement.[62]

This concept is attracting funding from a variety of sources. Since 2001, the Bernard Osher Foundation has been offering universities grants to establish Lifelong Learning Institutes. Typically, the foundation grants a university $100,000 as seed money to launch a lifelong learning institute, and if the institute shows promise, the grant is renewed. If the institute proves successful and sustainable, the Foundation provides an endowment gift of no less than one million dollars.

Rutgers University in New Brunswick, New Jersey established the Rutgers University Academy for Lifelong Learning (RU-ALL) with the help and guidance of the Osher foundation. The program is designed for citizens over fifty years old who want to continue their learning experiences and share knowledge with others. Like most of the lifelong learning programs, RU-ALL is a noncompetitive, noncredit education that is stimulating, friendly and informal, with no tests or grades.

The courses reflect the diverse nature of the lifelong learning programs. One class meets weekly as "Foreign Affairs Associates" to discuss and solve a particular foreign policy problem. Another, "Health Care for Baby Boomers," is a bit more pragmatic, as is the "Intermediate Art Workshop." Other courses study Western Culture, the Supreme Court and the evolution of Western science. The course "Broadway in Your Backyard" takes the participants to the local professional theatre, the famous George Street Playhouse, and provides them pre-performance lectures by actors, production and staff personnel.

Both the U3A and Lifelong Learning Institutes are currently aimed at the retiree and seasoned citizen. However, if we are to take the idea of personal and intellectual development seriously, we must expand this type of education to ages younger than fifty. After all, people of all ages will be taking those job sabbaticals and career hiatuses. So these programs should be accessible to all. Actually, the Learning Annex in New York has been offering minicourses to young and older adults in a wide variety of topics for several decades. However, many of these seminars are one-shot skill-building exercises which do not compare to the type of ambitious learning objectives that the U3As and lifelong learning institutes are famous for.

Eventually, a vast "personal enhancement" industry will arise to meet self-development needs of our entire society.

GIVING BACK: VOLUNTEERISM AND MENTORING
Volunteering seems to be one of the great American pastimes. Millions of people offer their services to a variety of organizations and causes that need individual who will donate their time and effort, and will do so for free.

The Superlongevity Revolution will serve as a big boost for organizations requiring many person-hours of unpaid labor. People who will either be on career hiatuses or are actually transitioning to full retirement will provide the organizations a veritable army of volunteers. On recent surveys many Americans are assuming that volunteering will become a natural and fulfilling part of their post-work lives.

I personally saw the power of volunteer work about ten years ago. The city of Morristown, New Jersey decided to rehabilitate its moribund theatre to a state that would enable the city to invite top classical, dance, comedy and popular acts into the city environs. The building's physical rehabilitation was performed with the help of a large cadre of volunteers, who swept the floors, painted and did whatever physical work was necessary to get the building in working order. Improvements have been made over the years in the building's structure and size. Now the theatre has no problems attracting top orchestras like the Budapest Festival Orchestra as well as pop performers such as Dennis Miller, Tony Bennett, the Beach Boys and the like. Volunteers continue to keep the Community Theatre running—they operate the box office, serve as ushers at performances and staff the concession stands.

The people who volunteer in projects around the country and the world are sometimes retirees who want to make a contribution to their communities, as well as working professionals and business people who have the need to give. Mentor programs have proliferated throughout the world—such programs often link seasoned professionals and retirees with young people, including elementary school age students who need help with reading or math or simply completing their homework.

We already looked at the experience of the retired and semi-retired professionals living in Callawassie Island in South Carolina who volunteered their time to help the local towns as financial advisers, remedial reading mentors, and fund raisers. Reading in various capacities seems to be an area needing volunteer work. One of my aunts worked for several years in a New York-based "reading for the blind" program, which specialized in providing books-on-tape. She started out as a sound engineer and eventually worked her way up to reader—at seventy years old she still retained her clipped, clear speaking manner required for tape transcriptions. Another person I know became involved in a literacy program for immigrants. She worked for months as a one-on-one instructor teaching English to a recent immigrant from Poland, a role she found extremely fulfilling.

Volunteering will become a bedrock activity as the Superlongevity Revolution adds healthy years to our lives. A report on work patterns in West Virginia stated findings that residents were very prone to volunteering. At Huntington West Virginia's "Faith in Action of the River Cities", a volunteer interfaith care-giving agency in Huntington, retirees make up more than half of its volunteer force. According to Executive Director Darlene Lowry, the retirees "have an awareness of the needs of the community." More importantly, she said, they know that the organization needs free labor, because they realize that groups such as Faith in Action are "providing services on a shoestring budget." One of their volunteers, a former newspaper reporter, drives elderly people to doctors' appointments and does their grocery shopping.

Many retirees and those in between jobs get out in their communities by working in senior centers, senior programs, Meals on Wheels, or are involved in church or community activities. According to one program administrator, "Volunteering to do something is meaningful and many retired workers sure have that spirit."[63]

Volunteering benefits not just the organizations and the people that they serve. The act of assisting others also provides benefits to those who do the helping. A two-year study of 128 volunteers between the ages of sixty and eighty-six, who were working with schoolchildren in Baltimore, Maryland, found that the people who volunteer were in better health, watched fewer television programs, burned more calories each week, and reported having more friends and acquaintances in their social networks when compared with a control group sample of people of similar age and socio-economic background.

Organizations such as the American Association of Retired Persons are well aware of the physical, social, and psychological benefits of volunteering. For this reason AARP actively encourages and fosters such altruistic activities. The AARP volunteer programs and activities cover a wide gamut, many of which exist for the expressed purpose of helping older people and others "maintain their dignity, independence, and sense of purpose."

The AARP Benefits Outreach Program has volunteers help older people with low or moderate incomes find public and private benefit programs that pay for their prescription drugs, groceries, doctors and heating bills, property taxes and more. In 2005, the program helped nearly 5,000 low-income older persons acquire benefits. 2400 AARP chapters in the United States and elsewhere serve as centers of community volunteerism. The chapters support and service mentoring activities, food and clothing drives and often combine with groups like Habitat for Humanity and Meals on Wheels. AARP also runs a volunteer-driven service called AARP Tax-Aide, in which volunteers provide free tax preparation services to millions of low and moderate income taxpayers, focusing on those age sixty and over. Over the last thirty-six years, an astounding 32,000 volunteers have worked in a variety of positions in the TAX-

Aide program.

One of their programs, AARP's annual "National Day of Service," is a testimony to the power of volunteering. One May 11, 2006, AARP turned out 32,000 volunteers and staff to provide key services and information to communities around the United States. The volunteers spent the day working at community-based organizations such as food pantries, senior centers and assisted living facilities. In Oregon, AARP teams worked with food banks to provide and deliver food for the needy, and in Michigan, these Good Samaritans staffed blood drives throughout the state. In Missouri, AARP volunteers made "friendly" visits to nursing homes, visually checking that the homes maintained safe and hygienic standards and practices. In Connecticut and Delaware, teams made modifications to ten homes occupied by senior homeowners.

Many corporations and non-profit organizations encourage their employees, most of whom are years away from reaching senior status, to donate their time for a variety of causes. I recently participated in a three-mile walk to raise awareness of breast cancer—several thousand employees and their families representing hundreds of corporations from New York and New Jersey made the hike to support this cause. Timberland, the boot shoe manufacturer, runs a program called Serv-a-palooza. Timberland employees in twenty-seven different countries give of their time to help communities in very direct ways—they renovate playgrounds and spruce up camp grounds. Two hundred company employees and guests in Zhuhai, China landscaped and painted the Fei Sha Elementary School.[64]

One *Wall Street Journal* article discussed some issues which people should consider when they are about to contribute their time to such altruistic activity.

According to John Gomperts, chief executive of Experience Corps, a nonprofit service organization based in Washington, D.C., "If you want [volunteering] to be a significant part of your life, then it's likely going to take some work to figure out the right fit."

Retirement consultants, non-profit executives and happily-placed volunteers quoted in the article advise that a person who wants to volunteer first identify what type of cause and activity they find inspiring. Mary Westropp, director of volunteer placement for Boston-based New Directions Inc., advises you to determine, "What really matters to you? Is it housing and homelessness? Human rights? Education? Do you have an interest in the fine arts?

Perhaps you should become a docent in a museum." In addition, experts warn that the volunteer might have to "start at the bottom."

They also suggested that you should be mindful of whether you want to get involved in something completely new. In their quest for novel experiences, sometimes people volunteer for positions and activities for which they have very little preparation and skill. Not everyone can build a pier, prepare someone's taxes or teach others to read.

The experts made a very good point about how much time a volunteer should expend in this activity. Even if you love the cause—tutoring children can be extremely emotionally rewarding—you still must determine what your priorities are. The personal development paradigm outlined in this chapter is not to be taken lightly—in a career that might stretch well over a century, the experiences we have during our hiatuses from careers is a critical component of the sum of our lives. The article describes Mr. Williams, an investment banker who retired in his fifties. While he volunteers in activities such as fund raising and job-training, he makes sure those activities do not end up ruling his life. Since he retired primarily to be with his family, his priorities are family number one, than volunteering activities and lastly a Chinese investment venture he recently started.[65]

The United States Government, through its Corporation for National and Community Service, seeks to encourage citizen altruism. The Corporation's program "Mobilizing More Volunteers" is attempting to increase the number of Americans who volunteer each year to ten million within five years, hoping to reach a total of some seventy-five million in 2010. The plan's stated goals are quite ambitious—provide mentoring services to three million additional children and youth living in disadvantaged conditions, and engage five million college students in service and an additional three million baby boomers in volunteering.[66]

STRENGTHENING THE MIND AND BRAIN

Possibly the most important component of the self-development process is the nurturing and strengthening of our minds and brains. In the next chapter we will look at ways breakthroughs in fields such as genetics, nanotechnology, and pharmacology will lead to a radical improvement in the functioning of the brain, as well as other parts of the body and the human shell itself.

However, regardless of how much modern science improves the brain's functioning, the actions of the brain's owner will go a long way in determining how efficiently the brain retains its vibrancy and agility.

Growing the Brain

Surveys have shown that our culture has several stock beliefs about the brain and how it functions. Do you share these beliefs? Answer "true" or "false to each item to find out:

1: You can't change the overall efficiency of your brain
2: People lose brain cells every day and they eventually just run out.
3: The brain doesn't make new brain cells.
4: Memory decline is inevitable as we age.

The majority of people answer "true" to the majority of these questions. The truth is that the more we learn about the brain the more we are fascinated with the capacity of this seat of cerebral activity to regenerate and rejuvenate.

Until only recently, most researchers believed that the human brain started out malleable, and as it matured over time, gained shape and intellectual muscle. This organ supposedly reached its peak of power and dexterity when the person reached age forty. After that, the brain began to slowly lose its cognitive power. By age sixty or seventy, the person's brain had lost much of its ability to retain new information—the person's "memory isn't what it used to be." As time went on, the brain's ability to process the information it already had was also impaired.

Through various laboratory tests and field experiments, we are discovering that this model is overwhelmingly flawed. For one thing, the "hardwired" brain was much more malleable than thought. The term "neuroplasticity" has come into vogue among scientists studying the brain. In the book *The Mind and the Brain* the authors Jeffrey M. Schwartz and Sharon Begley described a wealth of experiments showing that the brain could be rewired not only in childhood, as originally thought, but throughout the person's life. Equally promising was the fact that studies were clearly demonstrating that we can use our minds to actively engage the brain and improve its overall efficiency. [67]

As scientists reassess old results, they are even discovering that neurons do not simply disappear from the brain. According to Marilyn Albert of Johns Hopkins School of Medicine, "It used to be thought that normal cognitive decline occurred because of loss of neurons throughout the brain." However, studies with newer technologies such as the MRI demonstrate quite clearly that most regions of the brain, including the hippocampus, where our memories arise, or the frontal cortex, where planning and judgment take place, retain their neurons, suffer little or no loss of neurons. People at seventy and older create new neurons.

Neurologists and psychologists increasingly conclude that the brain's neuroplasticity enables it to rewire itself by fashioning new connections among its neurons and thus rewire itself. Even sensory input can change the brain, and the brain remodels itself in response to behavioral demands. Regions that we use most often literally expand—experiments have shown that in the busiest regions the neural circuits endure and enlarge. During what is currently seen as our "midlife" period, the years from thirty-five to sixty-five, our brains are much more malleable and have a much higher growth potential than science, and everyone influenced by scientific opinion, ever realized.

So what conditions and activities serve to stimulate brain growth? A clue comes from a study of nuns, the School Sisters of Notre Dame in Mankato, Minnesota. These nuns not only live long, but maintain their mental vigor into old age—their lifestyle was remarkable in its mental richness and stimulation. Researchers curious about the physical status of these nuns' brains examined the brains of some of these nuns after their deaths. They discovered in these brains something they did not expect: the characteristic of Alzheimer's tangles and plaques! The researchers puzzled over the nuns' ability to retain their mental powers despite the presence of Alzheimer's disease.

The neuro-scientists conclusions have profound implications for all of us. According to their findings, the Notre Dame nuns' lifelong mental activities conferred "neuroprotection" (which included the production of extra neurons and connections among them) that counteracted the effects of a dementing brain disorder. The nuns' mental activities—teaching, reading, researching and writing—ensured that the nuns would retain clarity of mind despite the presence of biological markers of a disease that we assumed should lead to neurological decline.

Research is also demonstrating that for many people not only does the aging process not batter the brain, it actually makes it better. As it ages the brain begins bringing new cognitive systems on line and increasing the cross-referencing between them in novel ways. Even if your memory cannot retain as much raw data as it could when you were a college student, your ability to manage information and make sense of it increases exponentially over time. "In midlife," says UCLA neurologist George Bartzokis, "You're beginning to maximize the ability to use the entirety of the information in your brain on an everyday, ongoing, second-to-second basis. Biologically, that's what wisdom is." [68]

One critical finding is that older brains deteriorate not so much because of their chronological age but because of the lifestyle of their owners. On average, when compared to younger people, the elderly tend to have fewer new experiences, be less physically active and socially engaged and live in less complex environments. All of these interfere with the brains innate propensity to produce new neurons and maintain neural circuitry. This is the problem with the current model of "retirement." According to research psychologist Denise Park of the University of Illinois at Urbana-Champaign, "The trouble with retirement is, there are not a lot of social or intellectual demands." She says that cognitive decline is rooted in the fact that "life becomes routinized" during retirement. [69]

Therefore, it is logical to conclude that whether we decline or improve during aging is within our control. I am reminded of a line from a Bob Dylan song-poem: "He not busy being born is busy dying." People themselves must determine whether or not they are willing to "grow their brains."

Unlocking Your Brain Power and Creativity

An article in *Time* magazine profiled two people, Barbara Hustedt Crook and Robert Strozier, who decided to collaborate on a daunting task, the writing of their first musical. They both had backgrounds in the arts, writing and editing in New York City, and Crook had experience performing, singing and piano. Still, creating a musical is a profound career leap. Crook started this right before her sixtieth birthday and Strozier began at age sixty-five. We usually think of the creative and performing arts as more of a young person's game, even if history shows that Brahms did some of his best work in his seventies and as mentioned writers like Barzun achieve great heights as they approach one hundred.[70]

Crook and Strozier, the budding playwrights, describe some of the advantages of creating at a later age. "I find that my brain makes leaps it did-n't make so easily. I can hear my inner voice and trust instincts and hunches in ways I didn't used to," Crook states. Stozier talks about the willingness to take chances at older ages. He revealed this willingness by saying, "At a certain age you either get older or you get younger. If you get younger, you venture out and take risks."

Since, as we've learned, the brain is a dynamic organ, the activities we engage in throughout our lives impact the brain's complex circuitry. Research consistently reveals that the brain responds directly to those activities and grows and strengthens that part of the brain necessary to carry out the activity, regardless of our age at the time of the activity. It allocates "neural real estate" in reaction to what we are using most, such as a videogame addicts' thumb, a Braille reader's index finger, a chess player's analytic ability or a linguist's language skills.

So how does one improve and revitalize the brain? Improvement can be achieved mostly through learning, in the broadest sense. According to Michael Merzenich, PhD, a neurobiologist at University of California, San Francisco, "The brain wants to learn. It wants to be engaged as a learning machine." This involves not just replaying well-learned skills that you've mastered in life, but also new skills and abilities, new hobbies and activities that require the brain to remodel itself. Staying mentally active throughout life is good advice. James McGaugh, PhD, a Dana Alliance for Brain Initiatives member at University of California, Irvine states that "We can make the brain work better simply by accumulating more knowledge, which builds more networks of connections in the brain."

Another Dana Alliance member, Duke University's Lawrence Katz, PhD, has developed a set of exercises called "neurobics," that encourages people to use their brains in non-routine ways. He focuses on among other things the routine activities of our lives, such as the route we take to work. Katz claims that taking this route becomes so automatic that you do it without even thinking about it. He suggests taking another route to your job occasionally. Why? Katz states that by taking a new route "your brain is forced to use its attention resources to do that very simple task." In simpler terms, by navigating through a different route you are making the brain think. Katz states that you exercise your brain by focusing "your brain's attention on what you're doing at the time you're doing it." Some of his other *neurobic* exercises include finding your keys or picking out coins in a purse by using your sense of touch rather than sight. These exercises can have certain effects on your brain by making it think differently.

When writing on my computer, I challenge my brain (and hopefully stir up the creative juices) by periodically forcing myself to operate the keyboard mouse with my left hand instead of my right hand as is my natural tendency. [71]

There are other more common sense methods of retaining brainpower. Experts advise people to perform physical exercise (especially aerobic exercise), engage in intellectually stimulating mental activity, eat a healthy diet, maintain social connections, including time with friends and family members, for example, learn to manage stress, and develop a positive attitude toward yourself and your world. I believe that in the Superlongevity Era people will follow in the footsteps of Stozier and Crook and engage in creative activities, like writing a novel, tackling a foreign language or learning to play a musical instrument.

One of the reasons that Nintendo, the Japanese game giant, is so successful is that it is constantly looking for new markets. One of the segments Nintendo would love to capture is the Baby Boomers, who might be worrying about losing their mental sharpness in their forties and fifties. Welcome to the world of *Brain Age: Train Your Brain in Minutes a Day!* Nintendo hopes to get American boomers to buy *Brain Age to* start doing its brain workouts. Of course, to operate the game each boomer will also have to purchase the 130 dollar Nintendo DS hand-held game machine, popular among teenagers but few of the older set. In early 2006 the game company blitzed the airwaves with ads showing a woman in her forties playing the game, writing her answers on the screen with a digital pen as the questions appeared in fairly quick order.

Based on the theories of a Japanese brain researcher named Ryuta Kawashima, the game looks at your answers and assigns your brain an "age," which Nintendo claims the game can reduce considerably through a series of digital training exercises—rapid-fire math problems, reading drills and language challenges. A second title, *Big Brain Academy*, will be released May 30.

Many of the exercises have appeared in different formats over the years, in newspapers, magazines, and on the Internet. One drill requires you to write the answers to twenty simple math problems. A second has you memorize and then write a long list of words. A third, the Stroop Test, in rapid succession, places in front of you the names of colors—"blue," "red," "yellow" and "black"—but each name is written in a color different from what the name signifies. (E.g. the word "blue" might be written in red type, the word "black" in yellow.) You are instructed to state aloud the color that the word is written in, not the word itself. Sounds easy? Believe it or not, most people initially give the wrong answer. If the word "blue" appears in red, most people say "blue," even though the instruction states that we are to say aloud the actual colorization of the letters of the word, in this case red. Most of us tend to read the name of the color as written, even though you know that you're supposed to say the color of the typeface that you are seeing.

Most people who play the game are essentially putting themselves through the same type of mental rigors they would encounter playing Suduku or other such games. These are fun mental exercises to regenerate the brain and hopefully stimulate it in parts that we have been ignoring.[72]

The Power of Meditation

For centuries, people have attested to the power of meditation, the very same technique practiced by monks and other religious contemplatives attempting to achieve nirvana or just get closer to their concept of God.

Many Westerners now use meditation to reduce stress—brokers and others working in high pressure environments have signed on to meditation training programs. Corporations such as Google, Deutsche Bank, Hughes Aircraft, Tower Co., a Washington-based development firm, as well as many other organization offer meditation classes to their workers. According to Jeffrey Abramson, CEO of Tower Co., 75 percent of his staff attends free classes in transcendental meditation. While these companies were originally interested in preventing stress-related illness and reducing absenteeism, they also have learned that meditation helps make employees mentally sharper.

Over the last decade or so researchers have scientifically demonstrated the powerful positive impact of meditation on brain activity. One 1992 experiment found that Nepalese Buddhist monks produced high-frequency brain activity called gamma waves during compassion meditation. Moreover, most monks showed extremely large increases of brain activity at levels never reported before in the neuroscience literature.

In recent experiments using advanced brain scanning technology, researchers are finding that meditation directly affects the function and structure of the brain, changing it in ways that appear to increase the attention span, sharpen the focus and improve the memory of the meditator. A 2005 Massachusetts General Hospital study showed that the gray matter of twenty men and women who meditated for just forty minutes a day was thicker than that of people who did not. And the subjects of this study were not Buddhist monks—they were Boston-area workers practicing a Western style of meditation called mindfulness or insight meditation. "We showed for the first time that you don't have to do it all day for similar results," says study director Sara Lazar. In addition, her research suggests that meditation may retard the natural thinning of that section of the cortex that occurs with age.[73]

Meditation delivers other benefits as well. Many people who meditate assert that the practice restores their energy, allowing them to perform better at tasks that require attention and concentration. It also seems to boost their emotional intelligence, their ability to get along with others.

If a person decides that she wants to incorporate meditation into her personal development program, she need not move to Tibet or join a commune. Some people get started by merely finding a "how to meditate" tip sheet on the Internet using a search engine. Others attend an instructional retreat such as the one week session offered by Insight Meditation Society (IMS) in rural Barre, Massachusetts or spend time at The Ashram, nestled in the Santa Monica mountains near Los Angeles.

There are other ways of developing the brain and increasing your creativity. A modern catalogue of mind expansion techniques include biofeedback, visualization, thought stopping, deep breathing, Yoga, and even hypnosis.[74]

Based on all we know about the potential of our brains to not only retain but actually expand its power as we age, it is obvious that the continued health and strength of our mental status is in our own hands. Our responsibility, then, is to challenge our minds on a daily basis and remain open to new ideas and experiences.

The activities that we are slowly adopting for our non-work hours, days, and months and years (when we are on a career hiatus) are increasingly designed to expose us to such novel experiences. And when we take courses that deal with subjects totally new to us, or work as a volunteer, or take an experiential travel excursion, we are resuscitating and refreshing our minds, and quite possibly our souls. That resulting mental sharpness in turn helps us retain the physical vibrancy and health of youth.

In the *Ageless Nation*, citizens will adopt personal development both as a core cultural value as well as a lifetime activity. Thank the Superlongevity Revolution for the many additional years which will be available to each of us so that we can spend time pursuing opportunities that will help us grow intellectually and spiritually.

chapter five

The Changing Family

In addition to work and education, the radical extension of the longer life span will radically transform marriage, childbearing and even the very structure of the family itself. Let's pose a number of tantalizing questions about how superlongevity will impact these institutions.

Will superlongevity encourage people to marry later or earlier than previous generations? Suddenly faced with the probability of living into their hundreds, will people opt not for singular monogamy but experiment with "sequential marriages"? Will longer lives encourage couples to hasten or postpone having children? Also, how will our ability to use genetic engineering to pre-select our offspring's height, eye color and intelligence fundamentally change the criteria by which we select our mate or spouse? Will tomorrow's parents attempt to create a new breed of superchildren?

The answers revealed in this chapter might surprise you. Let us begin with one of the more unexpected developments that I contend will result from increased longevity in the *Ageless Nation*.

THE REBIRTH OF THE MULTIGENERATIONAL EXTENDED FAMILY

One social trend, which I believe will develop as a result of the Superlongevity Revolution, is the rebirth of the multigenerational extended family. Multiple generations of a given blood-related family will not only be living at the same time, but they will gradually evolve into a working, functioning family unit. This trend will be contrary to the one of the last fifty or so years, in which people tended to live in relatively isolated mobile nuclear family units.

Before we look at the burgeoning statistics on the real growth in multi-generational housing and other trends, let me recount how I personally began to notice the beginning of this trend.

I first attended *The Fest for Beatles Fans*, or *Beatlefest*, as it was originally known, in 2000. The brainchild of Mark Lapidos, these conclaves have been going on since 1974 as a way to celebrate, study, and keep alive the legacy of the Beatles. The festival, which is held at various times of the year in the United States in New Jersey, Los Angeles, and Chicago, among other places, is the consummate celebration of the Beatles, featuring films, special guests, live concerts, an Art Museum and Art Contest, Flea Market, Discussions, Look-Alike and Sound-Alike Contests, Auctions, and a Charity Raffle.

Entering the Crown Plaza Hotel in Secaucus, NJ to attend my first such festival, I walked into a magical new world. People were congregating around musicians who had mysteriously coagulated in hallways and hotel lobbies into music groups playing, almost perfectly, various Beatles songs.

What struck me most was the diversity of age groups represented in the rooms and hallways. Standing around the impromptu concerts in the lobby and halls were people in their forties, fifties, and sixties; parents in their thir-ties and forties with children and teenagers; and couples in their twenties. At least half the people at these conclaves were not old enough to have person-ally experienced the Beatles phenomenon or the 1960s. But there is some-thing about the zeitgeist of those times, as epitomized by the Beatles music, films, books, and by the band's members themselves, that draw crowds which grow larger every year, whether they lived through those times or not.

The multigenerationality of this event serves a real function—the young people want to know what times were like and if their elders ever saw a Beatles concert. At their disposal are older family members to provide a "living his-tory" of the events of the time. Far from a "generation gap" existing at this event, there seemed to be a harmony between the generations. The common desire to understand, and keep alive, the spirit that was the Beatles spiritually link most *Fest* attendees, regardless of their ages.

A more visual representation of this multigenerational linkage emerged near the end of the Festival, at the "Battle of the Bands" event. Here, forty or so pre-screened groups, duos, and sometimes individuals sporting names like "Strawberry Fields" and "Lucy in the Sky" performed one Beatle song each in a contest for honors as the top performer. The performers range in age from twelve to as old as sixty or greater, with the majority of the bands in their late teens to early thirties. The age of the performers gives no clue as to their musical style—at times you have a more "senior" band blasting out raucous rock versions of Lennon & McCartney ballads and younger duos doing folk versions of the more dynamic Beatles tunes.

Common interest creates common grounds, regardless of our position in the life cycle. This was brought home quite poignantly at the 2004 *Fest.* Writer Peter Smith discussed his book *Two of Us: The Story of a Father, a Son and the Beatles,* which tells how he and his seven-year-old son were brought closer together through a mutual love of the Beatles. The son first discovered the Beatles when perusing his parents' old albums and cassettes. The father and son achieved a new level of communication in their voyage of discovery about the Beatles phenomenon, culminating in a pilgrimage by Smith and son to London and Liverpool to discover the roots of the Beatles experience. I sensed that many parents and children at Smith's lecture were feeling the same feeling of closeness to their children.[75]

One aspect of the Beatles music that helps this multigenerational communication is the fact that popular music itself does not separate people the way that music of twenty-five or thirty years ago did. The boomers could not imagine themselves sitting with their parents and listening to Big Band music of the 1930s and 1940s. But the rock music of the Beatles era and beyond does tend to sound very much like much of the music of today, excluding perhaps Rap or Hip Hop. Hence, even children, teens, and twenty-somethings enjoy listening to and playing Beatles music. (Many of my students join bands to recreate the sounds of Cream and Led Zeppelin, still considered the standard bearers of "real" metallic rock). Whatever divides age groups today, it is not the sound and cadence of music.

Multigenerationality's Benefits

The intergenerational connectedness I witnessed at the *Fest for the Beatles* is indicative of a trend I see emerging in a number of areas, including housing and travel. The revival of the multigenerational extended family in the Superlongevity Era is very good news. This type of family bestows on its members enormous financial, logistical, sociological and psychological benefits that are not readily available to those living in the current relatively isolated nuclear family.

Let's start by describing the physical status of the members of the multi-generational extended family in this new society. Based on the medical advances described so far, even at 125 years old the great-great grandparents in such families will be in a state of good health and be as physically fit as people are today in their forties and fifties. As we described earlier, "retirement" as we know it today will have become an anachronism—members of each generation of the family will be in their first or even their fifth careers, and still have incomes we associate with fully employed individuals. Some members of the family will also be on temporary job or career hiatuses and so have a good deal of free time.

The financial benefits of the multigenerational extended family extend from the adult child to the older parent. However, in this new paradigm, it will generally be the case that the great grandparents, who have been working and accumulating capital for a century or more, will be in a far greater position to help the younger members who have to support younger children. So these family elders can direct funds where needed to help the younger generations survive and thrive.

Also, the older family members, having worked in several fields for many decades, will have a plethora of job and career contacts that can help the younger generations find employment and funding for new businesses. Think of the power and influence of extended families such as the Kennedys and Rockefellers. These families still produce a large number of offspring, and have essentially organized themselves like political and business organizations. They are more than just families. Being born a Kennedy endows one with a wealth of political and social contacts developed by the family for more than a century. Instead of envying these families, the multigenerational extended family of the future will try to emulate the organizational style of families like the Kennedys and build social capital over time that can be shared with all family members.

Another advantage of having access to people considerably older than oneself is that these people become a veritable living history of events and times that today we can only read about in books or view on the *Biography* channel. They not only enlighten all those around them about the events, but often bring a unique perspective of times gone by that can help the next generation meet the challenges of current times.

Throughout my life, I have been lucky to be surrounded by "wise elders" who were intelligent enough, and sufficiently observant, to gain much from their experiences. One of my aunts, who recently passed away in her nineties, was already a working adult in the 1920s. She worked on Wall Street (which was rare for a woman back then) and experienced the stock market crash of 1929 first hand. She would describe the sheer panic in the eyes of brokers and stockholders, and the feeling of desperation wafting over the financial district during the weeks in that October. I myself have lived through stock market mini-crashes such as that of October 1987 as well as the bursting of the 1990s Internet stock bubble in 2000-2001. Because I had listened to my aunt's description of what a real crash "feels" like, I never allowed myself to engage in panic selling during these recent sell offs. While these were bear markets, they did not have the "feel" of the 1929 debacle that led in part to the economic debacle we know as The Great Depression of the 1930s.

I first developed an interest in my field, the impact of technological change, through talks I had with my grandmother. Over the course of several decades she observed how the introduction of the airplane, television, the automobile, radio, the movies and a host of other inventions created the world we live in today. As a very young baseball fan, I was thrilled by the stories about Babe Ruth and other stars told to me by relatives who had seen these legends play as far back as the 1920s.

University professors often serve as a sort of "historical memory" for students. As a management professor, I often deal with current issues impacting our economy. One of those is the recent spike in oil prices. Most of my students depend on automobiles (New Jersey has a fairly limited public transportation system), and are rightly concerned with the doubling of gas prices. Having lived through the gas crises of the 1970s, I try to provide perspective to my students and show the differences, at least for the time being, between the two eras. They express disbelief when I describe blocks-long lines of people waiting for gas, and the sheer desperation of not knowing if when you finally edged up to the pump it would just have gone dry. For some reason, the gas shortage experience has been expunged from our cultural memory. TV documentaries do not see the 1970s gas crises as a worthy or interesting topic.

While for the time being our society only has to deal with high petroleum prices, it is not inconceivable that we could experience at some point 1970s style gas shortages. I am sure that as a result of my cautionary tales, my students are persuaded that we could experience such shortages again. Hopefully some of them will avoid buying a gas guzzler and perhaps choose a high-MPG hybrid vehicle in the future.

There is another type of "history" which the wise elders of the multigenerational family possess. As we've observed, as a result of the Superlongevity Revolution, several generations of the same family will flourish simultaneously. These family elders, some who may be 150 years old, can make the younger family members aware of the roots and development of their family itself. True, today as part of school exercises children often draw comprehensive genealogical tables tracing their family's origins. Imagine how rich that history would be if the child has at his or her disposal living family members stretching back seven or eight generations.

Of course, there is a difference between history and what I label "nostalgia." Younger members are not necessarily interested in hearing the wise elders simply ruminate and reminisce about the good old days. What will get their attention, though, is any information that helps them make sense of their lives and their place in the flow of events. They also want to know how this information will help them navigate their way into the future. Remember, it is one thing to know about the past, but it is quite another to still be living in it. Younger generations will quickly sense the difference.

There are logistical benefits to the members of such families as well. In the next section we'll look at how the multigenerational extended family might also adopt living arrangements in which the members live in close proximity to each other. In such a situation, the older generations can baby-sit the great grandchildren when necessary. And the younger members can also be physically in position to help older generations of the family remain healthy and safe.

There is growing evidence that grandfathers are helping raise their children's kids. A survey of 1,353 parents performed by parenting Web site BabyCenter.com found that 72 percent had grandparents living nearby. Of those respondents, 77 percent reported that their children's grandfathers participated in child care duties. A *Wall Street Journal* article reporting the survey referred to these men as Mr. Grandmom. [76]

Some might ask why a multigenerational family unit will evolve in a society in which divorce has become more commonplace. The high incidence of divorce would seem to suggest that the family unit is becoming weaker and more fragmented, not more unified. True, the divorce rate in the United States is around 35-40 percent. (The oft-quoted 50 percent divorce rate is erroneous, based on a misreading of demographic statistics.) But the fact that divorce is so common, an experience makes the multigenerational extended family even more important. Although our society denies it, divorce has a devastating emotional impact on all involved. Study after study reveals how children are hurt emotionally and cognitively when their parents split.

I believe that a strong cadre of grandparents, uncles, aunts and cousins can possibly mitigate some of the more destructive aspects of the broken home phenomenon. In the two–earner family of today, when the couple splits up the mother, who most often must bring up the children, maintain the household and still pursue her career. Often in such situations, the husband becomes the "odd man out" in the emerging family paradigm. The parents of both ex-partners gravitate toward the grandchildren, and thus the remaining family unit. Regardless of their continuing relations with the ex-husband, many focus their holiday activities around the remaining children and thus the wife. What emerges is a new-style extended family unit in which all the grandparents provide the mother financial support and the children the needed emotional bonds. Most often, the children still celebrate all holidays and birthdays with their cousins, even if the cousins are the children of the ex-husband's brothers or sisters. The grandparents from both sides of the family also baby-sit when necessary.

According to Kent State University psychologist John Guidubaldi, grandfather involvement is crucial, especially in single-parent households. His study of 350 single-parent households revealed that when grandfathers are involved, children have fewer social problems, exhibit more confidence, and do better academically.

Technology Bringing Families Together

New communication and transportation methods will help bring generations of the same family together on a very personal level. Breakthroughs in communications technologies as well as faster and more accessible modes of transportation will make it easier for multigenerational families to function as a single unit.

Next-step technologies such as virtual reality and high-speed rail will enable the multigenerational family to remain an organic unit whose members can easily and frequently physically interact.

It is becoming easier for people of all ages to communicate via computer. The cultural template was established in a memorable moment in Stanley Kubrick's 1968 magnum opus, *2001: A Space Odyssey*, in which a scientist aboard a space station uses a picture phone to wish his daughter back home a happy birthday. Currently, this feat is a mere mouse click away for members of the multigenerational family.

Several developments help explain such progress. "Chat services," which allow instantaneous communication online, appeared in the mid-1990s as a way for users to exchange text messages instantaneously. Unlike emails, which we create, send and then wait for a reply, these chat services simulate real conversations.

These services have taken instant messaging to the next level by adding video options. This is possible, because web cameras dropped in price, and increasingly often are built right into the computer. Meanwhile, more families have high-speed Internet connections, which can carry the huge amounts of data that make video chats practical. A 2006 Nielsen/NetRatings study found that 95.5 million consumers in the United States now use such connections at home, a 28 percent increase in one year alone.

While most of these services are free, you can pay for extra options, including multiparty calling or the chance to record extended "video mail," which is simply email that contains film.

Such inexpensive and accessible videoconferencing is already facilitating multigenerational communication. An April 2006 *Wall Street Journal* article recounted how Steve and Linda Goldfarb, retired lawyers turned winemakers of Anomaly Vineyards in St. Helena, California, use their Webcam-equipped computer to wish their granddaughter, a toddler living in Los Angeles, California, a happy holiday. In a wonderful example of how people can expand technology well beyond the intentions of the inventors, Mrs. Goldfarb and the toddler have adapted the Webcam to a game which people used to play in person. Mrs. Goldfarb and her granddaughter actually play hide and seek using the Webcam. In the true spirit of multigenerationality, she videochatted with her son, a financial adviser in San Diego, and also bought a camera for her father, who lives nearby in Albany, California. "I use it a lot, even just to say hi," she says.[77]

One video-based concept that might catch on with the emerging multigenerational extended family is called the *Virtual Family Dinner*, the brainchild of Accenture Ltd. The technology consulting company's innovation would enable families to get together—virtually—as often as they wish. The concept is simple. A woman in New Jersey makes herself dinner, and when she is about to sit down and eat, the *Virtual Family Dinner* system's technology detects it and alerts her son and daughter-in-law in Atlanta, Georgia. The son then walks into his kitchen, where a small camera and microphone capture what he is doing. Both kitchens are equipped with speakers and a screen, which can be as large as a standard television screen. Cameras and microphones could be placed on top of a counter, television set or built into smart picture frames that capture what is going on in one family member's kitchen and display the information in another member's room. The mother sees the son and his wife eating, and they in turn see and hear his mother.

This kind of technology would enable the multigenerational extended family to retain a sense of intimacy and connection otherwise lost due to the physical distance between family members. Don Babwin's article "Set the Table, Pour the Water, Turn on the Camera: System would allow for meals with far-flung loved ones," which was syndicated by the Associated Press, discusses how according to Julie Locher, Assistant Professor of Medicine at the University of Alabama-Birmingham, who specializes in eating issues among older people, "To physically eat with others, to be able to do that, there are not only social benefits, but health benefits." We know, for instance, that older people who eat alone often do not eat sufficient amounts of the most nutritious foods. Some experts feel that an elder's isolation at meal time can trigger physical and mental problems that eventually can become life-threatening. Cai Glushak, a Chicago physician who runs a company that video-monitors patients, feels this *Virtual Family Dinner* concept would help the family keep an eye on the general health and well-being of the parents. For instance, they could tell whether the parents are looking too thin, combing their hair or wearing clean clothes.

Second Life, Inc. has pioneered an even more ambitious form of cyber-communication destined to be incorporated into family life whose locus of activity is found on their website. Second Life (SL) is a privately owned, partly subscription-based 3-D virtual world operated by San Francisco-based Linden Lab. Users, or "residents" as they like to be called, can visit and experience this virtual world like it is a real place. Like the computer game "The Sims," a user is represented by an "avatar", a cyber-body of his or her choosing. The SL software enables the user to guide his avatar through a 3-D landscape populated with hotels, pools, towns, ball fields and cafes built not by Linden Lab but by the people who inhabit it. (The Lab only provides the internet infrastructure.) You can talk and interact with other people/avatars, participate in individual and group activities and even construct objects such as houses. SL has been described as an animated version of real life—over time you become more familiar with the SL culture and learn the social skills required to interact successfully with others.

SL is growing by leaps and bounds. In early 2007, the average number of users in SL at one time numbers between ten and twenty thousand. Registered accounts grew from one million people in October 2006 to over two million by January 2007, due to both word-of-mouth as well as articles in the *Wall Street Journal*, *Business Week*, *Time*, and other national publications. This exponential growth is not surprising—anyone using Second Life will attest to the fact that SL is an engrossing, intriguing and possibly addictive simulation-based activity.

Annaless Newitz's article, "Second Life is Ready" in the September 2006 issue of *Popular Science*, discusses how SL is not only for residents wanting to play. Recently, several companies have built replicas of their conference rooms in SL so that far-flung employees can meet and exchange information, and even collaboratively build prototypes of real-world projects. Wells Fargo, Toyota, Nike and a host of other companies have now built their own branded "islands" within SL to show off and even sell their products. SL's conference rooms are excellent places to swap blueprints with a team around the world. Companies such as Wal-Mart, Intel and American Express are considering SL as their next corporate training site. And more than a dozen universities, including Montana State, have already started experimenting with SL as a teaching modality in which the professor and her students have real-time discussions and interactions in a simulated classroom.

Second Life could be a boon to family relationships. Families whose members are geographically separated because of jobs, lifestyle preferences or economic circumstances will have another tool for interacting with each other. Family members, including grandparents, parents, children, and cousins, as well as aunts and uncles, can get together in the realistic settings made possible by Second Life. Since SL technology permits users to create their own avatar (instead of using one of SL's pre-made "off the rack" anonymous avatars), people can design and represent themselves with an avatar that looks just like them. This should only heighten the realism of the SL family living experience. Grandpa Frank's avatar looks like, well, Grandpa Frank, Aunt Mary's like Aunt Mary, and my avatar looks just like me. To keep this all "in the family," the family's little corner of SL cyberspace can be password-protected.

The ways in which families can use SL to communicate and interact are only as limited as the imagination of the family members themselves. In fact, families can build houses, albeit cyber structures, in which the entire multi-generational extended family can live together on a permanent basis. Just the process of planning, constructing, decorating and modifying the house will itself become an ongoing family "teambuilding" exercise. Over time various family members (all of whom are represented by their avatars) can chat with each other in the rooms of their choice, play parlor games with each other, and eat at predetermined intervals with all or some of the members. The SL experiences of current residents indicate that over the next few years more and more geographically-challenged families will turn to SL-style cyberworlds in order to replicate the intimate multigenerational extended family living experiences that escape them in the real physical world.

Eventually, SL will become even more realistic. Currently, a person converses via keyboard— type in a statement, and it appears over the head of the avatar, as in a comic strip. Eventually new technology will allow people to speak into their computer—voice chat will replace the keyboard and the overhead bubbles as well as the dominant mode of communication.

In my opinion, the invention that will truly revolutionize multigenerational communication, when perfected, is virtual reality. This relatively new technology, also referred to as VR, enables the user to feel and believe that he or she really inhabits the world placed in front of him. This technology has evolved rapidly in the last decade. The user usually wears a helmet or light-weight stereo glasses through which 3D computer graphics are projected. The helmet is further equipped with head and hand tracking systems that make this particularly real. When the user turns his head, the landscape changes, as it would when surveying any scene, including a room, a street, or a playing field. Many new systems enable a person to experience tactile feelings, such as feeling the wind in his or her face as the individual drives a "virtual" convertible down a virtual country lane.

Virtual reality systems are being used by the United States Air Force in flight training and many hospitals are using VR to instruct budding surgeons in the performance of heart and brain surgery. VR is also being used in psychiatry to help alleviate the pain of combat-related post-traumatic stress syndrome in soldiers returning from Iraq.

VR technologies will add a more tangible and sensate "feel" to online interfaces. The grandparent and child, perhaps a thousand miles away, could meet in a virtual room, sit next to each other, hold each other, even play elaborate games of hide and seek with each other. VR users will be able to achieve a sense of intimacy hitherto unknown in technologically-based communications.

Over the last several decades, transportation has made it easier for people to enjoy face-to-face contact. Affordable and accessible plane travel especially has enabled family members who live far away from each other to enjoy holidays and vacations together.

Hopefully soon, the United States like many countries in the world already have, will construct a nationwide high-speed rail system. Trains that run 150-300 miles per hour will go a long way in enhancing the ability of family members who live in different states or countries to traverse the miles and share their lives together. France, the United Kingdom, China, South Korea, Germany and other countries have embraced this technology. The U.S. has a myriad of plans and proposals to build high speed rail. In a world of high gas prices and skittishness about flying, a high speed rail system would seem the perfect vehicle to bring us together. At 300 mph, a trip on the Acela train from New York City to Boston, Massachusetts would take no more than an hour, from San Francisco to Los Angeles, California, three hours.

And all this would be "local" travel, from train station to downtown train station, without the hassle of driving to airports, going through security and reconnecting to vans or cabs at the other end, all of which adds hours to the trip.

One new high speed train technology, the Advanced Vehicle Transport AVTrain (www.supertrain.com), promises to transport vehicles and their passengers in private quiet train compartments that are equipped with air conditioning, entertainment centers and restrooms. Drivers will enter a station adjacent to the freeway or roadway and then park their car. The car would be swiveled onto a shuttle which then will take off and eventually catch up to the train. The vehicle and passengers are automatically transferred onto a train while the train and shuttle are moving in lockstep. The high-speed train then will transport them to their destination, at which point they simply start their vehicle and drive away. AVT Trains will travel at 80 mph when cars are being transferred, up to 150 mph between stations and over 200 mph between cities.

How soon will the United States actually enjoy the benefits of super fast rail transit? According to U.S. Congressman Jim Oberstar of Minnesota, who, in 2007, took over as chairman of the House Transportation and Infrastructure Committee, high-speed rail is a priority item in the Congress under the new Democratic Party majority. In interviews, Oberstar seems to bring a sense of urgency to the issue, claiming that the U.S. has to "find a way to achieve that goal of high-quality, intercity passenger rail service." According to the new Transportation chairman, "The French have done it, Germany has done it, Spain, Japan have done it. ... Look at what the Chinese have done. They have just completed a rail line from Beijing to Lhasa, Tibet, with pressurized rail cars operating at altitudes in excess of twelve thousand feet."

He claims that we are lagging behind the rest of the world, because we "lack the will" to make the investments necessary to raise the standard for Amtrak to a world-class level. Oberstar envisions high-speed Amtrak train systems that can reach speeds of 125 miles per hour operating in the Northeast Corridor, and additionally a southern route, the high western route and a system connecting major cities in California. "On the East Coast, you have to think Washington D.C. to Boston in about four hours. ... We ought to be able to do 125 mph average speed in that corridor," the new Chairman opines. His vision for the Midwest is particularly encouraging. He speaks of establishing rail service in which a passenger could travel from St. Louis to Chicago in roughly two and one half hours. And he sees this integrated into international travel. "A passenger could buy a rail ticket to Chicago, continuing to (London's) Heathrow Airport. Bags would be screened, checked, sealed in baggage compartments in St. Louis. The train would take you right into the O'Hare (International Airport) air terminal, and you move directly on to your flight. ..."

As stated in Frederic Frommer's article, "J. Oberstar's Priorities: Amtrak Funding, Midwest High-Speed Rail," syndicated by the Associated Press, Oberstar says the funding for high-speed rail projects would come from both the individual states and the federal government, with "some sort of a revenue bond proposal." Oberstar wants to get this project moving quickly, by bringing "a group together who could flesh this idea out, put some financing proposals together, find ways to make a project of this nature happen."

However, even this "grand vision" tends to pale in comparison to plans for high-speed rail sprouting up around the globe. In 2007, Britain's Conservative Party wants the country to implement a grand plan for fast-train transportation that is anything but "conservative." In short, the Party is examining options for building up a high speed rail network in the UK that will compare to the expanding systems already operating in Continental Europe. Central to the plan is the construction of a conventional high speed rail network in the United Kingdom, with TGV-type trains running on traditional rails and linked to the Channel Tunnel, or the Chunnel. These trains would reach speeds of 180 miles per hour. More ambitious is the vision of building ultra-high speed inter-city rail links using magnetic levitation technology. The Maglev, already in use in China, is capable of reaching speeds in excess of 300 miles per hour.[78]

Other more daring proposals for super fast transport can certainly help families increase the amount of "face time" they spend with each other, not just on special holidays but throughout the year. Today's air transport has really not shortened distances over the last fifty years. With the introduction of commercial jet planes in the late 1950s, it was suddenly possible for the average citizen to traverse the U.S. skies in six or seven hours. However, that travel time has not improved much, and in fact, the actual time it takes to travel to many places has increased due to a variety of factors—airport security delays, the clogged flight paths between major cities and airport traffic gridlocks.

That may all change over the next few decades. Soon, believe it or not, you might be able to get anywhere in the world in one or two hours. Through the miracle of hypersonic flight families living on the east coast might be able to effortlessly travel to great-great grandma in San Francisco, leaving their house at 9AM and reaching her by 9 AM.....Pacific Time.

The idea of hypersonic flight has been around for decades. In earlier books I have described a variety of plans for super fast air transport. Although their design originally is for shuttling combat units to world trouble spots in record time, the resulting flying machines will also enable commercial travelers, including workers, tourists, and family members, to touch down anywhere on the globe in less than two hours.

NASA's $230-million, eight-year-long Hyper-X program was the centerpiece of experimentation in the hypersonic transport field. NASA's program tested a variety of innovative engines that will hopefully propel the next generation of space vehicles and, perhaps, civilian airliners. At what speeds would you be traveling? In 2004 NASA's X-43A Scramjet reached speeds of MACH 9.8, or roughly 6,800 mph, shattering the 6.8MACH speed record set only a few months earlier. The twelve foot, unmanned research plane is the prototype of planes that could reach an incredible Mach 15, which would cut an eighteen hour flight from New York to Tokyo down to two hours travel time.

Dave Axe's article, "Semper Fly," which appeared in the *Popular Science* January 2007 issue, discusses how the U.S. Marine Corps has suggested a method for reducing the time it takes to travel the 7000 miles from the U.S. to Southeast Asia to minutes, not hours. The proposal is called "Small Unit Space Transport and Insertion", but it is known by its acronym, SUSTAIN. Here is how Sustain would work. The vehicle holding passengers, known as a lander, would be mounted on wedge-shaped carrier aircraft. The lander would detach, climb, and accelerate with scramjet engines to 100,000 feet and then fire rocket engines to get above fifty miles over the earth. The lander, which would hold a dozen or so travelers, will float through space and reenter the atmosphere over its destination, for instance Tokyo, and land at that location. Because of the high speeds attained in orbit, travel between the U.S. and Japan would be reduced to less than two hours, travel within the U.S. to an hour or less.

Jet technology might also be applied to individual transportation as well. Late in 2006 Yves Rossy, a former Swiss army pilot and current Swiss airline pilot, demonstrated his personal winged jetpack. Rossy jumped from a plane over the Swiss Alps, deployed the pack's foldable wings, and lit up the pack's four small jet engines. He flew at speeds greater than 115 miles per hour, and even managed to climb slightly before opening his parachute to float to the ground. While Rossy's current design can only propel a person by jettisoning him from an already moving vehicle, he hopes to build a jetpack capable of lifting its pilot off the ground.

On January 1, 2007, in the middle of the Tournament of Roses Parade, America was treated to an intriguing glimpse into the future of such technologies. A man was lifted out of a box on the Oklahoma state parade float and then proceeded to fly and hover over the crowd by virtue of a jet pack strapped to his back. After his display of futuristic derring-do, the flyer returned to earth, and made a perfect landing on his feet. Then he walked over to the Oklahoma governor seated nearby and presented him with the state flag.[79]

A new era of high-speed land vehicles will also reshape interpersonal relationships, among spouses, friends and family members. Most speed limits for automobiles are still around 65 mph, unless one is traveling Germany's autobahn, where people routinely tailgate in the left lane at speeds of 150 mph or greater. But we know that cars can easily reach speeds of 200-300 mph. In 1997 the Thrust SSC, powered by jet engines, actually broke the sound barrier by traveling a mile in 4.7 seconds. If family members are ever to motor to each others' homes at such speeds, they will probably be doing so in "smart cars" and on "smart roads" which leave much of the actual driving to computers located both inside the cars and built into roads.

The next step in auto-transportation might be a form of the "flying car." Graduates of the Department of Aeronautics and Astronautics at the Massachusetts Institute of Technology are attempting to build a workable model of a car that also can take to the air, the Terrafugia's *Transition*. Terrafugia, which is a Latin name meaning "escape from the earth," was incorporated in 2006. The *Transition* is aimed at the trips that are too short to interest an airline but long enough to test the patience of the normal driver, treks between 100-450 miles. To avoid earlier "flying car" failures, the designers have decided that the best flying car should be a drivable airplane. The *Transition* would actually fall under the FAA's new Light Sport Aircraft category, which is easier to certify. Another company, Moller International Inc. in Davis, California, has been developing its elaborate high-tech *Skycar* for several years.

The main obstacles to the implementation of flying-car technology are not technological and economic (although the initial projected price of $148,000 might scare many) but logistic. All the traffic rules to which we have become accustomed would have to be changed—it would not be feasible for a flying car to suddenly land in the middle of a crowded freeway. And we would have to devise a way to manage the movement of hundreds of light aircraft hovering over that freeway—there are no roads or traffic lanes at one hundred feet above ground. However, we can expect to see these kinds of vehicles in our neighborhoods within the next ten years. [80]

Such super fast transport will make it easy for members of the multigenerational extended family to remain physically connected. If an uncle or grandmother is needed to watch the kids this afternoon, one can call 500 miles away and expect him or her to arrive within two hours. And the business trip 500 miles from home will no longer keep a working mother separated from her children for too long.

In this new age of high-speed transportation and instantaneous communication, no family member need ever be alone again.

Being There: The Advent of the Multi-Generational Households

The movie *My Big Fat Greek Wedding* was the hit of the summer of 2002. A low budget "small screen affair" produced on a shoestring budget, the film grossed over $300 million worldwide.

The plot seems simple. Thirty year old Toula Portokalos, an American of Greek heritage, works in her family's restaurant. While her family wants her to marry a "nice Greek boy," she falls for a Waspish high school English teacher. Her mother mediates the inevitable tensions between Toula and her dad, and they get married in a "big fat Greek wedding."

Even the producers were surprised by the film's huge success. People do not just want "family" movies—they also like movies that celebrate the family, and especially the multigenerational extended family. *My Big Fat Greek Wedding* is one such movie. *The Godfather* trilogy is another. In that film the tight family structure, with its loyalties based on blood relations that provided America with the vision of familial solidarity missing from our current social fabric. In a perverse way, *The Sopranos* is also a story about a multigenerational extended family finding its way.

Because of my research and interest in the effects of the *Ageless Nation*, what caught my attention in the *Greek Wedding* opus was not so much the plot-line, but the last scene that reveals the living arrangements that the couple has bought into completely. Various family members live on the same block, and maintain close communication with each other. Rather than resisting such an arrangement, the husband, who comes from a family without the warmth and loyalty of Toula's, embraces her family and their close-proximity living arrangements.

In the future, I believe the multigenerational extended family neighborhood, populated by financially secure and physically healthy individuals, could well choose such living arrangements. Even today, in Brooklyn, NY, nouveau-riche Vietnamese immigrants will buy a house, raze it and erect in its place a 4-floor building that will house multiple generations of their family.

It is only natural as people live longer that some of them will start to live together. Now when we have multiple generations of families alive, many will have the opportunity to choose a new living arrangement.

This trend is already well underway. According to the United States census there were 4.2 million households with three or more generations living under one roof in 2000. This represents a jump of 38 percent from 1990 (while two generation households were growing by just 8 percent). Although two-generation and one-generation households are far more numerous, (43.6 million and 57.5 million, respectively), they are not growing as rapidly.

By 2006, the media was beginning to notice this trend toward families living in multigenerational households. Articles on this trend suddenly appeared almost spontaneously in *Business Week, the New York Times,* and online media outlets. The reasons for the growth of the multigenerational household vary. In some cases, young couples move back in with one of the members parents while saving for their own home. In regions such as the northeast, some United States college graduates, often jobless and saddled with college loans, move back home while job hunting or getting themselves established. Recently divorced mothers and fathers take shelter with their parents to solve their childcare problems. Adults with dependent parents move into the parents homes or move the parents into their own homes in order to provide assistance to their parents. When a Century 21 survey asked respondents whom they preferred as neighbors, 51 percent answered "family."[81]

The benefits of the multigenerational extended family have been discussed earlier. I believe in the future form will follow function. That is, during the Superlongevity Revolution, we will choose multigenerational living arrangements in order to derive the logistical, economic and psychological benefits of multigenerationality as outlined above.

These current multigenerational households take different forms. Some homebuilders are building larger and more "complex" homes to satisfy the growing trend toward the multigenerational extended family. 75 percent of buyers took an option offered by Kirk Homes, "guest suite opportunities" that are obviously friendly to some form of multigenerational living. 85 percent of buyers of Kensington Homes added an optional second-floor bedroom and bathroom that could house guests, children and grandchildren. Concord Homes claims that 30 percent of its buyers are opting for intergenerational home features such as first-floor suites for people with elderly parents, as well as second-floor bedroom suites whose walls do not touch other bedrooms. This latter privacy feature is perfect for adult children returning after college, divorce, layoff, or other life changing events. Over the last several years every single-family home Chicago's CA Development has built includes multigenerational living features such as a walkout lower level with at least one bedroom, a full bath and a large recreation room with a private entrance. [82]

According to one article, builders are reporting that more people than ever are ordering two houses in the same development, one for parents, one for grandparents. One person with four grown children actually purchased an entire cul-de-sac to house various subunits of the family.

Whatever their form, the members of these households are already pioneering the multigenerational lifestyle that will flourish as the Superlongevity Revolution's influence extends itself throughout our society. Certain guidelines for making such households and communities successful are already evolving. People are discovering that everyone should develop an agreement about dividing the finances, chores, and living space among family members. Non-parent family members, grandparents, cousins, etc. should specify how much child care they're willing to do. All involved should recognize that the ultimate arbiters of proper child rearing are the parents. If family segments are living in the same house, issues around privacy must be discussed. Of course, if members live in separate houses in the same development or on the same block in a city or town, privacy issues are not as critical. Most experts agree that in this emerging household paradigm communication between the various family members is paramount. [83]

Travel: The Road to Multigenerational Communication

One proof that muligenerationality is an emerging trend is how intergenerational travel is increasing in the first decade of the twenty-first century. In fact, multigenerational travel is one of the fastest-growing segments of the leisure travel industry. According to a 2005 survey taken by marketing firm Yesawich, Pepperdine, Brown & Russell, of 1,655 travelers, 35 percent of grandparents reported having taken at least one vacation with grandchildren during the previous twelve months, a figure up from 30 percent in 2003.

Travel experts feel that the reasons multigenerational or intergenerational travel is increasing are rooted in the time we live. Everyone's busy schedule has made it increasingly difficult for people to connect with each other—even schoolchildren have schedules that would make a corporate executive quake—school, soccer, homework, ballet and a bit of a social life. Also, some feel that there has always been room for the family elders to have a relationship with the youngest generation. The child gains a sense of continuity knowing where the family has come from and where it is headed.

According to experts, such tours should appeal to kids and adults alike. They remind prospective travelers that children have limited attention spans,

so the tours of interest should most definitely feature lots of variety. They rec-
ommend booking through tour groups, because they tend to know what the
correct mix of events will appeal to both youngsters and the generations pre-
ceding them. And they say that people should be more ambitious in selecting
a tour itinerary. While once people planned intergenerational trips primarily
to domestic sites such as Disney World, now people are choosing to travel with
the whole family to exotic vistas like the Incan ruins in Peru, the Galapagos
Islands, or the Nile River in Egypt.

The travel site of one such company, Generations Touring, provides
insight into the richness of these voyages for the old and young, with tours
entitled "Baseball's Sacred Grounds," "Pura Vida! Costa Rica," "The Soul of
the Andes—Peru," and "Vietnam: Past and Present."

Some experienced "generational travelers" have come up with specific
guidelines they feel will help families successfully pull off a two week journey
that includes grandparents, children and parents, if not one or two other generation, cousins, and other relatives. For one thing, they find that children are
most open to such excursions at age 12 or 13, old enough to understand and
appreciate the richness of the experience, but not at the age yet when they
begin to tune out everything that their elders say and think. At a certain age,
around 14-16, it is just not "cool" to travel with, and show empathy toward,
older family members.

I am impressed by *Generations Touring* understanding of how people
one, two, or more generations apart relate to each other. As the company states
on its site: "We know you love your children and they love you, but we all
need a little space from each other occasionally." They offer a feature called
"Our Time Together—Time Apart." "Time Together" is the time the tour
operators establish for adults and children to spend with each other, both during the tour's scheduled events and during the free time families enjoy alone.
"Time Apart" gives the generations "a little space from each other." There
are nights on the tour when adults are free to do whatever they please, while
the kids are participating in kids-only activities supervised by a tour guide.

Elderhostel has international programs all across Canada, Europe and
Asia, for bookend generations. A Web search using the term "grandparent-
grandchild camps," will provide information on the leaders in organized, international "grandtripping" like *Grandtravel* and *Thomson Family Adventures*,
which plan trips from Turkey and Belize to Peru, China and England.

Some of these experiences are tailored specifically to a grandparent-grandchild travel experience, such as "Grands Camp" at the historic Adirondack Great Camp Sagamore in Raquette Lake, N.Y. At Grandkidsandme camp in Amery, Wisconsin, up to thirty campers bunk in dorm rooms overlooking Lake Icaghowan. Veterans of these camps consider it a way to build a bond between the generations.

Such multigenerational travel packages provide new opportunities for the old and young to enjoy the ultimate educational experience, learning about each other, and to free themselves of the myths each has about the other's age group. Too often the young and middle-aged see elders as out of touch, while the elders see younger generations as self-centered and discourteous.

It has been my experience traveling with various members of my family, at different stages of the life cycle, that some of the best times we enjoyed were those when nothing was on the agenda. I recently traveled to Georgia to see my niece, along with my sister, her daughter and my grand-nieces. The greatest communication took place at the end of the day, when we could kick back in the hotel, and freely discuss any aspect of life, family, sports, or whatever else came up. These, for me, are also the most memorable times.

One thing that has become clear to me is that the physical differences between the generations divide old and young as much as the differences in our generational experiences and relative perspectives. When children see an adult who is physically fit and active, the divide between the generations is reduced.

THE FUTURE OF MARRIAGE

There is no doubt the radically extended lifespan will have an impact on the institution of marriage and childbearing. The question is what kind of impact? Faced with a tremendously long life, will people postpone marriage and childbearing, or will they move the timetable for such event to earlier ages? Will people remain in a marriage their whole lives when that life extends to ages of 150 or greater? Let us consider the possibilities.

Timing Marriage and Childbearing When You Have All the Time in the World

With an extended life span, choosing to marry and have children early in life, or deciding that there is no rush to wed and procreate will be an important decision. When I discuss this with futurists or members of the public, they usually surmise that people will take their sweet time making these momentous life decisions. They commonly assume that men and women anticipating living so long will not feel pressured to start having children early in life. Rather, it is thought, they will choose to spend their teens and twenties pursuing the training and education needed to insure career success.

In my opinion, one could envision the Superlongevity Revolution creating a far different scenario, in which citizens of the *Ageless Nation* decide to marry and become parents relatively early in life.

Women would consider this option because there is growing scientific data suggesting that when it comes to pregnancy, the earlier the better. Statistically, a woman's chances for getting pregnant decline significantly by her mid-thirties. Also, the chances that the baby could be born with deficiencies increase with the age of the mother. One of those potential risks, according to Dr. Nadja Reissland, an expert in child development at Aberdeen University, is Down's syndrome.[84] Reproductive biologist Roger Gosden has stated that "deferring fertility is a gamble." According to Gosden, by age thirty-five "a woman will take twice as long to conceive as she would have ten years earlier." He adds that "despite the reassurances of prenatal screening and an overall decline by some 70 percent in fetal death rates, the risks for both mother and child remain stubbornly higher than for younger women."[85] Genetic biologists P. Astolfi, L. Ulizzi and L.A. Zonta, describe those risks: Fetal losses increase twofold with respect to mothers and children born to parents over thirty-five years old. The infants also exhibit a greater frequency of genetic anomalies.[86]

So when will the women of the *Ageless Nation* decide to wed and have children. Studies show that a woman is at peak fertility around nineteen and twenty years old. In this scenario, the woman might have two, three or more children over a five to seven year period. As recently as 1970, the average age of a bride in the United States was only around twenty, and in one of those months her age dipped to 19.7!

Even though the woman is at peak fertility in her younger years, the argument against her having children early in her life has been that in our society she will need an advanced degree to pursue a career, and thus should acquire her degree before even considering having children. But technology is making it easier to stay at home and pursue a degree. Distance learning, which we discussed at length in previous chapters, would enable a young mother of nineteen or twenty to earn her degree at home while taking care of toddlers. Furthermore, her husband could take a company or government sponsored career hiatus to become the principle childcare provider while his wife attends school. So people will be able to more easily pursue their careers while engaging in other activities including raising a family.

In fact, one could argue that a mother who is also a student would provide enormous intellectual stimulation to her children. After all, she will be undergoing extreme intellectual growth just at the time that her children are going through a critical period of their cognitive development. A mentally stimulated mother would naturally enhance the learning curve of her child.

At age twenty-five, when her children are in school full time, she might have completed both her degree and for instance an MBA, or other graduate degree and be fully ready to start her career.

Would her absence from the workforce during her early twenties impede her career? According to the *Wall Street Journal*, Dartmouth, Harvard and other graduate business programs are launching executive-education courses geared toward women who have put their careers on hold to raise families and are ready to return to the professional world. The new courses aim to help women overcome the big gaps in their resumes with job-seeking strategies and update them on changes in the field since they have been gone.[87] While this program is aimed at women with prior experience, it strongly indicated that business needs educated females to fill skilled positions in accounting, marketing and management regardless of her prior work history, and will wait for the talented woman to enter the labor force, whenever she is ready to do so. Companies such as Booz Allen Hamilton, Lehman Brothers, Deloitte & Touche, Merrill Lynch and dozens of others have developed new programs, including targeted recruitment, special retraining, mentoring and flexible scheduling, to woo back their female professional ex-employees who have become stay-at-home mothers.[88] In 2006, Sharp Corp launched a new scheme under which former employees could get their jobs back up to seven years after they quit the firm to raise their preschool children.[89]

Our young stay-at-home mother can also garner resume points as well as a college degree without walking out her front door. She might have already begun her career while bringing up her children. Again, with the miracle of electronics, even today women are starting successful businesses from home. As we have pointed out, eBay is a liberating force in the lives of millions. And now, a growing number of consumer products and services companies, such as Office Depot, Wyndham Hotels and Sears Holdings are outsourcing call-center job to people in their homes in the United States. Such jobs are a potential boon for people who care for children or elderly family members at home. Companies report that these in-home workers stay with the job twice as long as regular call-center workers.[90]

However, further complicating this debate are recent medical developments that might make it easier for women to have children at much older ages than currently possible. In coming decades fertility science might be able to counter the medical impediments to later-life pregnancies.

We already hear of women having children well into their forties in spite of the medical risks involved. Susan Sarandon had her child at forty-five. Other celebrities that fall into the "older mother" category are Jane Seymour, Jerry Hall and Madonna. The process of in vitro fertilization has allowed women in their late fifties and early sixties to give birth to children.

Science might enable us to break the very bounds of any limits to fertility and childbearing. A new field has developed, called ectogenesis, in which an artificial womb is used to grow an embryo outside the body of a female. The world was stunned in 2002 when Dr. Hung-Ching Liu of the Cornell University Centre for Reproductive Medicine and Infertility announced that she and her team had grown tissue samples out of cells removed from a human uterus. They then engineered the tissue to resemble the shape of a natural womb, and inserted human embryos into these tissues. The embryos nestled into the artificial womb's lining and started to grow. In order to stay within the United States legal limits of in vitro fertilization (IVF) legislation Liu and her team halted the experiment after two weeks.

As the womb is created from the woman's own endometrial cells, there is minimal chance of organ rejection. While Dr. Liu envisions artificial wombs as a way to assist women with damaged or diseased wombs to conceive to term, we can envision how people might turn to this technology in order to conceive a child at any time.

One can imagine the debate that will brew in our society over a technology that will enable us to raise an embryo from conception to full development outside of a human body

Dr. Yoshinori Kuwabara at Juntendo University in Tokyo is conducting research into a perhaps eerier approach to the "artificial womb." In this system tanks are filled with amniotic fluid maintained at body temperature, and the embryonic umbilical cords are attached to external pumps which regulate nutrient intake and waste outflow. In this system the fetus can develop in an environment free of disease, environmental pollutants, alcohol, or drugs which the mother may have in her circulatory system. Another advantage is that this system would reduce the chances of miscarriage and premature births by allowing the embryo to develop full term outside the mother's womb, transferred after the initial 17 weeks of implantation.[91]

For too many of us, this might evoke the image created by Aldous Huxley in his novel, Brave New World. In Huxley's grim future, children are engineered ("decanted") in massive factories.

Another technology that should expand the age at which women can conceive is being pioneered by a team led by Jonathan Tilly, a reproductive biologist at Harvard Medical School. He released a study suggesting that doctors could boost women's supplies of eggs and thereby help them bear children long after the normal onset of menopause. Biologists have assumed that female mammals are born with a limited supply of eggs that gradually declines with age. But the discovery of vast numbers of immature eggs dying in the ovaries of mice led Tilly's team to find what they claim are "hidden ovarian stem cells" they say can sprout new eggs to replace vanishing ones.

If these findings hold true in humans, women in their forties, fifties and sixties may be able to bear children. We could freeze a woman's stem cells at a young age and have them re-implanted at a later date. Cancer patients, often left infertile by chemical and radiation therapy, could put stem cells on ice before treatment, or drugs may be able to rev up old or damaged stem cells. Tilly has already found a molecule that boosts the number of eggs mice make. "I think it'll be in the clinic quicker than you can dream of," he says.[92]

Nature, however, is certainly providing the conditions for reproduction at earlier ages, and this alone might influence how early someone chooses to have children, regardless of the increased number of years ahead of them in which to do so. The average age of menarche, or first menstruation, had already fallen dramatically (from seventeen to about 12.8) between the middle of the nineteenth century to the middle of the twentieth—mostly owing to improvements in nutrition. (Menstruation is considered the technical start of puberty; the outward signs of sexual maturity usually come earlier.) Studies have also found boys developing signs of puberty (pubic hair, genital growth) a half year earlier than previously measured. [93]

Furthermore, a totally unexpected population trend could induce a cultural shift in favor of early childbearing, certainly in the developed world. After decades of rapid growth, world population will begin to slowly decline by the middle of the twenty-first century. In many developed countries, including Germany, Italy, France and Japan, population decline is already becoming a troubling issue. To reverse this trend, society could begin to subtly encourage earlier marriages and pregnancies, through government programs and media campaigns.

'Til Death Do Us Part?

This brings us to an even thornier puzzle, the question of whether the practice of monogamy—one man, one wife—will withstand the exigencies of time. When you tie the knot in the *Ageless Nation*, you are committing yourself, at least theoretically, to a relationship that could last more than a century.

How can you be sure about your compatibility with your projected spouse or partner that you are willing to commit your very long life to that other person? This is a conundrum for sure. However, let's envision how this might all work. In reality, it is not as daunting as you might imagine.

Even during the first stage of the Superlongevity Revolution, with its ever increasing life spans, the divorce rate has not exceeded 35 percent over the lifetime of marriages. In fact, we find that after ten years or so of marriage the chance that a couple might divorce is dramatically reduced. About 60 percent of all marriages that eventually end in divorce do so within the first ten years.

Certainly, in the United States the idea of marriage has almost universal support, even if one-third of us get divorced. According to sociologist Martin Whyte, "There's very little evidence of rejection of marriage as an institution." A reported 95 percent of Americans say they want to marry and think they will.[94]

Lest one imagine that the very expanse of life in the Superlongevity era will make it difficult for any one to remain with one spouse for the rest of his or her life, here are some reasons why monogamy will be invigorated even when marriages stretch across a century or more.

The best way of speculating about this question of whether superlongevity will impact the long term stability of a marriage is to ask why people divorce in the first place. The fact is that the more education a person has, the less chance they will ever get divorced. In the United States college graduates consistently have about one-third to one-fourth the divorce rate of non-graduates. There is debate about why education seems to act as a preventative to divorce. A good guess is that an educated couple, who statistically is better off financially than the non-educated, is less prone to experience financial difficulties, a major cause for divorce. Also, the more educated you are the more likely you are to have a fulfilling job and career. This level of self-satisfaction makes for a better relationship at home.[95]

In the next decades, we can be fairly certain that higher percentages of people will have college degrees than they do today. Hence, we can posit just from that statistic based on past reports of which we just spoke that more families will remain intact.

Perhaps a stronger reason for family stability is the predicted growth of the multigenerational extended family unit in the Superlongevity era. As we discussed, the members of this unit—generations of grandparents, uncles, aunts, cousins—will support the couple in numerous ways. We have already reviewed a number of these in which the family network can provide financial and career help as well as personal support and advice to the young couple. Also, the thriving couples that form the nexus of the multigenerational network will also serve as a role model to young couples.

There is another aspect of the Superlongevity Revolution that should also contribute to marital stability and hopefully bliss. The breakthroughs leading to our extended lives will also help us live that life as physically healthier, *younger* people. In the next chapter we'll look at the Ultra-human Phenomenon, in which humans are adopting a plethora of technologies to both expand their mental and physical capabilities. These technologies will not only dramatically enhance our physical appearance in the cosmetic sense. They will also open the door to *rejuvenation*, in which the eighty year old can look twenty five. Oftentimes the road to divorce begins with infidelity on the part of one or both of the spouses. One reason a husband or wife might have a fling is that the new paramour is better looking or younger than the spouse. We all age, and there are always younger and more attractive choices out there. But what if your wife or husband could always remain not just "youthful," but physically young (and just as attractive as any younger man or woman in the spouse's office or work area)? Why would anyone be "tempted by the fruit of another" when the tastiest dish is waiting for you at home?

Nevertheless possibilities other than lifelong monogamy need to be examined. Among them, is a chance that during century-long marriages partners might explore taking a marital hiatus of a half-year or so to refresh themselves and become a new and exciting person for the spouse, as well as for friends and family. Also, our society should explore in a mature and objective manner, what may be perceived by some as an opportunity for growth and not an escape from the relationship.

What might be the ultimate glue of these relationships is the well-documented panoply of advantages that accrue to both spouses. Married people live healthier and longer lives, by almost a decade, than single or divorced people. According to Maggie Gallagher, president of the Institute for Marriage and Public Policy, "married people are happier." Study after study documents that a generally happy person has less chance of getting ill than a depressed individual. Moreover, married people advance further in their careers and are wealthier than single folk. Such factors will not change, no matter how much we expand the human life span.[96]

DESIGNING CHILDREN IN AN UNCERTAIN WORLD

As we've noted, marriage, parenting, childbearing and rearing in the Superlongevity era will be more challenging than they ever have been. Other changes such as serial marriages, multigenerational households and more innovations are certainly on the horizon.

In addition, one of the critical technologies in the extension of human life span, the field of genetics and its practical application, genetic engineering, will also bring major changes in childbearing and in effect mate selection. Genetics will endow parents with the opportunity, and some claim the responsibility, to ensure that their children are born into this world free of the threat of a host of diseases. Moreover, parents will be able to genetically determine their children's height, weight, intelligence, in effect their total destiny, even before the child is born.

This new world of almost supreme power over children's genetic make-up will stem from the rapid progress made in genetic science and technology. The genetic revolution really accelerated in 2000, when Human Genome Project researchers completed the mapping of the genetic structure of the human body many years ahead of schedule. This project finished its mission earlier than expected because of the healthy competition that arose between government scientists working through the National Institutes of Health and a private concern, Celera Genomics under the guidance of the legendary Craig Ventner.

Having mapped the human genome, we are in position to uncover the link between particular genes and diseases such as Alzheimer's, Parkinson's, macular degeneration and many other maladies. Building on that knowledge will allow us to use gene therapy to cure genetically-based diseases. Through gene therapy, as Salk Institute Professor Inder Verma says, we can either "eliminate the defect, ameliorate the defect, slow down the progression of the disease or in some way interfere with the disease." Thereby we will extend human life.

In the future we will perfect the genetic engineering techniques to disarm and neutralize many diseases by placing beneficial genes into the cells of patients suffering from these maladies. Scientists are closing in on techniques that could let them safely repair almost any defective gene in a patient, opening the door for the first time to treatments for a range of genetic disorders that are at this point considered incurable.

Doctors using such techniques have already had some success combating pernicious maladies such as the SCID "Bubble-boy Syndrome." In 2002, researchers in Italy and Israel announced that they used genetic engineering techniques to cure children afflicted with the so-called "Bubble-boy" disorder, an inherited immune system disorder that forces sufferers to live in a tightly-sealed "bubble" or face death from exposure to ordinary microbes. The scientists injected the children with bone marrow stem cells that were altered to contain the enzyme gene missing in their genetic makeup. There was an initial euphoria about such results. Dr. W. French Anderson, a University of Southern California genetics pioneer, stated that the success with the Bubble-boy victims "proves our basic premise that if you can get enough gene-engineered cells into the patient it will cure the disease."

Unfortunately, after thirty disease-free months, the three youngest patients showed symptoms of leukemia. Although the new gene cured the disease in twelve patients, it went on to cause leukemia in three of them. It turned out that the foreign gene, in addition to producing the protein that vanquishes X-linked SCID, had the unexpected side effect of sometimes turning on a cancer-causing gene.[97]

In June of 2005, *Nature* reported that scientists at California biotechnology company Sangamo had developed a technique to get the body to recode the problem areas with the correct gene sequence without causing any harmful side effects to the patient's body. In another recent test in Frankfurt, Germany, doctors successfully used gene therapy to cure two men who suffered from chronic granulomous disorder (CGD), a condition that makes them almost defenseless against bacterial and fungal infections.

In 2006, two human trials were underway to test the effectiveness of gene therapy to overcome Muscular Dystrophy, the debilitating disease so prominently on display in America each year on the Jerry Lewis Telethon. These tests are being conducted in children at Columbus Children's Hospital and at the University of Utah. At the latter site, five year old Jack Knight was scheduled to receive a drug that scientists hope will restore muscle function by bypassing the genetic defect. Researchers are also claiming some success in using gene therapy to alleviate cystic fibrosis in many patients. [98]

It is exciting to imagine that genetic engineering will eventually eradicate a host of debilitating diseases such as Alzheimer's and the deadliest cancers. As we eliminate disease from the equation of human mortality, we increase the likelihood that our species will increase the life span into the 125-150 area.

But we are looking to genetics to do more than ameliorate the course of diseases such as MD and cystic fibrosis in those living and suffering with such maladies. Parents will soon have the power to go the next step—eliminate the possibility, before birth, of someone ever getting the disease. In a matter of decades, even years, we will be able to simply slip specific genes into human embryos. People could be engineered to be resistant to genetically-inherited diseases such as Cystic Fibrosis, Alzheimer's cancer, heart disease, AIDS and even mental illness.

And more excitingly, the final step would be to completely eliminate the disease-causing allele that in turn would eventually be completely eliminated from the gene pool in a few generations. An allele is a version of a gene that produces a different result when expressed in an individual. Fix or eliminate the allele, and you have removed the disease not only from your child but excised it completely from the family history.[99]

At the present time, although we have mapped the human genome, we have not yet discovered exactly what particular genes control what phenotype. But we are learning about the human genome much faster than we once thought possible. In 2006, the Translational Genomics Research Institute announced that researchers identified a genetic cause for epilepsy, which could lead to the development of medicines to treat epilepsy and autism.[100] The same week researchers at   Boston University School of Public Health announced that they had developed a way to use genetic variations to assess the stroke risk in individual patients.[101]

It is this particular aspect of genetic science that will fundamentally change the role of parents in their children's genetic destiny. Most prospective parents would want to use genetic science to eliminate the chance that their child could suffer from diseases such as cancer, autism, and epilepsy. Current prenatal tests allow us to identify only a few dozen different disease-causing genes. However, a process called "gene sequencing" will enable us to genetically test the unborn easier, faster and more accurately.

Moreover, the very techniques we use to identify genes implicated in the development of disease will empower us to do much more. But here is where the controversy comes in. Some ask why just rearrange our genes to prevent disease? If genetic engineering can pre-select for health, why can't we use it to "design" unborn children to be perfect in every way?

Soon, perhaps within the decade, parents will be able to identify every one of the thirty thousand or so genes their unborn child carries and the function of such genes. Combined with knowledge of what these genes do, this information will give parents an idea of a prospective child's appearance, intelligence, and personality. In deciding what traits a couple wishes their kid to possess, healthy non-carrier genes would be chosen. Parents can pre-select genes that will imbue their children with superhuman strength, flawless beauty or a photographic memory. Many of these children will live longer, and be healthier, stronger and more intelligent than any before them.

In a lecture at the University of California, Irvine in 2004 *Science* author Gregory Stock expressed the theory that soon everyone will have the ability to design their children. With the human genome now completely mapped, he observed, the ability to specifically determine the height, IQ, eye and hair color of one's child through scientific means will inevitably become widely available and affordable to the American public. We will also be able to determine our children's skin tone, height and facial structure, as well as health factors, athleticism and weight. They'll also be able to influence within certain limitations their child's IQ, personality and other mental traits. Parents will have almost Promethean power over their children's physical and emotional destiny.[102]

How would this work? In one scenario, a couple undergoing in vitro fertilization could use preimplantation genetic diagnosis (PGD) to completely screen the genes of the embryos they've created and select a few embryos for implantation on the basis of the traits they find. In his 1997 book *Remaking Eden*, Princeton's Lee Silver outlined the process. A couple goes into an infertility lab. There, they undergo an in vitro fertilization, which produces several embryos, each of which has its genes analyzed by PGD.

Here is where the scene becomes a bit unsettling. One can imagine the couple sitting in front of a computer screen which displays genetic "profiles" of the embryos they've created, plus computer-generated pictures showing the children and adults those embryos are likely to grow up to be.

In Silver's example, the parents click on one of the profiles and see the face of a potential child at age sixteen. They can see the shape of a nose, the color of eyes, the tone of skin, etc., all of which they would have encoded into the genetic structure of the child. The profile also includes the relative tendency to develop severe genetic diseases by delineating which genes the embryo carries and how high the risk is of developing more complex diseases like heart disease and cancer.

Silver claims that the parents will be in the position to increase the likelihood of their children developing specific personalities based on genetic selections. Do they want a lovely green-eyed, brown-haired girl, but with a high risk of heart disease and only average intelligence? How about a tall, athletic girl with perfect pitch but a tendency toward manic depression? Or would they prefer an average-sized boy with a high IQ, but slightly shy? Perhaps they want several children from several embryos.

In 2007 much of the public learned that a self-described "Human Embryo Bank," the Abraham Center of Life in San Antonio, Texas, had taken us a step closer to the world of "designer children" envisioned by Silver. The Center offers already created embryos for sale to prospective parents who can appraise the traits of the egg and sperm donors. To help the prospective parents make their embryo selections, the center provides photos of the male and female donors as adults and infants, in addition to medical reports and family histories.

On the Center's website, director Jennalee Ryan states that the donors have been given medical tests, and the embryos created by these donors have been "graded" medically in order to assure their quality. These are not just any donors. The males must have a college degree, but preferably should have earned their doctorates. Most of the female donors have at least attended college, she said. Although physical attractiveness is supposedly not a donor requirement, the sperm bank the Center contracts with is replete with sperm from attractive college graduates. The egg donors are also attractive, according to Ms. Ryan. Additionally, the center will provide pre-tested surrogate mothers.

Is the Center trafficking in "designer children?" The answer to this question depends on how one interprets the actions of the Abraham Center and the motives of the recipients. Ms. Ryan claims that clients do not "order up" babies tailored to their tastes. That is, prospective recipients do not provide her a list of desired donor characteristics. Rather, those interested can review detailed information about the Center's donors, including their ethnicity and educational background. As mentioned, clients can see the donors' pictures. The embryos are stored at various clinics affiliated with the Center.

To some, this differentiation smacks of pure semantics. The Center has been accused of brokering in "designer children," catering to couples looking for a made to order child with "perfect" characteristics. Immediately critics began calling the Center a "baby supermarket" and a "baby broker service;" some suggested that the Center's practices bordered on eugenics.

These concerns do not seem to discourage people from using the Center's services. According to Ms. Ryan, the Center has a long waiting list of recipients, and she asserts that each batch of embryos is "spoken for" immediately. This process will cost a couple anywhere from $8,000 to $14,000, which is considerably less than the price of an adoption.[103]

The debate about these so-called designer children heats up. On such issues the public has different views on the ethics of using genetic screening and manipulation to selectively shape the physical and emotional characteristics of their children. When it comes to purely medical applications, some favor genetics—73 percent favor using PGD to screen out disease. But Westerners are not very friendly to the idea of using genetic technology to enhance the unborn, which some ethicists refer to as Perfectionism. For instance, only 22 percent of Americans approve of using PGD to select desirable features such as hair color and intelligence.

Americans' attitude toward genetic engineering is even less favorable. 59 percent approve of using genetic engineering to remove genetic diseases. Only 20 percent of Americans approve of using genetic engineering to create desirable features in the unborn. Movies such as *Gattica* present an image of a society in the near-future in which genetic engineering is used to create a caste system made up of a ruling class of alpha-persons genetically programmed with superior intelligence and other desirable characteristics, and a lower class of lesser-endowed people who perform the drudge work of society.

Some surveys, such as one conducted by Johns Hopkins University Genetics and Public Policy Center, see a gradual shift toward more favorable attitudes about all forms of genetic enhancement of the unborn. This could be attributed to the old truism that "seeing is believing"—as we observe real couples using genetics to help their newborns, we are more likely to accept the idea of genetic enhancements. [104]

When the science behind genetic selection and manipulation is finally mastered, potential parents will be confronted with a host of ethical dilemma over what choices they make. Imagine a time in the near future where half the parents opt to genetically engineer their children to have IQ well above average, perhaps 130 to 140. These children will do well in school, ace their tests and dominate discussions in the classroom. Now imagine that you are a parent who decided for whatever reason to not interfere with nature. Your child is above average in intelligence, but his mental capacities pale by comparison to the whizzes in class, especially those programmed with photographic memory.

As he or she grows up, the child could resent you for not providing him or her with tools to adequately compete in the academic marketplace. Regardless of your explanations about the ethical considerations that led you to avoid genetic engineering, the child will be living with the consequences of what is essentially your choice to let chance determine his or her mental capacity.

Some ethicists have described even more complicated ethical dilemmas stemming from our future ability to choose our children's characteristics. Suppose, for instance, that one of those whizzes programmed for extreme intelligence secretly desires to be a sports star, and wishes you had actually endowed him with the height and strength to captain his school's basketball team.

Some children will know that they were "designed" to have a certain trait and end up resenting their parents for treating them as a lab experiment in which the child's destiny is controlled and scripted from the outset. They may feel that the parents left them no chance for individuality.

This "damned if you do, damned if you don't" aspect of genetic-engineering could provide the fodder for a host of psychological problems in the future, in which young adults will be accusing their parents of either: 1)not providing them with the characteristics to compete in this new world of "Ultra-humans," 2)controlling their destiny by providing those characteristics, or 3) providing them with the wrong set of characteristics—you made me an Einstein when I would have preferred to be a movie star. Of course since it is impossible to consult the child before birth the problem is irreversible decisions will be made at that time. If they are not, on the other hang, one can just imagine a young adult asking his parents "why were you unwilling to spend the money to buy me better looks or a longer lifespan?"

Issues of national security and competitiveness might trump individual ethical concerns when it comes to deciding whether or not to engineer the next generation. One technology pundit recently suggested that international economic competition might well determine the outcome of the debate in the United States regardless of individual's ideological or religious concerns. Like the nuclear arms race in the twentieth century, there may soon be a "eugenics race," as China and other nations promote the development of technologies to assure the smartest and most-productive future workforce in the world. Unless other nations keep up, a "smart baby gap" may be in our future.

At this point, according to polls, support for genetic technologies is much higher in Asia and other parts of the world. Majorities in several countries approve of the use of genetic engineering to select traits of children. However, in the future, America's natural competitive tendencies may triumph over ethical considerations in the drive to maintain its number one status economically, technologically and militarily. Such concerns may also prompt the government to loosen the regulatory restrictions on genetic science and its application.[105]

CHOOSING YOUR MATE

The breakthroughs in genetic engineering we just described could well change another area of human behavior related to interpersonal relations, that of mate selection. To understand how our ability to choose the genetic make-up of our children could transform, however slowly, the factors that influence our choice of lifetime mate. Let's look at the reasons behind our selection.

Most of us believe that we marry for love—it is the one decision in life which seems to transcend the more utilitarian factors that enter into the decisions we make about buying homes, choosing a college or purchasing a car. To most people, their memories of choosing a mate involve an experience filled with joy, emotion and overwhelming feelings of bliss, at times.

We fall in love with people whom we find appealing. But why do we find people with certain characteristics attractive?

One explanation comes from evolutionary theory. According to this school of thought, we are primarily concerned with the survival of the human species, and whether we are aware of it or not, most of our actions are aimed at insuring that our species will survive and thrive. We select our mates with the same goal in mind—we are attracted to people who we unconsciously perceive to hold the characteristics most favorable to the growth and development of the human species. So we look for mates based on their potential for their ability to first procreate successfully, but also to produce offspring with certain desirable characteristics, such as strength, intelligence, perceived general health and strong family health histories.[106]

Evolutionary biologists theorize that our perception of attractiveness, or "beauty," has been programmed into our brains through natural selection, or Charles Darwin's theory of the survival of the fittest. What we think of as physical "beauty" is a visual indication of how fit or healthy one is genetically and, through centuries of conditioning, our beauty preferences are thus governed by an evolutionary need to find healthy and fit partners and weed out less genetically fit sexual partners.

Applying Darwin's theory of sexual selection to the nature of beauty, modern biologists and psychologists contend that when a man reacts to a woman's "beauty," he is actually reacting to certain physical features in women that act as visual cues signaling her reproductive fitness, or quite simply, her fertility. This theory explains why men will prefer a woman who is younger and healthier—youth and health mean a greater chance for bearing (healthy) children, and more of them.

One finding might stun you. In study after study, men identify as "attractive" or "beautiful" women who, it turns out, have a waist-to-hip ratio of 0.7 (i.e. the waist measures 70 percent of the hip). Marilyn Monroe as well as every Playboy centerfold from 1955 to 1965 and 1976 to 1990 possessed this ratio of 0.7. Even though the Playboy models have become more slender over the years, their waist-to-hip ratio has changed only slightly. Even toy models evidence this physical characteristic. The famous Barbie Doll has the same 0.7 waist-to-hip ratio. Other studies show that men are generally attracted to women with large breasts. According to evolutionary biologists, the reason men are attracted to a woman with this bodily configuration is that the 0.7

ratio actually signals to them that this woman has strong reproductive potential. Recent studies bear out the biologists' explanation. Grazyna Jasienska, a researcher at Jagiellonian University in Krakow, Poland and her colleagues discovered that women with a relatively low waist-to-hip ratio and large breasts have about 30 per cent higher levels of the female reproductive hormone estradiol than women with other combinations of body shapes. What is special about this hormone, as demonstrated by two of the team, Peter Ellison and Susan Lipson at Harvard University in the U.S., is that higher levels of estradiol are indeed related to higher fertility in women trying to get pregnant. "If there are 30 per cent higher levels, it means they are roughly three times more likely to get pregnant," Jasienska, a human biologist, said in an interview with *New Scientist* magazine.

A woman with that waist-to-hip ratio also has high amounts of another female hormone, progesterone, which according to Jasienska should also translate to higher fertility.[107]

A plethora of studies showing that a host of characteristics we consider attractive, beautiful or sexy are the very same characteristics signaling that a person has high reproductive capabilities. Men, too, are judged by their physical appearance, although visual cues are harder to quantify. Many women prefer men who display signs of masculinity - think of Brad Pitt's large, chiseled jaw line. From the standpoint of evolutionary psychology, this makes perfect sense—studies have found correlations between a large jaw and high levels of testosterone, a male hormone that indicates good health in men. Deep-set eyes, prominent chins, facial hair and broad shoulders are also considered attractive and signs of sexual health.[108]

The likelihood of bearing healthy children is not the only reason we choose or reject a person as a potential mate. Many also look for mates that have combinations of characteristics that they want their offspring to have that will help them compete in the social and professional worlds—good looks, overall health and a sharp mind. A person might be physically attracted to someone and then slowly discover that the person is not very intelligent. In a society which values and rewards intelligence and creativity, a person might decide to choose another potential life partner. Also, one may think twice about marrying someone from a family whose members have a tendency to develop serious heart conditions or cancer.

I believe that the genetic technologies we earlier discussed will liberate us from such concerns when choosing mates. In a starkly new world of designer children and artificial insemination, one's genetic tendencies or "fertility health" would not be of serious concern. The genes a potential mate carries or the tendency to develop cancer, or whether you are short or tall will have little relevance. Technology will enable us to bioengineer our offspring endowing them with almost any qualities we desire, regardless of the parent's genetic limitations.

By using PDG, or simply slipping specific genes into human embryos, we could engineer our children for resistance to cancer, heart disease, AIDS and mental illness while bestowing on them beauty and intelligence.

Today many techniques including artificial insemination, artificial wombs, and a host of other technologies boost a woman's likelihood of conceiving a child. Many more will be discovered and perfected in the *Ageless Nation*. The propensity to bear children will depend as much on modern science as it will a woman's natural physical condition.

It is not inconceivable that over the decades, men's subconscious reaction to such cues as "waist-to-hip" ratio will therefore be diminished or disappear entirely. For example, why would a man continue to react to women primarily on the basis of a 0.7 waist-to-hip ratio that signals fertility when any woman chosen can conceive a child with the assistance of modern science? And why should anyone worry about what genes they carry when a host of technologies enable scientists to eliminate genetic flaws from our future family history.

In the *Ageless Nation*, thanks to genetic science and reproductive technology, the whole psychology of mating will change. This turn of events will certainly influence the criteria used to select spouses, and could prove to be quite liberating. Since people will be able to genetically engineer their offspring to have any qualities desired, they will be free to choose mates based on qualities other than their propensity to pass on desirable traits to their offspring.

In such a world we can concentrate more on the potential mate's personality, temperament, values, and a host of behavioral, occupational, social and moral considerations. Gradually, such characteristics will supersede the physical traits as a basis of mate selection.

Women, then, are very concerned about a men's interest in having children, nurturing them, and raising families. In the future, I believe genetics will enable us to design a person with any traits whatsoever, such personality traits will loom even larger in the choice of mate.

In fact, according to a recent University of Chicago study, women might have already started picking as mates men who do not have the highest testosterone level or physical traits such as above average height, broad shoulders, or other so-called masculine characteristics. A woman selects a mate not for perceived sperm count, but for what the woman perceives to be a man's willingness to have children and raise a family. The study, which was published in the *Proceedings of the Royal Society B: Biological Sciences*, claimed that women looking for long-term relationships are attracted to men who like children, and they can tell which guys might be interested in becoming fathers just by looking at their faces.

And personality traits are a matter of nurture, not nature. It still will be up to the parents to rear a child who will become kind, nurturing, and protective. We might be able to design a boy's or girl's facial features, but we will never be able to genetically determine the adult's facial expression. According to the University of Chicago study, man's facial expression tells the woman whether or not he will make a good father, a solid partner for the next century, and a wise patriarch of his multigenerational extended family. [109]

In the next chapter, we will look at how and why citizens of the *Ageless Nation* will have a great number of new and interesting traits to choose from.

chapter six

The Ultra-Human Mystique

The Superlongevity Revolution will not just involve the dramatic extension of human life. The technologies we develop to extend our lives, such as cloning and genetic engineering, are the very same technologies that will simultaneously transform our species from merely human to what I label "Ultra-human."

Imagine a world in which people have perfect hearing, sight which measures 20-15 or 20-10, perfect, resilient skin and a host of bionic additions, which provide human beings with "super-bodies." Some of these innovations will even endow people with photographic memories. "Smart pills" that can increase your concentration and enhance your memory are already being manufactured and are available, and more innovations will come.

Envision enjoying this cornucopia of medical enhancements in a body that is forever youthful. A forever young looking body will be attainable as long as men and women go for regular treatments for cellular regeneration, or utilize the latest breakthroughs in nanotechnology to strengthen and rejuvenate their skin.

In this strange new universe which is evolving around us, citizens of the *Ageless Nation* will use the creations of technology, science and pharmacology to expand their mental and physical capabilities and enhance their physical appearance.

Today, the many people who utilize a variety of ways to improve themselves physically are not consciously attempting to participate in a society-wide effort to take the next giant step in human evolution. They are merely trying to ameliorate some physical imperfections or perform better in sports, jobs and final exams. This concept of an ultra-human is the one we spoke of earlier when we discussed couples bio-engineering their offspring to be better looking, more athletic and smarter than the "child" would have been without the parents adjusting the genetic makeup of the embryo.

Now we shall explore how this trend toward "eternal youth" will affect our culture and our society.

A WHOLE NEW YOU
Part of the ultra-human phenomenon will involve people undergoing surgery to improve their sight, their looks and their hearing. Let's look at the various ways people are tuning in to the Ultra-Human revolution and the aspects of the human body they are trying to improve.

Super Vision
Several years ago, a woman I know had cataracts on both eyes that were worsening each month. She was constantly buying new lenses for her glasses to compensate for her weakening vision. Her optometrist told her that she would need surgery to eliminate the cataracts, but such surgery would have to wait until the cataract situation worsened. At their weakest her eyes measured 20-800 in one eye, and almost 20-1000 in the other. In other words, when she peered at objects twenty feet away, they appeared with the same fuzziness and lack of definition as would the objects 800 feet away for a person with normal vision.

As her eyesight deteriorated everything she saw was becoming increasingly fuzzy. Even while wearing her glasses, she could not read normal-sized text on a television screen no more than eight feet away.

Then she had laser surgery to remove one cataract. The surgery took only forty-five minutes, once anesthesia was administered and other pre-op preparations were made. After a few days the bandages were removed. A month later she had the cataract removed from her other eye.

In this operation the surgeon replaces the eye's lens with an artificial lens, which should provide the patient with perfect vision. The woman soon discovered just how perfect. One Sunday afternoon, soon after the operation, she and a friend decided to go to a nearby drugstore. As she pulled her car into the parking lot she was unsure if the store, which had an early closing time on the weekends, was still open. When she was approximately twenty feet from the pharmacy, she got her answer. She told her passenger that the store closed at 2 PM. Her passenger asked where she suddenly received this insight. The woman's answer stunned them both. From twenty feet away she could clearly read the store's schedule posted on the door, printed in numbers no more than one inch high. At that distance those letters should have been unreadable for anyone with normal eyesight.

What a way to discover that as a result of the cataract operation, her vision had not improved from 20-800 to 20-20. Her vision was now 20-10! You might say that she is now blessed with "super-vision." Even people with minor visual imperfections, with eyesight of 20-65, desire perfect, if not "super," vision. More and more young people with near-average eyesight are undergoing LASIK (Laser Assisted in Situ Keratomileusis) surgery to get that extra competitive edge. LASIK is a type of refractive surgery that reshapes the cornea of the eye in order to correct myopia, hyperopia and astigmatism. It is usually performed on an outpatient basis.

Only a decade or so ago such marvels would have seemed like a fantasy. However, they pale by comparison to the wonders that we will soon encounter. For instance, in the near future the blind will be able to regain their sight.

About 1.5 million people worldwide have a disease called retinitis pigmentosa, and 700,000 people in the western world are diagnosed with age-related macular degeneration each year. In both degenerative eye diseases, retinal cells that process light at the back of the eye gradually die.

Various devices, such as the artificial retina, have been developed to bring back some modicum of real sight to the blind. Although these are fairly primitive, their success and new discoveries indicate that within decades we should be able to return sight to the blind.

One such breakthrough has come at the University of Southern California's Doheny Retina Institute. Dr. Eugene de Juan Jr. and Dr. Mark Humayun have developed a miniature electrode array that can be implanted in the eye to replace a damaged retina. The array is attached by thin wires buried under the skin to a radio receiver that is implanted behind the ear. A microcomputer worn on a belt processes visual signals from a video camera and then transmits them to the receiver. The retinal array stimulates optical nerves, which then carry a signal to the brain. The signal is perceived as phosphenes, bright points of light. With correct stimulation, patterns of phosphenes can draw a picture in the mind similar to that on a stadium scoreboard, where pictures are produced by arrays of individual light bulbs.

They have tested this device on legally blind individuals, and the preliminary results have been "encouraging," Humayun said. "The brain can make a lot of sense out of crude inputs." Dr. Humayun claims that his next-generation implant should allow the bearer to "recognize a face and read."

Dr. Alan Chow of the University of Illinois at Chicago Medical Center has produced an implantable artificial retina. It is actually a silicon chip two millimeters in diameter—smaller than the head of a pin—and half the thickness of paper. It contains about 5,000 small solar cells, each attached to a miniature electrode on the back of the chip. Light falling on the chip will activate the electrodes, stimulating the optical nerves behind the retina. Chow has implanted the devices in six blind patients. "All of the patients have improved visual function, sometimes quite dramatic," he said.

The current status of these devices can be discerned from a profile that was recently reported in a Toronto newspaper. It told the story of Jens, a Canadian, who between the ages of seventeen and twenty lost vision in both eyes as a result of work-related accidents. Recently, when he was thirty-nine, surgeons in Portugal drilled a hole in Jens's skull and placed an array of electrodes on the surface of his brain. The electrodes are connected to a miniature television camera and a sophisticated computer that, together, have given Jens a rudimentary form of vision.

True, his current vision does not compare to his original sight. He describes his sight as "crude," but he observes that it is "a good improvement compared to being blind totally." At one 2005 meeting in New York Jens demonstrated his new sight by navigating through rooms, finding doors and even driving a car briefly, avoiding obstacles placed in his path.[110]

Eventually such devices might provide wearers above-average vision. Dr. Tanguay, an electrical engineer at the University of Southern California, is developing an aspirin-sized "ocular camera" that would be located just behind the pupil, in the small pouch where the eye's crystalline lens normally is situated. Tanguay says his camera's three-millimeter focal length will make objects appear crisp no matter how far or close they are, something even the physical eye can't manage. And he could use a sensor tuned to infrared light, the basis for night-vision scopes, so blind people could see in the dark.

One of his colleagues, biomedical engineer James Weiland, prefers the Bionic Man archetype. "You could hook our system up to an electron microscope and give someone super-vision," he says. He's only half joking.[111]

A New World Of Hearing

The improvements that have been made in bettering the lives of the visually impaired are less sweeping than the improvements we have made in restoring hearing to the deaf. For decades, the "hard of hearing" turned to such devices as hearing aids to regain their connection to the world of sound. Now the deaf can actually hear.

The cochlear implant first received approval of the United States federal government in 1984. At that time, there was much skepticism about the idea that a device implanted inside someone's head would suddenly restore his or her hearing. Early implants did not impress all critics. These devices threaded a single electrode into the cochlea—a pea-sized organ vital for hearing—to send crude signals to the brain. The deaf person was thus enabled to hear loud noises, such as that of a siren and to lip-read more easily.

Over the last two decades the technology has improved dramatically. Many people first discovered this wonderful breakthrough through mega-radio star Rush Limbaugh. In the late 1990s, within a four month period, Limbaugh mysteriously lost all hearing in both ears, possibly due to a virus. Because the ability to hear callers' comments and questions and immediately respond to them was critical to his success as a talk show host, his career was immediately placed in jeopardy. Quickly he decided to undergo cochlear implant surgery and was back on his radio show in a matter of weeks. His personal crisis elevated national awareness of the existence of this hearing miracle, and his discussions over the years of the benefits as well as the vicissitudes of depending on this type of device for his hearing has educated his public to the possibilities of bionic hearing.

By the time Limbaugh received his device, the implants permitted deaf people to hear speech more or less as it is spoken. But they do not work for everyone—studies have shown that people who have been deaf for a fairly long time may not respond to technology. And doctors feel that people who can effectively use hearing aids should go that route instead of undergoing an implant. These are unsuitable for people who are deaf for reasons other than a failure in the cochlea. According to the National Institute on Deafness and Other Communication Disorders, this would make about 250,000 of the million or more deaf people in the United States and many hundreds of thousands worldwide suitable candidates for implants.

While cochlear implants are not as expensive as artificial retinas, they do not come cheap. Typically they run more than $60,000 apiece, and many people who depend on the cochlear implant for their hearing feel that they would be better served with one such device in each ear. A recent article profiled an eight-year-old girl who is part of a small but growing number of deaf people who are getting cochlear implants in both ears. Her family decided to get their daughter an additional implant because having only one implant meant she had only one working ear. Her hearing was far from perfect— she couldn't tell where sounds came from, which forced her to rely on a sign language interpreter to follow and participate in discussions at school. Another problem was background noise, so much so that whenever she had discussions outdoors she couldn't pay attention.

Although her brain is still adjusting to the new mix of sounds coming through both ears, her parents feel that her hearing will eventually be acute enough so she can talk on a cell phone and even sing in a choir. Studies bear out the wisdom of the parents' decision. Research presented at the American Otological Society suggests that deaf children who get their second implant before age eight adapt to the device more rapidly and understand words better than older children. Moreover, a 2004 study by the Washington University School of Medicine in St. Louis found that children who only hear with one ear are significantly more likely to repeat at least one grade.

One major drawback is that insurers at this point are being less than cooperative in reimbursing patients for a second implant, claiming that research on the benefits of having two implants is "inconclusive."

More than 100,000 people around the world have implants, but the recipients tend to be rich or from countries with supportive health care systems. Things are changing quickly, however. The common infectious disease German measles is the number-one cause of childhood deafness in Indonesia. Doctors in that country are now being trained to perform the cochlear implant procedure so parents do not have to travel to Australia and other distant places in order to have their children fitted for the device. We can only hope that this diffusion of the technology increases. The World Health Organization (WHO) says there are 250 million deaf people worldwide, with two-thirds in developing countries. [112]

The Bionic Ear Institute in Australia is tackling the problem of deafness from a different angle. The organization is attempting to devise an implant for the inner ear that will literally shock damaged nerves back to health. In this medical scenario a small pump would shower the nerves with stimulating chemicals while electrodes excite the cells to keep them alive.

One can only wonder whether someday those with no hearing loss will desire access to some form of device that can provide them "super-hearing" as a way to hear distant conversations or improve the sound quality of music or other artistic productions, such as movies. The technology is certainly intriguing enough to attract the attention of those obsessed with becoming "ultra-human." [113]

Superstrength in a Second Skin

Another future possibility is one which will replace our muscles with an artificial component which is more durable, flexible and stronger than our natural muscle. Developed by Yoseph Bar-Cohen, a physicist at the Jet Propulsion Laboratory in Pasadena, this material is driven by a little-known material called electroactive polymer. It has an unusual property-when it is stimulated by electricity or chemicals, it moves, expanding, contracting, curling, pushing and pulling. It is springy, durable, quick, forceful and quiet. Because electroactive polymers share these qualities with human skeletal muscles, they have been labeled "artificial muscle."

At this point, the ultimate end-use for such electrical polymers is to replace up to half the planet's one billion electric motors— engineers are developing artificial-muscle-powered devices, including a knee brace that prevents injuries and tiny pumps to deliver drugs.

But an even more ambitious goal lies ahead: to replace the actual muscle. Bar-Cohen claims that, "In this material, we have the closest to real muscles we ever had." So researchers are looking at a variety of medical devices that would be implanted in or attached to people's bodies. These include artificial-muscle-powered prosthetic arms and legs, an artificial diaphragm to help people breathe and a pumping device to assist diseased hearts.

Decades from now, scientists talk of plastics that could replace or augment any muscle in the body. Of course, such muscles would initially be utilized to replace damaged muscles and limbs, the most obvious first candidates being military personnel, firefighters and the like. However, we can imagine athletes hankering for a stronger and more durable version of their original limbs. Sounds farfetched? Who could envision thousands of people injecting themselves with *botox*, essentially a poison, in order to eliminate a few facial wrinkles?[114]

All this is part and parcel of the Ultra-Human phenomenon; the relentless drive to push the human body into a form that is smarter, faster, more durable and even just better looking. We will deal with this dream—to create a body that is for all practical purposes "forever young"—in detail later. Let me just touch here on one aspect of this drive to look youthful, improving the look and feel of human skin.

The line between therapeutic improvements of damaged skin and cosmetic skin enhancement seems to be blurring. One substance, introduced by research scientist Burt Ensley of Sedona, Arizona, demonstrates this perfectly. Ensley, formerly of biotech giant Amgen and now a self-described "serial entrepreneur," has transformed a product originally developed to help heal wounds and to regenerate tissue into a commercially sold cream that could be used to slow the aging process. His concoction, DermaLastyl, contains elastin, which gives skin its elastic quality. As we age, our bodies lose elastin, and consequently the skin becomes saggy, droopy and wrinkly. This product temporarily restores elastin—initial testimonials to the product have been glowing. Actresses and models seem to be gravitating to it.[115]

Skin regeneration and rejuvenation might also emerge from completely different fields. Many are looking not to cosmetic-based therapies, but such cutting edge fields as stem-cell science to eventually re-invent practically all parts of the body. One promising area comes from new research into organ regeneration being performed at Harvard University. Led by Glenn Larsen, the chief scientific officer at Hydra Biosciences in Boston, these scientists are developing protein-based drugs that encourage the re-growth of muscle tissue that has died after a heart attack. What is more amazing is that patients themselves will be delivering these regenerative protein molecules into their bloodstream by using a device such as an inhaler or supersonic drug gun.[116]

Once these scientific techniques are developed and perfected, it is possible that we will be able to restore full health to any organ, including skin and muscle. When these techniques become affordable and available, most citizens of the *Ageless Nation* will be able to employ such technologies to make themselves look younger, more handsome or more beautiful.[117]

And This is Just the Beginning

A *Popular Science* 2005 issue entitled "Superhuman" gave the readers a glimpse into technological and pharmaceutical breakthroughs that will help us achieve this status in the near-future. They opined that regardless of what the drug or technology is originally created for, healthy people co-opt it to make themselves stronger, faster or smarter. Follow this trend far enough, *Popular Science* claims, and we reach the fully augmented human. I wholeheartedly agree.

The research under way in bioengineering laboratories worldwide to alter our bodies promises to bring us closer to the achievement of the Ultrahuman much faster than skeptics might imagine.

By 2008 or 2009, we might have an artificial heart that can last up to five years, longer than the one to two year lifespan of the current heart. Abiocor, the manufacturer, thinks that this state-of-the-art artificial heart, which currently fits only 50 percent of the male population, will be 30 percent smaller and fit most men and 50 percent of the women.

In six to ten years, if researchers at the University of Southern California are successful, arthritis sufferers and stroke victims might regain movement in their paralyzed limbs. How? The Bion, which measures one hundredth the size of an AA battery, is already being used to strengthen muscles of people in these groups. In clinical trials, doctors inject this 16-millimeter-long capsule of electrode-capped glass into the limb's lifeless muscle. The patient activates the battery to mimic nerve impulses. The muscle then contracts in response. They hope to make this system fully automatic.

Earlier, we discussed bringing vision to the blind. But we will also be able to improve vision for those not visually impaired. We can all improve on our current eyes, especially in terms of the colors we "see" with our eyes. Humans have three color-producing cones in our eyes—red, green and blue. Ten or fifteen years from now, if work performed by scientists at the Medical College of Wisconsin bears fruit, we will be retro-genetically engineered with genes for a fourth cone in our eyes. This one would enable us to see new hues that we can't even imagine right now. Imagine what a different world this would be if we could see into this "fourth dimension."

We know that one way to maintain a healthy lifestyle, and thereby increase our lifespan, is to stay lean and fit. However, the real question is how can you maintain a satisfying diet and achieve this svelte and fit body? Some would say by imagining that you are full even when you are not. Transneuronix in New Jersey has created a pacemaker that is helping test subjects lose 25 to 40 percent of their body fat. The pacemaker emits mild shocks that relax and expand the upper part of the stomach. The brain then interprets the distended stomach as feeling full. (The magazine lyrically labeled this treatment "Shock Therapy For the Gut.")

University of Pittsburgh researchers are working on what to me is an impressive innovation, the world's first implantable lung, a "high-fiber lung" due out in about five or ten years.

As they age, many people have problems remembering names, faces and even wedding anniversaries. Ten years from now, people will be able to acquire a microchip memory like the one neural engineer Ted Berger of the University of Southern California is developing. In his device, a microchip will send signals from one healthy brain cell to another, bypassing damaged tissue that would otherwise block the message. At first, his artificial hippocampus will most likely be marketed predominantly to Alzheimer's patients to help them regain the ability to form memories. The next in line will be the merely forgetful. Let's face it, though. We all would like to ace our SATs and Bar exams, and who would not want to have a photographic memory as a tool to use in achieving professional success in any field? Once the chip is perfected, we are all getting one, for ourselves and our children. [118]

Speaking of ways to enhance the working of the human brain, let us take a quick look at the methods thousands of people are employing to gain competitive edges in the battle to be smarter and quicker.

BRAINPOWER AND THE PROMISE OF COSMETIC NEUROLOGY

Nothing characterizes the Ultra-Human Phenomenon more than the efforts to radically enhance and expand human intelligence. The increasingly complex world makes it important for each of us to become smarter. The sheer amount of information people are expected to retain in order to succeed in school and perform their jobs increases exponentially every decade. Let's look at how our species will go about becoming the little Einsteins, Salks and Mozarts that our civilization needs in the exciting but very demanding future.

Smart-Pill Mania

Already, many people—students, soldiers, executives—are choosing to boost their minds via a whole new generation of pharmaceutical products known as "smart drugs." In fact, a new term has entered the lexicon to describe this aspect of the Ultra-human Phenomenon, "cosmetic neurology" or nip and tuck for the mind.

Interestingly, the drugs in question were not originally developed to help people pass tests. The first generation of mind-enhancing drugs was intended to treat brain and other disorders, but they quickly have been adopted by people from across the social spectrum because of their ability to enhance performance.

One of these drugs, Adderall, was originally created for people with attention-deficit disorder. Provigil, the commercial name for the drug modafinil, was developed to counter narcolepsy, a nerve disease which induces its victims to fall asleep uncontrollably. Through experimentation and possibly merely by accident, students and others with access to these drugs discovered that this class of drugs helps them concentrate, remain alert, maintain their focus and memorize and retain information. Thus students working on complex term papers and pulling all-nighters before exams covet the drug.

Even Ritalin, originally intended as a treatment for children and adults with hyperactivity problems, has moved into the mainstream as a memory enhancer. It has since been co-opted by students to help them concentrate. A study in the U.S. last year revealed that 20 percent of healthy American college students use Ritalin before exams

The word has spread quickly that such drugs are helping millions of people to improve scores on scholastic tests, including the SATs. In a recent four-year period Adderall sales went up 3,135.6 percent, and Provigil went up 359.7 percent. In May 2005, the Partnership for a Drug-Free America reported that among kids of middle school and high school age, 2.25 million are using stimulants such as Ritalin without prescriptions. That's about one in ten of the twenty-two million students in those grades, as calculated by the United States Department of Education. Half the time, the study reported, the students said they were using these drugs not so much to get high as "to help me with my problems" or "to help me with specific tasks."

And these drugs represent only the first primitive, halting generation of cognitive enhancers. Memory drugs will soon make it to market if human clinical trials continue successfully. Although the memory compounds being raced to market by four United States companies are initially aimed at the severely impaired, such as early-stage Alzheimer's patients, researchers expect the market for memory drugs to rapidly extend into the part of the population not suffering from major cognitive disorders. This would include the more than seventy million baby boomers who are tired of forgetting what they meant to buy at the shopping mall and then realizing they've forgotten where they parked their cars, too. Or students who think such drugs could help them gain a few hundred points on their SATs.

Some 4.5 million Americans suffer from the horrific symptoms of Alzheimer's disease; at least four million are afflicted with mild cognitive impairment, a precursor to Alzheimer's; and more than ten million have age-associated memory impairment, which means their memories are far below average for their age.

But here's the rub. The forty or so companies, including corporate giants such as Eli Lilly and GlaxoSmithKline, Pennsylvania-based Cephalon (which already has Provigil in its arsenal), as well as smaller companies such as Cortex Pharmaceuticals, that are pursuing pills to boost sagging memory have two distinct markets. There are those suffering from debilitating diseases such as Alzheimer's, and another much larger market, the general public that wants to enhance its intellectual abilities, who want Viagra for the brain.

These companies know that there is what some politely describe as an "off-label market" for drugs like Provigil. According to James McGaugh, a neuroscientist at the University of California at Irvine, "Companies won't tell you this, but they are really gunning for the market of non-impaired people—the forty-four-year-old salesman trying to remember the names of his customers."

One prominent neuroscientist, Anjan Chatterjee, calls this next stage the era of cosmetic neurology. "Prospecting for better brains may be the new gold rush," he says. This is due in part to the progress scientists are making in creating pills that enhance memory and intelligence is dazzling. In the past twenty years, scientists—aided by advances in computing, brain imaging and genetic engineering—have made significant progress toward understanding the biochemical systems that regulate cognition and emotion. This knowledge has raised the possibility of manipulating those systems more powerfully and precisely than ever before.

Many scientists, especially those outside the United States, are endorsing the removal of restrictions on such drugs to make them available without prescription. For instance, medical support for these intelligence enhancement drugs came from Sir David King, the British government's chief scientific adviser. According to King, smart drugs to make people think faster, improve their memory and reduce tiredness will be commonplace within twenty years. In 2006 King told ministers at a presentation in Downing Street that a new generation of brain-enhancing chemicals could be given to healthy people to enhance their lives. He said these new substances could even be used to treat mental disorders and fight drug addiction.

Andrea Malizia, a consultant senior lecturer in the Department of Psychopharmacology at Bristol University, is calling for Donepezil, a treatment for Alzheimer's disease, to be more accessible. Donepezil has a "remarkable impact" on a wide range of functions, including memory, concentration and the ability to learn, she says.

If modafinil is the "first true smart drug," it certainly won't be the last. There are dozens more "cognition enhancers" in the pipeline.

In 2005, an expert panel appointed by the United Kingdom government identified fifteen molecular pathways in the brain that are under active investigation as targets for cognition enhancement. All are being developed to help people with cognitive impairment such as memory loss due to Alzheimer's, but many will turn out to have positive effects on normal, healthy brains, and end up being guzzled like coffee.[119]

While we can expect a major debate over the use of such smart pills to erupt in many countries across the world, their use has been for the most part "under the radar." As of now, smart-pill use has not yet achieved widespread attention and has not been the focus of much data collection aside from the previously noted studies.

Richard Restak, a Washington neurologist and president of the American Neuropsychiatric Association, says that these drugs go unnoticed in the media because they are not infamous for being abused recreationally and they are not being used by people with diseases. They are used by ambitious students who want to get into good schools. Campus health center reports omit discussion of smart-pill use because, according to Restak, "This is not the kind of stuff that you would overdose on" easily. And Provigil has a pretty good safety record." He observes about these types of drugs, "If you go a little over you get wired up, but it wears off in a couple of hours."

Reports on these substances have remained fairly low key because they have not been linked to any major health problems. However, in 2005,

Canada pulled a form of Adderall off the market as a result of sudden unexplained deaths in children with cardiac abnormalities. In another case Provigil use has been linked to a decrease in the effectiveness of birth control. All of these drugs come with a raft of side-effect warnings.

Nevertheless these drugs are perceived as much more beneficial than harmful overall. Restak claims that, "We're going to see it not only in schools, but in businesses, especially where mental endurance matters." He can visualize a boss saying to a manager, "'You've been here fourteen hours; could you do another six?" Restak says that, "It's a very competitive world out there, and this gives people an edge."

We know that Provigil enjoys widespread use in the military. Because soldiers and pilots are often sleep-deprived during missions, the military wants them to use cognitive boosters that work better than today's amphetamines. In one study on helicopter pilots, it was discovered that modafinil could keep pilots alert with only eight hours of sleep in a three day or longer period. The French government indicated that the Foreign Legion used modafinil during certain covert operations. And studies have shown that donepezil dramatically increased the memory of pilots during flight training.[120]

The Coming Debate over the Smart-Pill

We can foresee a virtual battle breaking out between those who want to enhance their abilities pharmacologically, and government officials and others who feel that using drugs for purposes other than they were created for is downright wrong (unless they approve of the new use, of course). FDA rules prohibit the development of drugs just for enhancement.

Part of the uneasiness about the new enhancement pills is the way that they are reaching the general population and how people then use the drugs. It all begins when the pharmaceutical company develops a medication to treat a recognized physical or mental illness. At a certain point people realize that the drug can help healthy users too. Then some doctors prescribe the substance to patients "off label," that is, for purposes other than the ones recognized by the Food and Drug Administration. Then students and others use bootlegs of therapeutic drugs. Some college students take Ritalin to help them ace exams and Provigil, a sleep-disorder medication, to stay awake during class and intense study periods.

Even Eric R. Kandel, a pioneer in the research leading to the development of such drugs, is shocked by the idea that powerful elixirs like the ones he is developing might rapidly trickle down to ambitious college kids. Kandel, founder of Memory Pharmaceuticals, won the 2000 Nobel Prize in medicine for his research on the physiological basis of memory storage in neurons.

"That's awful! Why should they be taking drugs? They should just study! I think this is absurd," says Kandel. "What's so terrible about having a 3.9? The idea that character and functioning and intelligence is to be judged by a small difference on an exam—that's absurd." He went on to say, "I went to Harvard. I like Harvard. It ain't worth it."[121]

However, comments and messages that students and others posted about one *Washington Post* online story dealing with the growth of smart pill usage suggest that Kandel's views are out of synch with the realities of competing in today's academic and business marketplace. Getting a 4.0 grade point average and parleying that GPA into admission to Harvard or other elite schools is obviously a goal the current generation finds worthwhile. And some will take whatever steps necessary to realize that dream, even if those steps include Provigil.

Most of those responding online to the article voiced overwhelming support for using drugs that would enhance one's ability to perform well in school and work. The messages also paint a picture of the fiercely competitive nature of today's academic and professional environments. One writer endorsed the use of smart pills because, "In our competitive culture it is starting to become necessary to get in to Harvard or hold a 4.0 in order to get the good high-paying jobs; C grades (which should be "average" on the grading scale) no longer cut it." In contrast to Dr. Kandel's position, this generation feels that it is important to get admitted an elite school.

Another poster discussed the relationship between college GPA and the job that students will eventually be able to obtain. The poster stated that high grades lead to admission to better colleges, which leads to getting that elusive high-paying job. He quoted an executive of a Fortune 100 company, who said that "smart people can learn anything, and that's who they try to hire." The writer closes with a definitive statement on the issue. "With that said, I would definitely take these pills."

We can even see the genesis of a cultural and generational clash over the acceptability of using these drugs. One student states, "I love how old people think that kids use these drugs because they're lazy. Apparently they're out of touch with what teachers expect nowadays." He asserts that school nowadays involves an "insane amount of long thesis papers and grueling comprehensive exams." He concludes that, "If the pill helps and it can't hurt, I say go for it."

There was also a torrent of personal testimonials to the efficacy of various smart-pills as study companions and memory enhancers. One person claimed that he had been taking Adderall and Provigil for three years. Before taking the drug he was getting Ds & Fs and was suspended from school. The drug enhanced his memory and concentration to the point where he now gets As & Bs and was readmitted to the university. One mother asked her son, a pre-med student at UCLA, if he had heard of Adderall. "He told me that just about everyone he knows at UCLA takes it in order to get through the extreme demand of classes and finals," she wrote.

Adderall and Provigil usage is not confined to students. For instance, concert pianists take propranolol, a hypertension and angina medication, to ease pre-performance jitters.

In the near future, the drug companies will enter this debate to legitimize wider use of smart-pills. In a preemptive strike against further government prohibition of enhancement drug use, Cephalon has already submitted to the FDA a supplemental application that would give physicians freedom to prescribe Provigil for lesser sleep problems, such as shift-work drowsiness. Cephalon realizes that even without that approval, those pulling all-nighters account for a growing portion of Provigil's 200 million dollars in annual sales.

In addition, people who are prescribed some of these drugs for problems such as depression sometimes discover its potential as a "smart pill." One forty-three-year old woman was so incapacitated by severe depression that she had to go on disability. She calls Provigil a miracle drug! "It improved my concentration and memory and best of all I am eager to get on with my day with energy I haven't enjoyed in years." The woman was fairly ebullient in her claim that "I have found my life again with Provigil." A twenty-three year old, who has struggled through school most of his life because of a poor memory, is tempted to try smart pills so he can finally finish his college degree. Like others, he is defiant in the face of the medical and government establishments' resistance to the widespread use of smart pills and other enhancers. "I don't even care if they end up being illegal," he says. "If they can help improve my memory, help me focus and enhance my brain function, then I'm all for them and I can't understand why anyone would be against them."

Some defend the smart pills as a way to improve society in general. One articulate web-messenger sums up this position succinctly:"If our society were to embrace these drugs as the acceptable norm, think of how far our society can come. Think of the productivity....thousands of years of evolution, fast forwarded in a single pill....isn't that what medicine is about anyway?"

Although dramatically outnumbered on this particular message board, the naysayers weighed in with their own opinions, many which we could imagine the medical authorities voicing. Some mentioned the addiction and dependency problem that we associate with most drug use. One even objected to the title of the article, "Smart Pills," calling the title irresponsible. As far as she was concerned, taking an unprescribed pill is in itself a form of "substance abuse," regardless of the purpose and efficacy of the drug.

The illegality issue, and the hysteria often associated with the notorious "war on drugs" was brought up in a few of the online comments. One supported the idea of taking a pill to help you study, but was on his high school's hockey team and feared failing the school's drug test. This is a concern. In August 2003, US track star Kelli White tested positive for modafinil after winning two gold medals at the World Track and Field Championships. She was taking the drug to combat narcolepsy, but the IAAF, the sport's governing body, classifies that medication as a stimulant and stripped her of her medals.

One person recounted how he was arrested, put in jail, held on 5,000 dollar bail and put on three years probation. He now has a felony conviction on his record, and has paid thousands of dollars in legal fees. His crime: possession of one Adderall pill.

Reflecting a touch of Puritanism, it was claimed that such pills would "make it too easy" to be intelligent and perform well in school and at your job. Some even think taking smart pills is a form of cheating, not as bad as cheating from someone during a test, but certainly gaining an "unfair advantage over those who choose not to compromise their morals." One high school junior feels that such drugs threaten his position as a top student. He says, with some justification, that since he has worked diligently to claw his way to the top of the academic heap, he does not want his position "challenged by someone who is on a pill with no actual aptitude in fields of intelligence."[122]

While such pills evidently improve attention span and concentration, no one is claiming that they will level the playing field to the extent our "top student" fears. Nevertheless, they will enable many to achieve goals that were unattainable without the intelligence enhancement capabilities of such wonder drugs. Schools and universities are by their nature competitive. Regardless of how much students learn and know, an inevitable hierarchy of talent and skill emerges. A brilliant student can score nearly perfect on the SATs, and still find himself out of the running for admission to Harvard or Stanford because someone else earned a perfect score on the same test. Utilizing the pharmaceutical approach to getting a good grade is considered cheating, or at least cheating someone else who did not use a drug to enhance cognitive efficiency.

This situation changes, however, in the context of the work world. Yes, working in a corporation is competitive. But from the employers' point of view, a high-performing workforce ultimately contributes to the organization's bottom line. A shipping firm, for instance, wants its truckers to drive their routes at maximum efficiency, which means alertly and quickly. I want all my managers and salespeople to excel in the performance of their jobs and if I am a dean, I want all my professors performing top-notch research, getting published and excelling in the classroom.

My point is that most organizations would not mind if their employees were using Provigil to maximize output or some other drug to enhance their memories, unless of course there were health risks associated with taking the drug. It is possible that corporations might become friendly witnesses to the efforts by drug companies to expand the uses of smart pills when the debate begins to simmer over the next few years.

Support for expanded use of smart pills, I believe, will be generated by the majority of the public who simply want an edge in today's competitive marketplace. The numerous online responses to the Post article told stories of people who had to discontinue their careers, schooling, and jobs, not for lack of intelligence, but because of their inability to give the full level of concentration required in this competitive world. I believe it will eventually be seen as almost unfair, even heartless, to deny people a way to become smarter. And it will be perceived as harmful to prevent people from contributing their utmost to their society and their employers.

Electronic Wizardry

There are other perspectives on how to boost brainpower that make the pharmaceutical approach seem almost primitive. Ray Kurzweil, whom we spoke of in Chapter Two, is a leading light of what is broadly labeled the *Transhumanist* school of human development. He thinks that over the next several decades, we will so change the very structure of the human brain that the use of drugs to enhance its operation would be superfluous.

Kurzweil believes that our current brains are essentially limited and relatively fixed in design. By 2030, we will use nanotechnology to change and transcend the basic architecture of the brain's neural regions, modifying their structure and function.

To understand, let us return to those ultra-tiny nanobots, or nanorobots, that we said would be used to clean our bloodstreams and repair and rejuvenate our cells. Kurzweil has another job for them to do—these nanobots will play a key role in expanding our minds through the merger of biological and non-biological, or "machine," intelligence. In the next twenty-five years, Kurzweil speculates science will discover a way to augment our one hundred trillion relatively slow interneuronal connections with high-speed virtual connections facilitated by the use of nanorobotics. As these nanobots do their job, our brains will be operating at exponentially higher speeds. Forget Provigil or any of the other wonder drugs cooked up in the labs of GlaxoSmithKline or Merck. Our reconstructed brains will greatly boost our memories, pattern-recognition abilities, and overall thinking capacity. As Kurzweil sees it, these brain implants based on massively distributed intelligent nanobots will overcome our current architectural flaws.

That is just the beginning. Kurzweil envisions our reconstructed brains as being capable of communicating with each other, as well as with powerful artificial-intelligence computer networks, sort of a souped-up Internet system to which we are connected, wirelessly I assume. We will be downloading and uploading information on a continual basis.[123]

Kurzweil's vision is highly speculative. Many scientists are not sure that such a restructuring is viable, let alone desirable. In an earlier book, *The Future Factor*, I suggested that Kurzweil's vision of the future human, enhanced or not, was more machine than human. In fact, to me, his neural connection network seems more like the Borg, those robotic worker-bees that routinely terrorized Captain Picard and his crew on *Star Trek: The Next Generation*.

That is not to say we will not someday use some form of electronics to boost our brain power. Some imagine that in as little as ten years from now you will be able to visit a "brain spa" to get a temporary boost in your intelligence quotient via a variant of something called "transcranial magnetic stimulation" (TMS). The TMS delivers microsecond pulses of energy a few centimeters into its wearer's brain, inducing electrical activity in brain cells. Neuroscientist Mark George and colleagues at the Medical University of South Carolina, as well as other researchers, have found that such pulses delivered via a helmet connected to a TMS machine can increase the pulse-recipients' reaction time on tests.

Studies have shown that such painless electrical zaps to key areas of the brain reduce depression. They hope that TMS therapies administered to someone who has taken a smart pill could boost a person's intelligence immeasurably.[124]

Will a combination of cybernetics and electronics someday endow human beings with telekinesis? If researchers at Brown University and Cyberkinetics in Foxboro, Massachusetts succeed, within ten or fifteen years we might be able to acquire a brain implant that will enable us to communicate with machines. Seems "futuristic"? Well, it is. In the researchers' scenario, a microchip implanted in the motor cortex just beneath the skull will intercept nerve signals and re-route them to a computer, which will then wirelessly send the command to any of various electronic devices, including computers, stereos, even electric wheelchairs.

Intelligence and memory might not be the only object of the "cosmetic neurology" industry. Ramez Naam, author of *More Than Human: Embracing the Promise of Biological Enhancement* claims that over the next few decades, "We could create new drugs to sculpt or alter any aspect of human behavior: infatuation, pair-bonding, empathy, appetite, spirituality, thrill-seeking, arousal, even sexual orientation." James Hughes writes in *Citizen Cyborg* that "the heritability of happiness…suggests that there could be future drugs and gene therapies that jack our happiness set-point to its maximum without negative side effects." Transhumanist philosopher David Pearce says that drugs could be invented to chemically crank our dopaminergic systems so that "undiluted existential happiness will infuse every second of waking and dreaming existence."[125]

Happy drugs? If we are in the middle of a debate over pills that improve our test scores and work habits, imagine the *sturm und drang* that will engulf pharmaceuticals that help maintain a state of mental euphoria 24/7.

Regardless of the attempts to limit the use of and access to drugs that make us smarter, quicker, happier and more efficient, Guideline #5 to the future still holds: "Build It And They Will Come: If You Create Something That People Perceive As Beneficial, They Will Want It, Find It, And Use It." Of that we can be absolutely certain.

FOREVER YOUNG: THE PROSPECTS FOR REJUVENATION AND ETERNAL YOUTH

Perhaps the Ultra-Human enterprise's most far-reaching benefit is the possibility of living one's very long life in a perennially youthful and healthy body. This may even be a more precious commodity than creating brilliant minds and photographic memories? Most people would trade their fortunes to be eternally youthful and attractive. In popular fiction, characters have sold their souls for such a treasure.

Rejuvenation will have a tremendous impact on social relationships, and will introduce a countless number of intriguing scenarios and possibilities in the way that we will live our lives. Before we explore these scenarios, let us look at some of the breakthroughs which will enable us to live a very long life as a physically young person.

The Many Fountains of Youth

How will we get to the point where the human being would be blessed with a life in which he or she would live in a state of eternal youth. How is this at all possible?

Actually, some of the technologies that we discussed earlier that are involved in the life extension process are the same ones that will help us to live in a permanently youthful state.

The 2003 President's Council on Bioethics report dealt with the ethical, political, social and economic impacts of a variety of life extending and life improving scientific breakthroughs. They stated that we are approaching a point where we could conceivably achieve "ageless bodies," as one of their report's sections was titled. The advances in biotechnology and other fields are bringing us face to face with the possibility of extended youth and substantially prolonged lives. They stated that the "prospect of possible future success" of these new breakthroughs is sufficiently probable that society should begin to consider the "profound and complicated questions" regarding rejuvenation. [126]

For many people, the idea of bodily rejuvenation brings visions of a surgeon applying the knife to reshape part of the body. Cosmetic surgery has of course helped us to remain looking physically young. According to recent studies, 124,514 facelifts alone were performed in 2002. Thousands subject themselves to liposuction operations or have breast implants procedures to enhance their appearances. Lasers and other high-tech devices used quite effectively, if only temporarily, shave years off patients' outward appearance. By the 1990s, more than 50,000 board-certified plastic surgeons actively practiced in the United States and many more world wide.

Rejuvenation, or achievement of the true "ageless body," goes well beyond the merely cosmetic approach of twentieth century reconstructive medicine. A host of cutting edge technologies promise to soon enable us to live our entire lives physically young and healthy.[127]

The most accessible of these techniques is caloric restriction. At this point CR is the only technology which has irrefutably been shown to stop aging, and to imbue those utilizing the technique profoundly "youthful" existences throughout their very long lifetimes. Numerous studies on mice, worms and various mammals and primates have revealed that a reduction of food intake to about 60 percent of normal has a significant impact on the animal's lifespan. It also retards or completely stops the rate of decline of the animal's neurological activity, muscle functions, immune response and nearly every other measurable marker of aging. Studies in mice and rats suggest that CR helps these animals run greater distances and to maintain "youthful" levels of activity at ages when non-restricted animals of the same species are either dead or "retired" from full activities.

As discussed earlier, if we develop drugs that mimic the impact of CR on cells, we could soon have at our disposal a method to live a very long life in a very youthful state.

Telomere research is an additional method that can add to living a long life in a youthful state. Since the mid-1980s, researchers have known that telomeres—which form the tips of chromosomes—can shorten over time as cells divide. When this protective tip shortens, eventually the cell stops dividing and then dies. Telomerase, an enzyme, influences the erosion and shortening of telomeres.

Studies in the 1990s strongly suggested that telomere length correlates with cell aging. Telomere erosion has been associated with wrinkling of the skin, age-related muscular degeneration, and atherosclerosis. Some scientists are reasoning that if we prevent the shortening of telomeres we can slow the aging of cells. Once we learn to keep the telomeres healthy, that is, prevent them from eroding, the cells theoretically could keep dividing and stay "young."

The ultimate tool in the rejuvenation enterprise will be nanotechnology. This possibility was first suggested by E. Kenneth Drexler in his *Engines of Creation*, penned in the 1990s, that "molecular engineers will eventually combine improved biochemical knowledge with improved molecular machines, learning to repair damaged tissue structures and so rejuvenate them."

Aubrey de Grey, a Cambridge University scientist who writes on life extension, sees a major role for nanotechnology in this century. De Grey claims that "nanotechnology seems likely to play a major role in the more sophisticated interventions that will be required to maintain youthfulness." According to de Grey, biotechnology can take us just so far in the rejuvenation process. He thinks we will turn to "non-biological tools," especially nanotechnology, to repair cells and eradicate cellular damage. We will discuss his theories in detail in Chapter 10.

When will all this happen? Drexler's timetable has this innovation occurring in the latter part of the twenty-first century. Thus, many people living today can look forward to nanotechnology overtaking their aging process and delivering them safely to an era of cell repair, vigor, and indefinite life-span.

We will have much to say about nanotechnology, as well as other rejuvenating technologies, in the final chapter on immortality. As the Bioethics Council stated in their report, our quest for both eternal youth and eternal life emanate from the same set of desires. "Taken to its extreme," the Council stated, "The underlying impulse driving age-retardation research is, at least implicitly, limitless, the equivalent of a desire for immortality."

Living in the World of the Forever Young

Many of us pretend that appearances are not important, that we accept people for who they are, for their characters, senses of humor and a host of other qualities that transcend the purely physical.

Sociologist Kurt Lewin always said that if you want to understand how any system truly operates, be it a society, organization, religion or any value system, change it! Yes, mess something up and you will know exactly how it truly worked and how important that "something" really was, to you, your life, and your world.

One of the most important outward characteristics influencing how we react to each other is our perception of each others' ages. We react differently to a person based on whether he or she is child, teenager, young adult or a senior citizen. We might accord more respect to someone older than ourselves, or take a bit more seriously a statement of a person from an adult age group over that of a younger person.

We use our perception of age to guide any number of social interactions, including who we will date, marry and choose as our friends. So what will happen to the myriad of experiences when we can no longer trust our physical perceptions of a person's age, when someone we perceive as the picture of youth, is older than we thought?

When we do finally discover the fountain of youth, when a cellular manipulation can radically transform a person into any age desired, Kurt Lewin's principle will enjoy its true flowering. We will have eliminated one of the most elemental components of our society, its age structure. No, I'm not saying we will have magically reduced the number of years a person has already spent on the planet. That is logically impossible. Rather, we will have removed the possibility of knowing how old a person is strictly on the basis of his or her appearance. For all practical purposes, we will eliminate age as a social reality.

Let's engage in a few "thought experiments" to see how we would adjust to a world in which everything we thought we knew is suddenly and immutably turned upside down.

Imagine in the dawning of the Superlongevity Revolution you will be between thirty and forty years of age. You meet a woman or a man who appears to be about somewhere between twenty-five to thirty years old, and according to currently accepted criteria is considered extremely handsome or beautiful. You date this person for about a month, and based on the interactions, and let's face it, the person's devastating good looks and physique (your friends never cease telling you what a catch this person is), you are starting to think that this individual is Mr. or Mrs. Right. Sexual intimacy only heightens the passionate feelings you have for this person.

You have never asked this man or woman her age, and neither has your partner inquired about yours. And why should age be important, you reason? Age is of no consequence when two people are in love—it is the inner person that really matters.

Suddenly you discover this gorgeous young woman or man is eighty-five years old. Upon learning this, you will probably go through several stages of reaction—disbelief, bewilderment, resentment, even disappointment.

So what will be your next move? Before you respond that you might consider terminating what has become the best relationship you have ever had because of the "age difference," let me establish some other criteria. You have been born into a new period in which people have little or no experience with or first-hand knowledge of "physical oldness." Becoming eighty-five, one hundred, or 120 in this period will just mean that you have spent more time on the planet, not that you look older. Breakthroughs in cellular regeneration, nanotechnology, and CR pharmaceuticals will have made traditional images of physical old age obsolete, something you read about in a sociology text book or learn about on the History Channel.

In this new social environment, discovering that you are dating a man or woman of eighty-five, whose physical appearance is that of a gorgeous twenty-five year old, should not be any more jolting than discovering any number of unusual background facts about your potential soul mate. It shouldn't be any different than finding out she was once a beauty pageant winner of he is the widower of a famed movie star.

However, in exploring the "forever young" aspects of the Ultra-human phenomenon with the interviewees for this book as well as with a variety of audiences, including those in Internet chat rooms where such topics are discussed, one of the recurring beliefs I encounter is that regardless of how perfectly modern science can restore an 85 or one hundred year old body to the state of a beautiful twenty-five year old person, that person would still inadvertently betray his age by the topics he chooses to discuss, the terminology or slang he uses, his attitude, and his frame of reference. One Internet respondent stated quite emphatically that "anyone speaking to you for any length of time would begin to realize you really are a kid or just a septacentarian trying to pose as one." According to the writer even if the young-looking oldie tries to "fake naive enthusiasm, pretend a lack of experience and get hip to current youth subculture," a younger person would soon discover his age.

Many of us intuitively agree. However, others in the chat group refuted him by mentioning that many netcitizens fake their identities, including their sex and age. It is not uncommon for people to create what are known as "avatars," physical cyber-representations of themselves, and have their avatar interact with other avatars in various cyber settings, such as simulated cafes, parks, homes and even at the poker table. Some men even assume a female identity, or an older person represents himself with an avatar that appears twenty-five years old.

The writer states that if someone chooses an avatar that does not reflect her or his age or sex, "the only way you'll know how old a person is, is if the person tells you or if you are astute enough to garner clues of how long a person has lived from the person's writing style or philosophical tendencies." In fact, he states that after fifteen years of participating in various online communities, few people have guessed his age. "If people share common interests and goals, and the variable of physical appearance is removed or distanced from the equation, age becomes much less of an issue." Or not one at all!

Another internet participant sees this close similarity between gaining a rejuvenated body in real life and assuming an avatar in cyberspace. "In a future consisting of people whose bodies are, in fact, akin to internet 'avatars' in function and purpose, then a similar situation to the online one will develop," the writer claims. As in the cyber-avatar experience, "people will gain respect and interest from others based on their interests, demonstrated abilities, and personality traits. "

Consequently, he says, our society will become more of a meritocracy. Institutions will no longer discriminate on the basis of age, since everyone will look young. He does worry, however, that in the beginning the rich will have a distinct advantage not only in having initial access to the rejuvenation technology but in their ability to afford better looking outer-shells. He fears that "some custom physical 'avatars' are bound to be more expensive and capable than others, especially in the beginning when only the very wealthy are likely to have access to them." You could buy the Mercedes or Ferrari-quality outer-shell, but I could only afford the Chevrolet version.

When considering the societal impact of the introduction of the new rejuvenation therapies, many futurists and sociologists assume that anyone who can afford treatments such as a cellular regeneration program will purchase them. However, the consumers will base their decision on a number of factors. First, of course, is the affordability issue itself. I am reminded of an old Twilight Zone episode which dealt with an elderly couple, in their eighties, living in a future where such rejuvenation therapies are available, for a price. In an almost O'Henry-esque plot twist, the couple has enough money for only one such operation. They decide that the husband will get the operation. As one can imagine, the resulting disparity in physical states—he comes out looking like a twenty-five year old body builder while she remains a wrinkled, stooped old lady—tests their marital relationship mightily. The story ends with the husband deciding to go back to his older physical state—his marriage was more important to him than physical youth and overall health.

Eventually such operations will be within the financial reach of all citizens. However, there is a possibility, and this is very speculative, that some people will resist undergoing such transformations in age, even if the benign State offers all citizens this opportunity for free. Rejuvenation could affect your relationship with those who know you, including lifelong friends. "You'll fall into a younger age group based on appearance," one respondent writes, "Because people who are 'naturally' younger will more likely respond on the basis of appearance." They will assume that you'll have whatever fashionable preoccupations and interests that generation is involved, "even if you don't."

While you are busy becoming accepted into one age group, your relationships with your true peers could suffer. "Your present friends, still sixty-plus, will perhaps instinctively begin to regard you as less relevant to what they perceive as reality. They know that it is still "you," but if physical appearance still affects how people perceive others, your "un-rejuvenated" friends, even those who have known you since high school, could start having problems relating to the "new you."

One of the most jarring aspects of rejuvenation, however, will be people's perceptions of themselves. At least in the early stages of the introduction of this technology, people will be undergoing rejuvenation procedures such as cellular regeneration or nanotechnological therapies after they have gone through a significant portion of the aging process. As rejuvenation becomes more of a routine, perhaps a century from now, citizens of the *Ageless Nation* will simply undergo some form of treatment, perhaps telomere-based, that simply stops the aging process at twenty-five or thirty. But until that time, it will be commonplace for people to choose to become rejuvenated at sixty, seventy, eighty or one hundred years of age. To an extent, for better or worse, our image of ourselves as people is based on what we see in the mirror. It would be certainly wonderful at age seventy to one day find a sparkling young image reflected back at you in the mirror—how could you not feel younger, happier, and more vibrant (especially since you have rejuvenated all organs, and you are as strong and healthy as a twenty-five year old?)

However, you might start wondering who exactly is that person staring back at you in the mirror. Inside, you have the same mind, soul, personality, and habits, but you are seeing reflected a visage and a body you have not seen for some time. Confronted with this stranger in the mirror, will you be as alienated from yourself, at least initially, as your lifelong friends have become? Can you still relate to yourself when you look like someone you have not resembled for half a century or more? And most futurists assume that you will choose a body resembling your own physical status at age twenty-five. However, why just settle for the physical look of your body at twenty-five when modern cellular rejuvenation technology enables you to transmute your body into a state that is the very picture of physical perfection itself. The difficulty of becoming acclimated to the "twenty-five year old you" will be multiplied exponentially if you choose to look like someone completely novel.

Representing yourself with an avatar in cyberspace is one thing. You can always walk away from your computer or delete your avatar. For better or worse, the skin, body and overall appearance you choose via the rejuvenation process will be with you forever. And eventually, it will be you forever.

Beware: Age Envy Ahead!

Most people generally agree that there are benefits and disadvantages of being either old or young. We associate youth with vibrancy, strength, health, good looks, and of course, potential. Being older usually implies certain life advantages: you have more money, experience, knowledge, power, career and social contacts, and confidence. If you retire, you can generally enjoy a comfortable life of post-career leisure and personal development.

Up to this point in time, the fact that young people tend to have less money, power and security than older people tends to be beautifully balanced by the pure unadulterated advantage of, well, being young. Society is more likely to equate "being young" with being glamorous, attractive and sexually desirable. It seems almost as though nature has devised the ultimate fair trade-off between being young and old.

However, that balance of advantages and disadvantages will be dramatically upended when it becomes the norm to undergo physical rejuvenation procedures.

A rejuvenated eighty year old will bring to society's table a complete menu of desirable characteristics. He or she will have power, a lifelong accumulation of wealth, social connections, a wealth of knowledge, and enjoy all this in the body of a thirty year old. I can imagine the resentment that a twenty-five year old will harbor toward an eighty year old man who has the temerity to look as young as and possibly more attractive than the young stud. Remember, rejuvenation means exactly what the word implies—this will not be an "old guy" trying to look young. It will be a long-lived individual who is physically thirty years young. Will young men have to worry about bringing a girlfriend home in the fear that his gorgeous "young" grandfather might be visiting? Is there a chance she might prefer this "hot young guy" with an accumulation of eighty years of wealth and "life smarts" over his poor grandson?

The ability to appear young despite chronological age should certainly upset the balance of power in the television and movie industry. Imagine an actor with the physical features of Brad Pitt or Tom Cruise with the years of accumulated thespian experience of noted actors Sean Connery or Sir John Gielgud (and with a loyal audience built over half a century). What "age" role would this eighty year old stud play? The kindly old doctor? The young lothario? And will the ages depicted in the movies of *Ageless Nation* make any sense whatsoever in terms of our 2007 lifecycle?

The fact that rejuvenation could endow a person with exceptional strength, speed, and physical dexterity would have a tremendous impact on sports. We can imagine the eighty-year old Ultra-human biogeneticist or circuit court judge re-careering as a wide receiver for the New York Jets. (Since his college days are a half-century behind him, he would have to sign on with the team as an "undrafted free agent.")

Will intergenerational envy become a social issue? I believe it is a moot point. I am sure that most people will decide to undergo rejuvenation as soon as the technology becomes available, the social consequences be damned!

chapter seven

Making Superlongevity
a Reality

Alcor, Elixir Pharmaceuticals, Agensys, Arius Research, Corus Pharma, MedImmune and Celera Genomics are companies on the cutting edge of the Superlongevity Revolution.

While these companies are not recognizable names to most at the present time, they are making society's hopes for reaching the goal of a radically extended lifespan possible. The firms are critical components of what I label the "Superlongevity Industry." They form the nexus of the scientific thrust.

In the Superlongevity Industry, such companies and some individuals are researching and developing technologies and products that will enable us to live longer, healthier lives. Pharmaceutical companies, biotechnology companies, as well as other organizations and individual practitioners researching the aging process populate this industry, as do companies involved in cloning, cryogenics, tissue research, genetic engineering, bionics and stem cell applications.

Bankrolling many of the existing players in the Superlongevity Industry are a group of venture capital firms, the sine qua non of market success. Among them are OrbiMed and ARCH Ventures. They are the main mechanism by which smaller start-up biotechs can research their products and get them to market.

Collectively such organizations as the American Academy of Anti-Aging Medicine, the Methuselah Foundation, the Immortality Institute form part of what I call the "Superlongevity Lobby." They will play significant roles in our species' achievement of superlongevity. These organizations have different missions. Some exist as clearinghouses for information on medical break-throughs. Others run conferences that bring together scientists, futurists, policy planners and companies from the superlongevity industry. Some are activist oriented, hectoring government, industry and the public to support the goal of superlongevity and accelerate funding for medical research.

Together, the Superlongevity Industry and the Immortality Lobby are helping to make extended life a reality. This chapter, though not an exhaustive list of all companies and organizations helping to bring superlongevity into existence, examines the dynamic nature of the growing support for humans living a very long life.

THE SUPERLONGEVITY INDUSTRY

Many types of organizations will help create the science necessary to improve the human condition both for altruistic reasons and economic ones.

The Superlongevity Industry is comprised of the latter. We will look at the companies and organizations that create the product and those that underwrite the entire life extension venture.

Biotechnology: An Engine of the Superlongevity Revolution

Throughout this book, we have discussed many of the breakthroughs in the field of biotechnology that are helping to save and extend human lives.

The term *biotechnology* represents any technology based on biology, especially when used in agriculture, food science and medicine. According to the United Nations Convention on Biological Diversity, biotechnology is a technological application that uses biological systems, living organisms or derivatives thereof, to make or modify products or processes for specific use.

Others define biotechnology as the manipulation of organisms to do practical things and to provide useful products. Included here is the directed use of organisms for the manufacture of organic products, such as beer, milk products, and skin. Biotechnology is used to recycle, treat waste, clean up sites contaminated by industrial activities (bioremediation) and even produce biogenetically modified crops. It is also the science behind the building of biological weapons. Other applications of biotechnology do not use living organisms. Examples are DNA micro arrays used in genetics and radioactive tracers used in medicine.

The worldwide biotech industry is gargantuan, with revenues in 2005 exceeding sixty billion dollars for the first time in the industry's thirty year history.

That year biotech sales surged 18 percent according to the financial firm Ernst & Young.

Biotechs are an extremely attractive investment target—industry companies managed to raise $19.7 billion in capital last year, marking its second-highest tally since the 2000 bubble.

The Biotech sector is being helped by its sales of pharmaceutical products. Drug sales, with a big boost from Medicare coverage, are expected to keep rising for the next ten years, and biotechs are expected to get the lion's share of that increase. In the United States, spending on prescription drugs is projected to more than double between 2004 and 2015, to 446 billion dollars from 188 billion dollars, according to the Centers for Medicare and Medicaid Services. Drug sales were expected to jump 7.7 percent in 2006 alone, and to grow between 8 and 8.4 percent annually through 2015, according to CMS.[128]

Let's examine some of the major players demonstrating the power of biotech to cure disease and extend life. Over the past twenty-five years, one company, Amgen, has become a leading human therapeutics companies in the biotechnology industry. Amgen pioneered the development of novel products based on advances in recombinant DNA and molecular biology and launched the biotechnology industry's first blockbuster medicines. Amgen's product pipeline demonstrates that the company has pursued an aggressive program for fighting a host of diseases and conditions, including asthma, pain, various types of cancer, anemia, obesity, post menopausal osteoporosis and other forms of bone loss and rheumatoid arthritis. Anti-anemia drugs Epogen and Aranesp account for about half of its sales, which totaled around thirteen billion dollars in 2006. Enbrel, another leading drug, treats rheumatoid arthritis and is one of the best-selling drugs in this multi-billion-dollar market.

Firms in the Superlongevity Industry usually partner with other companies. Amgen has done this as well. The firm has marketing alliances with Hoffmann-La Roche and Japanese brewer and drug maker Kirin, among others. Amgen has been acquiring other biotechs. It recently acquired Abgenix, a firm that manufactures human therapeutic antibodies, for about $2.2 billion.

Genentech is another big player in the superlongevity game. Rituxan, which treats non-Hodgkin's lymphoma, is a billion-dollar blockbuster drug. Its latest approved cancer therapy, Avastin, treats colon cancer by choking the blood vessels that nourish tumors. Genentech features other oncology products, such as lung cancer killer Tarceva and breast cancer treatment Herceptin. The biotech company also makes the cystic fibrosis drug Pulmozyme, cardiovascular therapies Activase and TNKase, human growth hormone Nutropin and the asthma drug Xolair, which it developed with Novartis and Tanox. Hoffman-La Roche owns 56 percent of the firm. Genentech, like many biotechs, has undergone tremendous growth over the last five years, with almost eight billion dollars in sales in a recent year.[129]

Other major biotech companies in the Superlongevity Industry are Med-Immune, Celera Genomics, BioReliance Corp., Gene Logic Inc. Digene, Martek Biosciences Corp, Igen International Inc and United Therapeutics.

Many of the innovations in biotechnology drugs emanate not from the large companies such as Merck and Pfizer, but from smaller biotechs. Moreover, the drugs that "Big Pharma" companies do develop eventually lose patent protection. It is estimated that between 2006 and 2011 one hundred billion dollars worth of branded drugs will lose patent protection. In other words, Big Pharma needs new drugs. One of the easiest ways to get those drugs is to license them from smaller companies. While big companies like Merck could buy such companies outright, licensing is less risky.

During one week in March of 2006, two such deals were consummated. Pfizer, the world's biggest drug maker, signed a deal with the German drug maker Noxxon Pharma AG for a worldwide license on the company's Spiegelmer technology to develop weight loss drug NOX-B11. And Merck signed a deal with French biotech NicOx SA to collaborate on a new treatment for high blood pressure, which alone is a thirty billion dollar industry. [130]

Sometimes the relationship between Big Pharma and the smaller biotechs seems less than friendly, if not out and out hostile. In 2006, giant Eli Lilly & Co, an Indianapolis drug maker got into a squabble over patent rights with Ariad Pharmaceuticals a Boston-area biotech. Earlier, Lilly had brought out two drugs, Evista, for the prevention and treatment of osteoporosis in postmenopausal women, totaling one billion dollars in 2005 sales, and Xigris, for the reduction of death in patients with severe sepsis, with 214 million dollars in 2005 sales.

Ariad sued Lilly, but not for the drug patent. Ariad had not patented Evista or Xigris. However, the company did patent a method of treating disease by regulating a certain type of cell activity. A jury agreed, and slapped Eli Lilly with a whopping 65 million dollars in damages, ruling that two drugs from the larger company had infringed Ariad's patent. The smaller biotech, which had been bleeding money throughout 2005, got an even better present from the jury: it decided that Lilly would have to pay Ariad a 2.3 percent royalty on future sales of Evista and Xigris until patent expiration in 2019.

Lilly is trying desperately to get that court decision overruled. Not unexpectedly, Ariad CEO Harvey Berger stated at a news conference that he was "delighted at the outcome" of the original trial. Reacting to Lilly's indignation over the suit, he vowed to "prevail at the bench trial."

Right after the jury handed down its decision, California-based Amgen, the biggest biotech in the world, went into lockdown mode. The company took a pre-emptive measure to strengthen its patents on Enbrel and Kineret, both rheumatoid arthritis treatments. Fearing that these two drugs might be the next target of an Ariad lawsuit, Amgen filed for declaratory judgment to legally define their status.[131]

Most companies in the biotechnology area started relatively small. However, one never knows which company will be the next Amgen or Eli Lilly. It is quite remarkable what smaller companies are able to accomplish considering their financial limitations.

One such company, deCODE, headquartered in Reykjavik, Iceland, is a biopharmaceutical company applying its discoveries in human genetics to the development of drugs for common diseases, and considers itself a global leader in gene discovery. deCODE's population approach and resources have enabled it to isolate many of the key genes related to ills from cardiovascular disease to cancer. These genes provide the company with drug targets rooted in the basic biology of disease.

The "population approach" the company refers to is in itself quite amazing. It somehow convinced over half of the adult population of Iceland— more than 100,000 volunteer participants—to provide genetic samples as well as family and medical histories to help deCODE determine the genetic origins of a host of diseases. This is a massive project, which includes sifting through a genealogy database covering the entire present day population and stretching back to the founding of Iceland, an event which took place more than 1000 years ago.

The company currently has eight lead programs in drug discovery and development, including three in clinical trials, and is broadening its pipeline through gene and target discovery work on fifty of the most common diseases. DeCode is also leveraging its expertise in human genetics and integrated drug discovery and development capabilities to offer innovative products and services in DNA-based diagnostics, genotyping, bioinformatics, structural biology, drug discovery and clinical development.

They are working quickly to develop drugs to attack and eliminate disease and expand the human life span. In their pipeline are genetically derived drugs aimed at such maladies as heart attacks, arterial disease, asthma, pain, vascular disease, diabetes, schizophrenia, and obesity.

Quite an achievement for a company that few people besides Icelanders and industry specialists even know exists!

Stem Cell Mania

The superlongevity industry also includes the companies and laboratories attempting to make use of stem cells. These are cells in the body that have the amazing capacity to develop into many different cell types in the body. They serve as a sort of repair system for the body, and are believed to have the capacity to divide without limit to replenish other cells as long as the person or animal is still alive. When a stem cell divides, each new cell has the potential to either remain a stem cell or become another type of cell with a more specialized function, such as a muscle cell, a red blood cell, or a brain cell.[132]

Because stem cells can potentially be used to repair specific tissues or to grow organs, most biologists and medical researchers feel that the science emerging from stem cell research will change the face of disease management. Much work has yet to be done, but reports out of the labs show that stem cell therapy will someday be used to cure a host of neurological diseases, including Alzheimer's.

In June 2006, an astonishing discovery was announced. For the first time, researchers enticed transplants of embryonic stem cell-derived motor neurons in the spinal cord to connect with muscles and partially restore function in paralyzed animals. The mice, which had been unable to walk, were at least able to hobble around their cages once the stem cells connected with these neurons. The study demonstrated quite plainly that similar techniques could eventually be used to treat such disorders as spinal cord injury, transverse myelitis, amyotrophic lateral sclerosis (ALS) and spinal muscular atrophy in humans.[133]

In terms of its current money making ability, the stem cell industry is years behind Big Pharma and the biotech companies in spinning off drugs.

Although the research on stem cells demonstrates that the field is rife with potential cures for a host of diseases, there is much debate over whether companies in these fields can be immediately profitable.

"People get excited when there are scientific advancements like this, and you need that excitement to get investors interested in companies like these," said Noble Financial Group analyst Ben Weintraub. However, he cautioned, "the road from an advance such as the one just mentioned into human medicine could take at least ten years."

Such discouraging words have not dampened the hope of companies such as Geron Corporation, StemCells Inc., Aastrom Biosciences Inc. and ViaCell, Inc. that their research into the mysteries of the stem cell will someday pay off. Also, as we will see, many of these companies can acquire seed money from venture capital firms that share their same vision about the tremendous promise of this field.[134]

Let's revisit two companies brought up in Chapter Two. Geron Corporation, located in Menlo Park, California, is extremely active in developing cell-based therapeutics based on differentiated cells derived from human embryonic stem cells. The company is hoping to use such technologies to tackle spinal cord injury, Parkinson's disease, heart disease, diabetes, osteoporosis and various blood disorders. Importantly, Geron holds licenses to intellectual property covering core inventions and critical enabling technology.[135] The other, Advanced Cell Technology boldly states in its literature its mission to be "the first to commercialize the most profitable applications of regenerative medicine." Two biotech legends, Dr. Robert Lanza and Dr. Michael West, head ACT's research team on using stem cell technology in the fight against cancer and cardiovascular and autoimmune diseases of various types. The company owns or licenses over 300 patents and patent applications related to the field of stem cell therapy and allied areas.[136]

Despite its lofty ambitions the Superlongevity Industry is fraught with risks and opportunities. After all, this is a field whose ultimate goal is one that is desired by most people, to remain alive and healthy for as long as possible. However, as is the case in stem cell technology, one can never be sure when and if a particular path to this goal will be viable or profitable.

Stem cell technology as a profit-making field has its solid boosters. The Red Zone Network, a small financial services analysis company, sees stem cell therapy as one of the most promising fields in medical history. One of their reports mentions that the early phases of legal stem cell research have already provided many major medical landmarks in such areas as skin transplants, spinal cord replacements, cures for diseases, such as Leukemia and Parkinson's, and repair of damaged organs.

Red Zone is referring to another roadblock that this industry must contend with. The Bush administration banned the use of most stem cells derived from embryos. In spite of the predictions of dire consequences of this decision, researchers are discovering that adult stem cells, derived from the patients themselves, are extremely useful, as mentioned above. We will discuss the politics of stem cell research at greater length in Chapter Nine.

The Red Zone group feels that the stocks of top stem cell companies could potentially offer investors profit opportunities. They even arranged a conference call where potential investors could listen to, which featured some of the leading experts in the field. Among the guests were Dr. Christopher Thomas Scott, director of Stanford University's Program on Stem Cells and Society and Ann B. Parson, contributing science journalist for The New York Times and Boston Globe.[137]

No one doubts that stem cell technology will be a major contributor to the Superlongevity Industry. The question is more a matter of "when."

Cryonics: A Future Temporarily On Ice

Suppose you were to discover that you will die within the next year of a disease for which science currently has no cure. Reading the scientific journals and newspaper reports, you learn that most scientists are certain that within the next fifty to one hundred years, the technology will be available to remedy your malady. Perhaps the solution will emerge from stem cell research, biogenetics or nanotechnology. You fret that the only reason that you need die from this disease is the bad luck of being born a few decades too early.

According to many scientists, all hope is not lost. A relatively new technology, cryonics, offers you an alternative to permanent mortality.

Cryonics is the preservation of legally dead human beings or pets at very low temperature (below -200°F, -130°C) in a state that will be viable and treatable by future science. The hope is that science will be able to restore them to life, youth and health. As a caveat it should be mentioned that even its most ardent supporter refer to cryonics as a "speculative" life support technology that seeks to preserve human life by future medicine.

Although small in comparison to the biotechnology or pharmaceutical industries, cryonics is, by its very definition, an established player in the Superlongevity Industry. The two major players in the cryonics fields are the Alcor Life Extension Foundation[138] and the Cryonics Institute.[139]

Because of laws safeguarding patient privacy, it is fairly difficult to get lists of those actually in cryonic suspension. As of March 2006, Alcor had 789 members on their list for future cryopreservation, and seventy-four patients in cryopreservation. In May 2006 the Cryonics Institute took in its seventy-fourth patient, a seventy-nine year old woman who was a victim of breast cancer. The *Wall Street Journal* reports that some one thousand members of the "cryonics movement have arranged to have themselves frozen in liquid nitrogen at the hour of their demise."[140]

We know the names of some of the more famous people who are cryonically preserved. Recent news headlines informed the world that renowned ex-baseball player Ted Williams was taken to Alcor immediately after his death by his son John Henry. Some other family members objected, claiming Williams wanted to be cremated, not placed in suspension. In December 2002, the matter was settled and Ted Williams remained at Alcor. Two years later, John Henry succumbed to leukemia, and now he too is in suspension at Alcor. The first person cryonically preserved with intent of future resuscitation was one Dr. James Bedford, a psychology professor and member of the family that founded Bedford, Massachusetts. He was cryonically preserved (frozen) on January 12, 1967 in Glendale, California at age seventy-three. Fereidoun M. Esfandiary, the man credited as the founder of the "Transhumanist" philosophy, is also in cryonic suspension. Ironically, he had had his name legally changed to FM-2030, the numbers referring to the date he would turn one hundred. He fully expected science to have cured all diseases by that date—if he could live that long, he said, he could live forever. Also in suspended animation is Jerry D. Leaf, who was the Vice President of the cryonics organization Alcor Life Extension Foundation, and President of the cryonics service firm Cryovita, Inc.[141]

What are the costs of cryo-suspension? Alcor quotes prices of $150,000 for whole body suspension, while the Cryonics Institute claims that they can do the job for $28,000. The varying prices reflect different methods of payment. Since these companies are preserving the "members" for an indefinite period, they want to invest part of the fee to create veritable annuities which will pay for the maintenance costs of suspension ad infinitum. Actually, most middle class people can afford this treatment via a well-structured insurance policy—this is not just the plaything of the Bill Gates crowd.

While the number of "patients" and candidates for cryo-suspension totals only a thousand, one can easily imagine this number growing dramatically in the future. After all, the word is finally getting out to the public that break-throughs such as those discussed in this book are making it more possible that we will be able to cure many diseases that are currently killing us, including many forms of cancer and heart disease. The more members of the public are convinced that the cure for their diseases are only a decade or two in the future, the more likely they will be to take the plunge and undergo cryonic suspension.

Venture Capitalists in the Mix

As we brought up earlier, the Superlongevity Industry would not stand a chance of reaching its lofty goal of radical life extension without the help of venture capital, the lifeblood of economic growth and expansion. Several companies actually specialize in the investment in the areas of health technologies and life extension.

One of the largest venture capital firms in the superlongevity arena is OrbiMed, based in New York City. Founded in 1989, OrbiMed focuses on the global health sciences industry, from small privately-held firms to large multi-national companies. It has over five billion dollars in assets under management across a family of venture capital funds, hedge funds and other investment vehicles. Like many firms that invest in healthcare, it has among its partners a scientist familiar with biotechnology, Michael B. Sheffery, Ph.D. Sheffery was formerly head of the Laboratory of Gene Structure and Expression at Memorial Sloan-Kettering Cancer Center.

Its company literature is indicates that OrbiMed is one investment company that comprehends the enormity of the Superlongevity Revolution, and intends to capitalize on it. Two factors are coming together to create a perfect climate for the health sciences industry: demographics-driven demand for better healthcare, plus the innovation-driven supply of new therapeutics. As a result, the number of profitable biotechnology companies has grown from one in 1986 (Genentech) to sixty-three in 2006, and an estimated eighty-five by 2007.

Humankind's discovery of the structure of DNA and the cracking of the genetic code are notable recent breakthroughs that will open the floodgates of new discoveries. Like many of the investment firms in this field, OrbiMed believes that such discoveries include new "blockbuster" drugs in development all over the world that will be available for treating diseases such as cancer, Alzheimer's and diabetes. Such fundamental breakthroughs could eventually transform the health sciences. Moreover, as OrbiMed states clearly, companies engaged in the pursuit of tomorrow's innovations, and those that invest in them have the potential to profit handsomely. From OrbiMed's perspective, the key life sciences fields in this environment are biotechnology, pharmaceuticals, diagnostics and medical, dental and surgical devices such as kidney dialysis equipment, cardiovascular stents and orthopedics.

Since 1993, OrbiMed has been an active investor helping to start, nurture and commercialize some of today's most successful health sciences companies. OrbiMed raised thirty million dollars in 2000 to finance a company, Given Imaging, which makes a capsule containing a tiny video camera that patients swallow as a means of diagnosing digestive-tract disorders. Today, Given Imaging is valued at close to a billion dollars.

The companies in the OrbiMed current investment constellation reflect their broad vision of the future of the life sciences industry. One, Agensys, located in Santa Monica, California, develops targeted cancer therapeutics based on novel antigen discoveries. Toronto-based Arius Research endeavors to discover novel anticancer monoclonal antibodies. Corus Pharma of Seattle, Washington targets respiratory and infectious diseases. Based in Woodlands, Texas, Sapphire Therapeutics is a biopharmaceutical company that produces promising compounds for treatment of oncologic and metabolic diseases. [142]

Another venture capital firm, ARCH Venture Partners invests in the development of seed and early-stage technology companies that have the potential to grow rapidly into successful businesses. The venture capital firm, which specifically looks at companies that are co-founded with leading scientists and entrepreneurs, concentrates on bringing to market innovations in information technology, life sciences, and physical sciences. One of their strategies is to tap into geographic markets they consider underserved, and then concentrate on actively supporting the region's venture community and area entrepreneurs. They have offices in Albuquerque, Austin, Chicago and Seattle.

Organizations such as ARCH look for companies with broad technology platforms that can become the leading companies in their fields. They especially like companies that have the potential to create new industry. ARCH's track record is impressive, being an early investor of superlongevity-oriented fields such as gene therapy, genomics, new immunotherapy techniques and bioinformatics. They are also aware of how innovations evolve and gestate out of the university science environment. Hence, many of their portfolio companies in the life sciences originated in laboratories at institutions such as University of Michigan, the University of Chicago, Harvard University, Stanford University and the Massachusetts Institute of Technology.

ARCH's nose for innovation and commercial potential has helped them become active investors in some remarkable companies. San Francisco-based Achaogen, Inc. is a pioneer in therapeutics for combating the increasing bacterial resistance to antibiotics. ARCH has provided seed money for Elixir Pharmaceuticals, Inc. of Cambridge, Massachusetts, which is actively involved in the discovery of therapeutics that slow or counteract age-related diseases and conditions. GenVec is developing gene therapy for cardiovascular disease and cancer. Another of its Cambridge-based companies, Magen Biosciences, Inc., is developing therapies to improve the health and appearance of skin and hair. Selective Genetics, Inc. of San Diego, CA is working on gene-based therapeutics for tissue repair and regeneration. Trubion Pharmaceuticals, Inc. of Seattle, Washington is developing small molecule therapies to combat autoimmune and inflammatory diseases.

Many of these venture capital firms are awash with cash to spend. MPM Capital, the world's largest dedicated investor in life sciences, has over $2.1 billion to invest globally in superlongevity-related fields such as biotechnology, medical devices and biopharmaceuticals. One of its investment mechanisms is the BioVentures family of venture capital funds.

MPM targets biotech companies that cover the gamut of technologies and scientific breakthroughs that are fueling the Superlongevity Revolution. Acorda Therapeutics, Inc. is involved in finding novel therapies that improve neurological function in people with multiple sclerosis, spinal cord injury and other disorders of the central nervous system. Ceregene, Inc. is working on treatment of neurodegenerative disorders using gene therapy. More than a few of their portfolio companies are involved in pain management therapies of one type of another, including Kentucky-based Xanodyne Pharmaceuticals, Cerimon Pharmaceuticals and Neuromed Technologies, located in Vancouver, British Columbia.

One of the companies MPM Capital has invested in is ViaCell, Inc., which is involved in cutting-edge stem cell research. The company describes itself as engaged in "sourcing, developing and commercializing cellular therapies to address cancer, cardiac disease, diabetes and infertility." But they are working on ways to isolate, purify and expand the populations of stem cells. It currently has a licensing agreement with Amgen and is involved in research collaboration with Genentech. Its commercialized product Viacord is a leading brand in the cryopreservation of umbilical cord blood stem cells. It is also developing a product that when ready will offer women the ability to preserve their fertility through the cryopreservation of human eggs.[143]

Oxford Bioscience Partners (OBP) is also heavily bankrolled, with close to a billion dollars in capital committed to various ventures. OPB specifically targets start-up and early-stage, entrepreneurial-driven companies in the bioscience and healthcare industries. Obviously, the risks and rewards are more pronounced when pursuing such a strategy. To make as accurate an assessment as possible when selecting investment targets, OBP wisely has included on its partnership team scientists with backgrounds in biotechnology. Dr. Alan G. Walton, a senior general partner, had previously been the CEO of a public biotechnology company and also had experience in seed investments in university-related projects. One of their investment managers, Omar Amirana, M.D., was Vice President of Business Development for the Cardiology Division at St Jude Medical. The other partners have decades of investment experience in the life sciences field.

The companies in their investment portfolio reflect this level of expertise. Cyberkinetics Neurotechnology Systems, Inc., based in Foxboro, Massachusetts, builds direct brain-computer interfaces to treat individuals affected by paralysis or neurological disorders. Two of their companies are very well known. Human Genome Sciences, Inc. is a well-known entity that identifies and commercializes genes for human therapeutic development, and Geron Corporation develops and commercializes therapeutic and diagnostic products for oncology and regenerative medicine. Illumina, Inc. of San Diego, California, develops tools for large-scale analysis of genetic variations and gene function. Elixir Pharmaceuticals, Inc. of Cambridge, Massachusetts, is a drug discovery company developing therapeutics to treat age-related diseases, with a focus on metabolic diseases such as diabetes and obesity. VaxInnate Corporation of Cranbury, New Jersey and New Haven, Connecticut develops prophylactic and therapeutic vaccines, basing its technologies on research and discoveries of leading scientists from Yale University.

Bringing Industry, Science, and Venture Capitalists Under One Roof

In October 2002 the first Anti-Aging Drug Discovery and Development Summit was held in San Francisco, California. The purpose of the conference was purportedly to discuss scientific aspects of the aging process and evaluate efforts to discover and develop anti-aging therapies in aging intervention. Although the conference featured presentations on such erudite subjects as "Aging Drug Development, the New Biotech Frontier," "Lifespan Extension—The Genes, the Hormones and the Drugs" and "Caloric Restriction, Gene Expression Profiling and the Aging Process," other sessions reveal an additional focus of the conference. Listed boldly were talks on "Prospects for Venture Capital Investment & Returns in Aging-Intervention" and "Regulatory Environment."

Now organizations and conferences exist that bring together venture capital, scientists, policy planners and everyone involved in the health industry. One of the largest is BIO, the Biotechnology Industry Organization, formed in 1993 from the merger of two small Washington-based biotechnology trade organizations. Today it is the major advocate for the biotechnology industry. It also provides business development services to member companies, such as investor and partnering meetings.

Although the companies under BIO's tent are not exclusively involved in "anti-aging" science, biotechnology will play such a strong role in radical life extension that organizations such as BIO are a key part of the superlongevity industry. More importantly, BIO and other such groups provide a powerful role model for how one goes about garnering support for an industry, as their April 2006 international conference in Chicago clearly demonstrates.

Over 19,479 people from sixty-two countries attended the conference. Representatives of hundreds of industries exhibited there, including Genentech, Amgen, Human Genome Sciences, Inc., deCODE, Pfizer, Merck, Siemens and a host of other powerhouses in the biotech area. BIO really knows how to corral the big names to maximize public awareness of the conference as well as to announce to the financial community that the government and most of corporate America supports the biotechnology industry. Among the speakers were former United States President Bill Clinton; Mike Leavitt, Secretary of the Department of Health and Human Services; the CEOs of Biogen, Baxter and Abbot; former CIA Director James Woolsey; famed former basketball star Magic Johnson; Chicago Mayor Richard Daley as well as Neil Cavuto, FOX network financial anchor. In addition, about a dozen state governors at that time, including the governors of Illinois, Alabama, Michigan, Missouri, Ohio, Kentucky, and Kansas, attended. President George W. Bush's brother, Governor Jeb Bush of Florida, as well as a possible presidential candidate Gov. Mitt Romney of Massachusetts was also there.

The BIO Business Forum was an on-going three-day program which provided a vehicle for biotechnology and pharmaceutical companies, academic research institutions and most importantly investors from all over the world to gather in one physical location. There these parties could meet one-on-one to discuss business and possible investment opportunities. It could accommodate over 10,000 one-on-one on-site meetings, business development-focused Company Presentations.[144]

One can only imagine the number of deals that were finalized as well as the number of new ventures that were initiated as a result of this conclave of venture capital, science-based companies and policy makers from all level of government.

SUPERLONGEVITY'S SUPPORTING CAST

As we've seen, industry is feverishly pursuing the dream of superlongevity as it simultaneously pursues its need for revenue and profits. While these companies and venture capitalists are helping the cause of superlongevity, support from other sectors is needed if the Superlongevity Revolution is to reach fruition. Radical life extension is not just a process; it is also a cause, one that naturally generates moral, ethical, legal, economic and social issues. To succeed, superlongevity, like all original and earthshaking ventures, requires backing from all aspects of society.

There have always existed groups of one type or another that supported the general concept of public health. The United States government has a Surgeon General who periodically wags his finger at the American public warning the citizenry of the dangers of smoking and unprotected sex and exhorting us to maintain a low fat diet "rich in fruits and vegetables." Organizations such as the March of Dimes and the Muscular Dystrophy Association have raised money for medical research to overcome disease. Other organizations, such as the American Breast Cancer Foundations, encourage research to cure diseases and actively exhort people to take measures to prevent the onset of disease or to detect the disease while it is treatable. The constellation of organizations that collectively comprises superlongevity's supporting cast transcends the scope and intent of the organizations. They are literally prodding society, industry, government and the public to create, or allow to emerge, the conditions under which the human species can reach life spans of 150 years plus.

While the biotechnology and pharmaceutical companies are working on methods that will extend the life span, this supporting cast has emerged to accelerate the progress that we have made so far. It has a number of important roles to play.

These organizations first and foremost are developing and presenting the arguments for superlongevity. In that sense, they are providing a counterbalance to the forces and other assorted naysayers that regard with suspicion the creation of a world in which people live to 150 or 200 years.

These organizations also provide a forum for ideas from people and organizations on a number of issues related to this new concept. What will life be like when people live to such ages? How will superlongevity impact society, religion, politics, families and our culture? Will people have to work longer to support themselves and their extended families when we finally achieve superlongevity?

Some of these organizations are champions of one or another technology to achieve superlongevity and even immortality. The World Transhumanist Society, the Singularity Now organization and the Methuselah Foundation fall within this definition.

Many of these organizations distribute their information to the press and offer the media and organizations guest speakers to heighten public awareness of the superlongevity and increasingly, the Ultra-human, phenomena. Others cover a wider and more inclusive set of activities, including raising funds for anti-aging researchers in universities, hospitals and non-profit institutions. Some provide information to the medical field on how to begin a practice specifically attuned to anti-aging medicine.

Certainly proponents of other breakthrough technologies can only envy the financial and moral support that superlongevity is receiving from government and foundations. The United States space program languishes, as NASA budgets stay stagnant and the public and press become disenchanted with the program's progress. In 1969, after Neil Armstrong landed on the Moon, the expectation was that within another decade or so American and other countries would be establishing colonies on that orb, and certainly landing on

Mars. Over thirty-five years later, the manned space program consists of shuttling astronauts to and from an Earth-orbit space station.

Relatively few public-based organizations exist to marshal public support for greater funding for more ambitious forays into space. The National Space Society and the Planetary Society do what they can to get our species to take the next big step into the cosmos, but they boast only a few thousand members.

By contrast, what I label as the "Superlongevity Lobby," dedicated to the achievement of the lofty goal of radically extended life spans, is a vast and growing network of organizations and associations. This lobby is helped by the fact that superlongevity is a natural attraction for most people. After all, most of us wish to live a healthy and happy life, and no one really wants to die. Health and longevity are not the hard sell that space travel has become. Space enthusiasts evidently have to convince the public of the benefits of colonizing space and exploring the universe, and worse have to convince the electorate to pay for this enterprise out of their already overtaxed pockets.

We will look at various pockets of the nascent "supporting cast" that is helping propel our species more deeply into the Superlongevity Revolution.

Shaking The Money Tree
Without the funding to pay for equipment, personnel, and related expenses research would not get done. While industry has its revenue streams from the profit it makes on its various products as well as venture capitalists hungry to share in that bounty, many independent and university researchers have to depend on grants and donations to set up their labs and conduct their investigations. That is why a key member of superlongevity's supporting cast is the sector that either directly funds anti-aging research or raises monies from a variety of sources for distribution to scientists and laboratories searching for ways to radically extend life.

Founded in 1981, the American Federation for Aging Research (www.afar.org) serves as a perfect example. AFAR is based on the principle that research into the fundamental processes of aging, or biogerontology, will help extend healthy life and cure age-related diseases. Using privately funded grants and other administered programs AFAR has showered a hefty eighty-seven million dollars on more than 2,100 talented researchers to help them in their careers in aging research and geriatric medicine. AFAR has a multifaceted mission in its effort to serve as a catalyst in the Superlongevity Revolution. This hard-driving federation uses its funds to build a cadre of new scientists in aging research and geriatric medicine and also offers scientists and physicians opportunities to exchange new ideas and knowledge about aging at conferences. It also uses its funds to inform the public about health-related issues such as medical breakthroughs that can extend our lives (and asks the public for contributions, as well.) AFAR also partners with companies such as Pfizer and Merck to fund researchers in various aspects of biogerontology.

Established in 1936 and with an endowment of around eleven billion pounds, the Wellcome Trust helps many of the charities and granting agencies supporting research in the superlongevity area. This is an independent trust established by Sir Henry Wellcome, who co-started the famous pharmaceutical company Burroughs Wellcome & Co. The foundation supports research in areas critical to life extension: immunology and infectious disease, populations and public health, neuroscience and mental health, physiological sciences and molecules, genes and cells. It is the United Kingdom's largest non-governmental source of funds for biomedical research, investing more that half a billion dollars a year in biomedical research. While the Wellcome Trust claims in its literature that it supports largely "pure science," research that while adding to understanding of health and disease has no immediate application, the real products resulting from that research over the years are mind-boggling. It lists as some of the successes achieved through Wellcome Trust financial support the sequencing of the human genome, development of the antimalarial drug artemisinin, creation of pioneering cognitive behavioral therapies for psychological disorders and the establishment of the UK Biobank.

The last of these will prove an important tool in the achievement of radical life extension. After years of planning the UK Biobank was finally a reality in 2006 as a way to improve the prevention, diagnosis and treatment of cancer, heart disease, diabetes and many other serious conditions. This visionary project will gather and store medical data and material on half a million volunteers aged forty to sixty-nine. Each participant agrees to donate a blood and urine sample, have blood pressure and other standard measurements taken, and will complete a confidential lifestyle questionnaire. Over the next twenty to thirty years approved researchers will be permitted to use these resources to study the progression of major illnesses. It is reminiscent of deCODE's cataloguing of genes of Iceland's inhabitants. This Biobank will enable scientists to study in depth how the interplay of genes, lifestyle and environment might affect the risk of developing specific diseases.[145]

In the US governmental support should be considered a key component of the monetary support for the life extension mission. The National Institute of Aging (NIA) supports research and research training related to aging, especially into areas such as the basic biological, neuroscientific, behavioral and social research on aging, as well as intervention studies and clinical geriatric research. NIA, through its Intramural Research Program, conducts research in its laboratories in Bethesda, MD and the Gerontology Research Center in Baltimore, Maryland. However, most of NIA's research is "extramural," supporting research institutions such as universities and hospitals. Some of its most important research examines the biological mechanisms underlying the aging process to "enhance and extend the human health span." It also supports the Baltimore Longitudinal Study of Aging (BLSA), which began in 1958 and is America's longest-running scientific study of human aging.[146]

A group of foundations have pooled resources to support the Paul B. Beeson Career Development Awards in Aging Research. The intent was to create a dynamic new cadre of physician-scientists capable of developing breakthrough research in the area of superlongevity, and who would also be committed to mentoring and teaching the next generation of physicians about the care of older adults. With the help of the NIA, the size of the award is around $600,000 to $800,000 for a three to five-year period. NIA and the American Federation for Aging Research currently share administrative responsibilities for the program, with AFAR conducting the Beeson annual meeting. Recent areas researched include risk factors in developing Alzheimer's disease, long-term outcomes of caring for a disabled spouse, methods of reducing geriatric depression and genetic factor in aging.[147]

One of the more ambitious anti-aging funding groups is The Ellison Medical Foundation (EMF), started by Larry Ellison, the founder of computer-industry giant Oracle. The EMF supports basic biological research in aging to increase our understanding of aging processes and age-related diseases. Some examples of basic research include work dealing with the impact of telomeres on longevity, the role of genes in senescence, how "paternal age" effects fetal development, how free radical production affects health, how changes in neural networks affect cognitive aging and the underlying gene dynamics of age-related memory decline. The recipients are usually situated at prestigious research sites, such as the University of Pennsylvania, the Children's Hospital of Philadelphia, M.D. Anderson Cancer Center and Johns

Hopkins University. Senior Scholar awards provide funding up to $150,000 per year for a four year period. [148]

The number of foundations mobilizing financial resources to radically extend the human life span is increasing. Much of this impetus emanates from the research itself. The more we discover about the role genetics can play in controlling or eliminating diseases, the more we learn about how caloric restriction extends the lives of lab animals and the closer we get to mastering nanotechnology, the more encouraged we are to pour money into research that will "finish the job" and develop the science that will make real superlongevity a reality.

There has been some criticism of this type of philanthropy. Some worry about a potential over reliance on the generosity of the wealthy. The Bill and Melinda Gates Foundation, which many perceive as already setting much of the world's agenda on combating diseases in developing nations, had its coffers increased considerably when Warren E. Buffett gave their foundation thirty-one billion dollars, most of his fortune. Nicolas de Torrente, Executive Director in the United States for Doctors Without Borders, which provides health care in developing countries, has asked "What happens if they change their mind or de-emphasize something?"[149]

Some also claim that there is some evidence that governments cut spending on disease and medical research if they believe that philanthropies are taking care of a problem.

In spite of such concerns, most researchers and small laboratories are grateful that many of the super rich spend considerable portions of their wealth on improving the human condition.

Championing Superlongevity

Every cause needs its champions, its promoters, to heighten public awareness of the cause and to mobilize public action to ensure the success of the cause. As a plethora of scientific and technological breakthroughs have made superlongevity ever more attainable, numerous organizations have sprung up to accelerate the process by encouraging pro-superlongevity public activism. They want people to organize, and write their congressional representative, even the President in order to move us closer to the dream of superlongevity.

The organization Alliance for Aging Research has a full-pronged approach to the issue of furthering the cause of superlongevity. It exhorts its

members and the general public to lobby, write, call and otherwise communicate with their representatives on the state and local levels to lobby on a host
of issues related to life extension. They make the process extremely easy from
their website. This organization is a pro when it comes to legislative action. In
fact, their online "Advocacy Toolkit" should be a model for political action of
any stripe. They show you how to send a letter to a person in power, set up a
meeting with a legislator, make phone calls to key people in the legislation
process and join with other groups and organizations that feel the same way.

The issues in which the Alliance for Aging Research are most interested
range from the need for more geriatric training, to increasing the money for
research on arthritis, Alzheimer's and degenerative diseases and the legalization of therapeutic cloning. They fully explain the issues, their reasons for the
stances taken and why they have shaped their legislative agenda on all measures in just the way they have.[150]

An extremely proactive and effective organization in the anti-aging
lobby is the Life Extension Foundation (LEF). Although it was incorporated
in 1980, its founders have been writing about and financially supporting anti-
aging research since the 1960's. In its effort to extend the human life span,
LEF has developed research programs to identify, measure and develop
advanced, new therapies to slow, reverse and, ultimately, eliminate the deterioration associated with the aging process. Many of their therapies are in the
"holistic" or natural vitamins area—sales of these products support their other
research objectives in life extension technologies.

One web-based organization, The Longevity Meme, encourages people
to take a variety of actions to support and help bring about the Superlongevity
Revolution. They provide their members and the general public an easy three-
step approach to make this possible: stop damaging one's health, adopt a better diet and lifestyle, and support medical research. The Longevity Meme
provides common sense tips for its members to achieve the first goal, such as
stopping smoking, refraining from drug use, increase the amount of exercise
in one's life, and visiting a doctor for a physical. In terms of a better lifestyle,
this organization errs on the side of calorically-restricted diets, not the therapy
of choice of everyone in the superlongevity movement, but certainly an
increasingly popular one.

In fact, it is in the area of CR that this organization feels that its members
ought to take an activist stand. It is their position that speaking out in favor of

medical research is just as important as practicing present day healthy life extension to ensure that superlongevity is achieved. The Longevity Meme feels that the fields of aging and serious anti-aging research are poorly funded, and the public is largely unaware of the possibilities offered by this research. Some politicians and bioethicists oppose many of the more promising branches of medicine. The organization's solution is speaking out in favor of better medicine, and trying to prevent legislation that slows or criminalizes vital medical research.

The Immortality Institute (www.imminst.com) is a nascent organization not only attempting to organize public support for superlongevity but also for immortality. Their mission statement is quite clear about its goals. "The mission of ImmInst is to conquer the blight of involuntary death." The organization hopes to serve as an umbrella organization in this drive to achieve human physical immortality. This Institute wants to serve as a platform for the "exhibition, exchange, debate, and creation of concepts and methods toward that end," and also serve to disseminate information relevant to the achievement of human physical immortality. While this might seem grandiose, lofty goals such as human life extension need a bit of hubris to ever get actualized. This organization was able to publish a noteworthy book, "The Scientific Conquest of Death," a compendium of original essays by some of the leading researchers of the life extension movement. A second volume is in the offing.

The Immortality Institute uses press releases and other media to get the word out to the public on important discoveries and research initiatives. Their website and meetings also serve as a focus for much discussion and idea exchange about life extension that can be the basis of activist synergy in the future.

Training Physicians in the War on Aging
Some organizations aim their efforts at increasing doctor participation and training them to practice in the growing anti-aging medicine field.

The American Association of Anti-Aging Medicine (A4M) is one of the leading organizations involved in certifying and training physicians and health care professionals in the anti-aging field. The A4M's 2006 World Congress on Anti-Aging Medicine held in Chicago drew upwards of 4000 of the most influential physicians, medical researchers, scientists, educators, industrialists, investment bankers and journalists from around the world.

The goals of this organization are multidimensional. It wants to create an environment in which skilled academics and clinicians can work to combat aging as a disease. A4M recognizes that in the process of helping humanity the organization is also contributing to the creation of a rapidly expanding multi-billion dollar industry. According to the A4M literature, their many conferences then become the "place to be" center point for what they consider the "real players" in anti-aging medicine, the next great primary care medical specialty. One annual conference no longer satisfies the needs of industry and venture capital to mine this rapidly expanding field. In 2006 A4M ran international conferences in Paris, France; Orlando, Florida; Chicago, Illinois and Las Vegas, Nevada.

Although A4M started out rather humbly in 1993 with just twelve physicians, it has grown into a worldwide international medical society represented in more than seventy countries. The organization is also involved in training. Its academy has trained over 30,000 new physicians in its hands-on scientific, academic, and clinical areas. It also provides educational training programs, seminars, videos, website, textbooks, and outreach programs to over one 100,000 health professionals. A4M also runs board certification programs for those wishing to specialize in anti-aging medicine. On its website, which gets an astounding fourteen million visitors per month, the organization also delivers to the general public a wealth of information on anti-aging medicine and technologies.

The 2006 conference brochure reveals the depth and breadth of this growing anti-aging movement, and how A4M has commandeered much of the public, media and industry focus on the movement. Hundreds of presentations by doctors and scientists cover a broad range of topics related to the anti-aging phenomena. Participants can sit through and learn from sessions on topics such as "Anti-Aging Therapeutics from Europe," "Toxic World: Influence on Health & Ageing of Pollutants: A Wake-Up Call," "New Techniques for Cancer Prevention and Early Detection," "The Genetics of Brain Aging" and "Exercise Prescriptions for Adult Rehabilitation and Anti-Aging." John Gray author of *Men are from Mars, Women are from Venus*, presented a talk entitled "The Mars & Venus Diet & Exercise Solution."

Many European doctors are realizing the commercial and medical potential of the anti-aging field. In 2006 the first European Congress on Anti-Aging Medicine was held in Vienna, Austria and England hosted the third annual Anti-Aging Conference in London. The latter featured as a keynote speaker noted best-selling author Dr. Deepak Chopra who lectured on alternative medicine, as well as A4M founder Dr. Ronald Klatz.

Such organizations have their fair share of critics. Some scientists are turned off by the idea that at some of the meetings the organizations are less than selective when it comes to which companies exhibit their wares. Less reputable sectors of the "anti-aging" business community, those pushing commercial pills and potions alongside potentially serious ventures, are seen as tainting the entire anti-aging field.

Choosing a Road to Superlongevity

There are many groups who champion one type of technique or method over all others to reach superlongevity, and they will do whatever they can to get their message out to the public.

An excellent example is the Calorie Restriction Society, which attempts to convince people that they will live longer by eating fewer calories. Since 1993, the Calorie Restriction Society is dedicated to understanding and promoting the Calorie Restriction (CR) diet. Their methodology is straightforward. They endeavor to provide basic information about practicing CR, act as a contact point for anyone interested in CR (they run several active email groups), pursue basic research in CR through long-term human studies and work with the media to inform and educate the public. They got a big media break in 2002 when the *Wall Street Journal* ran a front page article on their organization and caloric restriction.

They also organize regular conferences on the topic of CR. In April of 2006, they held their fourth scientific CR conference. In 2005, they published a book based on caloric restriction principles, The Longevity Diet, which Amazon.com has often placed in the Top Ten of its "Movers and Shakers" list.

The Society's basic tenet, that solid research demonstrates quite clearly that a calorically-restricted diet has the potential to dramatically increase life expectancy, is gradually beginning to penetrate into the general mass media. So their efforts are beginning to bear fruit.[151]

Another organization that promotes a particular scientific methodology that can radically extend human life is the Foresight Nanotech Institute. Foresight is the leading think tank and public interest institute on nanotechnology.

Foresight was not specifically established to promote superlongevity. Founded in 1986, Foresight was the first organization to educate society about the benefits and risks of nanotechnology. The tireless efforts of the Institute and its founder Kenneth Drexler have turned nanotechnology from a little-known concept to part of the public lexicon. However, today the Foresight Nanotech Institute is a key player in the Superlongevity Revolution, because nanotechnology, once perfected, would not only become a critical tool in achieving superlongevity, but could conceivably become the foundation of human near-immortality.

Now Foresight is turning its attention to guiding nanotechnology research, public policy and education to address the critical challenges facing humanity. The organization is now dedicated to ensure the beneficial implementation of nanotechnology. It has expanded to over 14,000 individuals, including scientists, engineers, artists, policy makers, business people, investors, publishers, ethicists, interested laypersons and students from grammar school to graduate level, as well as a growing number of corporations from across the United States and the world.

Foresight takes its responsibilities very seriously. It endeavors to provide information about the benefits and possible uses of nanotechnology through public policy activities, publications, networking events, tutorials, conferences, roadmaps and prizes. They get their opinions out through op-eds in major newspapers and media appearances.

Anyone who hopes to see superlongevity become a reality can only cheer on Foresight and wish them all the best as they endeavor to bring the nanotechnology enterprise to fruition. When we can control the behavior of the atom to the point that we can use individual atoms as building blocks of body parts and virus-killing nano-robots, we will know that the Superlongevity Revolution has finally arrived.[152]

A curious addition to the immortality lobby is the transhumanist movement, an eclectic collection of people representing a diverse set of backgrounds and disciplines. One organization known as the "World Transhumanist Association" describes itself as an "international nonprofit membership organization which advocates the ethical use of technology to expand human capacities." The goal of transhumanism is to "support the development of and access to new technologies that enable everyone to enjoy better minds, better bodies and better lives."[153]

Helping humankind achieve radical life extension is a key goal of the transhumanist movement. They are also committed to the general improvement of the human condition, as they see it: including enhancing genetic and cognitive abilities, prolonging life, enhancing positive psychological and emotional states, anticipating the effects of what they label "evolved consciousness" on interpersonal relationships, re-defining life forms and multiplying forms of consciousness.

This last point about "re-defining life forms" might seem a bit unusual, if not disconcerting. The statement reflects that fact that over the last few years the transhumanist world has come heavily under the influence of the ideas of Ray Kurzweil, who we have mentioned previously. Kurzweil has specific ideas about how humankind can achieve superlongevity and potentially immortality. In his future scenario, humankind will reach near-immortality through the evolution of the species into a human with cybernetic components (e.g. chips implanted into the brain enabling constant communication with the worldwide web.) We will look at Kurzweil's theories in more depth in the final chapter dealing with the immortality question.[154]

Transhumanists credit the birth of their movement to F.M. Esfandiary (aka FM-2030), an Iranian-American futurist who first laid the receptive groundwork between a future marriage of man and machine in the 1960s and 1970s with books such as *Are You a Transhuman?* Considered a fringe movement for many decades, since the founding of the World Transhumanist Association in 1998 it is beginning to gain members with chapters throughout Europe, America, and now in places such as India, Beijing, Tokyo, New Zealand and practically every country in South America. They hold annual conferences, which bring together those sharing that philosophy. While the organization's official membership numbers under 4000, their influence is being felt in the media and now in academia— in 2006 Stanford University Law School hosted a conference on Human Enhancement Technologies and Human Rights."

Another tireless promoter of immortality is Cambridge biologist and computer specialist Aubrey de Grey. Suffice it to say the Mr. de Grey's 7 stage plan for re-engineering the human body, labeled SENS (Strategies for Engineered Negligible Senescence), has received world wide coverage, including a long interview in late 2005 on the CBS program "60 Minutes." While his method for achieving human superlongevity is widely debated, his appearances, media blitzes and speeches at events sponsored by groups such as the World Transhumanist Association serve to increase public awareness of the possibility of a radically extended human life span. We'll look further into de Grey's theories later in the book.[155]

Together the companies comprising the Superlongevity Industry, the venture capitalists and foundations supporting those companies and private researchers, and the many groups and organizations serving as superlongevity's "supporting cast" are spearheading our rapid entrance into an exciting new era in which we will all enjoy much longer and healthier lives. If the leaders of these companies and groups are correct, that era is almost upon us. This means that society must begin now to prepare for the transition into what will prove to be a time of cataclysmic change.

chapter eight

Preparing for the Future

As we've seen, medical breakthroughs in fields such as genetic engineering, stem cell research and nanotechnology that will enable us to radically extend the human life span are occurring at an accelerating pace.

Radical life extension will rock our society and all its institutions, including businesses and employers of all types, government, the media and educational institutions. No individual or family will be untouched. And as we shall see, our beliefs about age and the lifecycle will be challenged as never before.

As sweeping as these changes will be, our institutions and society as a whole still have time to make the adjustments necessary to survive and thrive in the Superlongevity Era. In this chapter, we will examine in depth what transformations are on the horizon and how we can meet them.

PERSONAL RESPONSIBILITY IN THE SUPERLONGEVITY ERA

Before discussing how our schools and businesses must prepare for the cataclysmic changes wrought by the impending Superlongevity Revolution, let us look at the steps each citizen of *Ageless Nation* must take to navigate through this new age.

The challenges will be enormous as we talked about earlier—we will be required to plan our careers in a world in which work lives can stretch a century. And to take advantages of the breakthroughs making long lives possible, we will have to become mini-experts in the innovations of the scientific and medical fields.

As my mother told me when she escorted me to my first day of kinder-garten, "Think of it as an adventure."

Plan Your Career Life Cycle

Previously in this book, we saw how drastically the human life cycle will change as the Superlongevity Revolution accelerates. We have also discussed how our careers will follow serendipitous routes involving training, first career, job sabbaticals, retraining, career continuation, career hiatus, retraining/ schooling and re-careering.

Let's review the career cycle. Let us sit in on a typical career planning seminar held in the near future. The trainer asks you to fill out a form in which you must indicate your career plans for specific life stages. The life plan as outlined in this form covers a period stretching 140 years, and as the introductory statement at the top of the form clearly states, "assume for the purposes of this exercise that you will, as well as your friends and family, live to that age as a vibrant, healthy individual in a relatively young body." You are aware of the phases mentioned, including re-careering and hiatuses, but you notice that one conventional stage of life is not accounted for on the form. Where, you ask, is retirement on the career planning document? It is this phrase we now address.

Over the last century, most individuals living in industrialized, developed countries have come to expect, or at least hope, that at some point in their lives they will enter into a phase we label retirement. For decades bookstores have been awash with books and magazines dedicated to advising people on how to spend these post-career years.

However, as the Superlongevity Revolution progresses and life spans continue to increase, the career lifecycle will be so altered that retirement as we know it will most likely disappear. After all, people will be in the peak of health at ages sixty and seventy making the idea of totally withdrawing from the workforce of little sense from a personal or financial point of view. They might change careers, but why stop working altogether when they still have the ability to earn a substantial amount of money.

As we've looked at before, periodically people will probably take career hiatuses, possibly for fairly long periods. Hence, we will still find some "expert" guidelines to enjoying "happier retirement" applicable to these inter-career breaks.

One bit of advice traditionally given to potential retirees that is certainly useful to those considering a career hiatus is to "think ahead." While people today often poorly plan the timing of their retirements, the hiatus concept is by definition a planned event. Experts also advise retirees to "value their time," another solid suggestion I would expect those taking a hiatus to have no problem adopting. They will know both the length and purpose of the hiatus, as well as their career and life direction after the hiatus period ends.

Experts today warn potential retirees that they could experience a lowering of their standard of living once they stop working. I have always been a bit mystified by this caveat. After all, anyone who plans early enough for their leisure years should have more than enough money to live, travel and enjoy the finer things in life, especially since they have already made many of their major life purchases.

I believe that with similar planning most hiatus-takers, who will only be temporarily out of the work force, should be able to enjoy their between-careers period without worrying about money. One way people have been able to live well after they retire is by buying "annuities," even if they have standard 401Ks, IRAs and pensions as long term financial safety nets. As career hiatuses get more popular, I believe, banks, insurers and other institutions will make financial programs available to members of the general public that will be specifically tailored to the hiatus periods. They will be fashioned in such ways that people will be able to live on that income as if they were working.

Today, people who remove themselves from the workforce for whatever reason face more than financial pressures. When we asked retired professional baseball and football players what they miss most about "the game," these ex-heroes of the diamond and gridiron invariably responded "I miss the guys." Many retirees suddenly realize that the workplace provided them with social networks of organically connected people working for common goals. For many people the sense of belongingness they found in the workplace is hard to replace in their post-career world.

One useful suggestion made by retirement expert Prof. Andrew Oswald of Warwick University, U.K., is to "invest in friendship." Oswald states, "My candid advice to aging Americans would be to use your hard-earned cash to invest much more in friendships than in material items." If you plan to live for 140 years or more, you probably want some solid companions along for the ride. The longer we live, the more important having friends becomes, regardless of our career status. A person contemplating a career hiatus of even a year will enjoy that time more if he can spend some of it with friends and family, and perhaps make new acquaintances as well.

As the lifespan increases to 120 or more years, most people will get the message that the conventional retirement planning process is becoming as obsolete as the very idea of complete retirement itself. People are retiring between the ages of fifty and sixty when we are at the cusp of a medical revolution that might extend their lives for several decades. Do they really want to spend the next hundred years golfing? And have they truly developed a financial portfolio that can provide a livable monthly income into the latter part of the twenty-first century?[156]

At my training sessions, speeches and in my university courses, I ask members of the audience to describe their own life plans, I am always surprised how few have thought much farther than beyond the next one or two years. Occasionally I encounter students with five-year and ten-year plans, but this is a rarity. And often even the longer plans are focused only toward career issues, not taking into account personal events such as marriage or children.

Total life planning in the emerging Superlongevity era is one of paramount importance. It is not easy for people to plan for a career, and a life, that will be longer than anyone in history has yet experienced. However, as I have pointed out, the transition will occur at a pace slow enough that we can adapt. In fact society has adapted to the Stage I extension of the life span from forty years or so to almost eighty. Earlier in this book, I have tried to convey the many directions and shapes of this new lifestyle which will form our futures in the *Ageless Nation*.

Hopefully the educational and employment institutions will do their parts to educate their students and employees about this new reality and get them thinking about and planning for the complexities of life in the Superlongevity Era.

Becoming Your Own Primary Care Provider

As the Superlongevity Revolution accelerates, the mantra of every citizen of the *Ageless Nation* should be "live longer so you can live longer." Or a variant of that might be, "the longer you live, the longer you'll live."

This phrase will be an apt description of the human condition in the twenty-first century and beyond. Within two decades, most experts believe, science will finally make it possible for all of us to live incredibly long. They also believe that medical wonders will enable all of us to experience true physical rejuvenation. Our job, then, is to stay alive long enough to enjoy the fruits of the veritable cornucopia of life extending miracles.

We mentioned earlier that Ray Kurzweil takes 250 supplements a day to slow his aging process, but that is not all he does. Kurzweil does not take too many risks with his life. For instance, he doesn't tailgate—since he plans to live forever he certainly is not going to risk immortality, because he is a few minutes late for a meeting.

He also drinks eight to ten glasses of alkaline water, and ten cups of antioxidant-rich green tea daily. On a regular basis, he keeps a record of forty to fifty fitness indicators, including his "tactile sensitivity," and makes adjustments as needed. While many people think his health regimen is excessive, he calls it "effective." His regimen is working—he is rarely ill, and although he is chronologically in his late fifties, his "real" age has been measured at around forty. He feels he has slowed down the aging of his body considerably, both visibly and at the cellular level.[157]

Each of us needs to take responsibility for his or her health. We need to become medical detectives on a quest to discover what foods, medical technologies, and lifestyle practices will best insure that we live long enough to live forever. While you might think that Kurzweil has the advantage of knowledge gained from being intimately involved in aging research, he wants to spread this knowledge to the public. His book, *Fantastic Voyage*, presents the reader with a very accessible program for achieving a similar level of health.[158]

The idea is not to follow every health and diet fad that comes down the road, although many of them are based on simple principles of good nutrition. Rather, we should all become lifelong health experts, and we should do this from our earliest ages. Parents should attempt to take back from the fast food merchants the control and direction of their children's eating habits. Preaching to your children, however, is not productive if your own diets tend to be high in carbohydrates and empty calories.

Caloric restriction has a major role to play in increased longevity. The public is only beginning to hear about the seemingly miraculous experiments in which mice on low-calorie diets for their whole lives are living to the equivalent of 140 human years. While this may sound like the usual advice to cut back on calories for weight loss, caloric restriction is only tangentially aimed at losing weight—it is meant to radically slow the aging of the body by making it work less hard processing foods.

One book which offers a health regimen that incorporates caloric restriction is Dr. Maoshing Ni's *Secrets of Longevity: Hundreds of Ways to Live to be 100*. Based on Oriental medicine techniques he uses in his practice, one of his primary guidelines for achieving a long life is the "three quarters rule." Dr. Ni realized that most of the centenarians he surveyed made a practice of leaving the table when they are three-quarters full.[159]

Another general rule is to get all the medical tests doctors suggest, plus some you think you might need, and also a periodic full medical examination. Mammograms, colonoscopies and prostate examinations do in fact save lives.

Perfect health does not come cheap. Because of that fact, people are turning to what is being labeled "medical tourism" to get the medical treatments and bodily enhancements they want but might not be able to otherwise afford. The *Confederation of Indian Industry* estimated that in 2006 close to half a million foreign patients traveled to India for treatments as varied and complex as neurosurgery, bone marrow and kidney transplants, dental implants and joint replacement. A dental implant performed in India costs half what it would in Australia. South American dentists undercut US dentists by 20 to 50 percent. The cost of some medical treatments in Asia can be one-tenth of those in Europe or the United States. Some people are traveling to Singapore from Western countries for cardiac bypasses.

To lure patients to foreign medical offices and hospitals, many doctors package the medical care with vacation-style extras. For instance, you can visit Thailand for a cataract operation and spend a week on the beach at Phuket. Another package bundles a visit to South Africa for cosmetic surgery with a safari. Others can travel to the Middle East for complete medical care at a luxury destination.

As the Superlongevity Revolution advances, expect more people to seek the best in medical service anywhere they can find and afford it. For instance, by 2010, Dubai will operate the largest international medical centre between Europe and South-East Asia, which will include a branch of the renowned Harvard Medical School.[160]

While it has always been advisable to eat nutritious foods, get tested for potential maladies, and get the best medical attention wherever you can find it, now there is an added impetus to remain healthy. For the first time in history, it is very possible that if you can stay alive for a few more decades, you could be around for the next two centuries.

Everyman As Scientist

In both *Seizing the Future* and *The Future Factor*, I strongly expressed my belief that for the human species to achieve true scientific and technological progress, it is important for everyone, not just scientists and professional technologists, to become involved in the scientific enterprise. Non-scientists must transform themselves from average citizens to producers of science and technology. The non-scientist, I stated, "must participate in its (science's) creation."

At the time I wrote these books, the concept sounded outlandish—after all, the Internet, that broad distributor of information, was only in its infancy. And scientific knowledge was almost the exclusive domain of professional scientists, making them veritable high-priests of the professions and keepers of sacred knowledge.

Today, that has all changed. Communications media such as the internet have made it possible for people to access journals, reports, news accounts, plus a wealth of other material pertaining to diseases, research and possible cures. The computer itself enables scientists as well as non-scientists to even experiment on any idea or object without moving from their screen, such is the power of three-dimensional imagery and the emergent technology virtual reality to replicate experiments that previously required access to a physical laboratory.

In the mid-1990s, when these two books were written, I saw how an early version of my concept of "Everyman as Scientist" had become reality in the AIDS crisis. At that time many AIDS activists saw their friends and family members dying before their eyes and were dissatisfied with the medical professions lack of progress in finding any real therapy for this horrible disease. The activists mobilized themselves as well as members of the medical profession to accelerate the research process. Many became familiar with the various types of AIDS-related research, and often served as intermediaries among researchers often working in isolation from each other, informing each group of the other's progress. The efforts of these groups are often credited for the accelerated pace at which many life-saving and life extending anti-AIDS drugs were introduced, including first AZT and later so-called AIDS "drug cocktails" increasingly used in the early 2000s.

The concept of "everyman as scientist" was popularized in the visionary 1993 movie *Lorenzo's Oil*, which depicted the painstaking labors of the parents of a child stricken with a neurological disease to find a cure for the ailment on their own. They refused to accept the medical establishment's contention that no cure existed for their child's malady. In the film we see the couple establishing a worldwide personal and electronic network of patients and researchers, and eventually supersede the efforts of the medical establishment to fight this disease. Astonishingly, the couple, with little if any medical or scientific background, discovered a concoction of ingredients that could help alleviate some of the disease's symptoms. Then they built a lab to manufacture the "medicine," which became known as "Lorenzo's Oil." Throughout the movie, the doctors and specialists were telling the couple that this therapy was useless, even as some of the other children taking oil were either improving or staving off further physical deterioration.[161]

Today, patients and their families are forming action groups to tackle various diseases in every way they can. One of the more important patient movements is the growing role of the public in developing biospecimen banks for rare diseases. These banks, which can include tissue samples, blood, spinal fluid or other specimens along with clinical data about patients, are critical to medical research on various maladies. Such banks offer researchers a way to test new drugs, study the disease's biology and are seen as the optimum way of finding new targets for experimental drugs.

Patients have taken the matter into their own hands to create their own banks mostly out of frustration with the inability of drug companies to develop such research storehouses. Individual centers may not see a sufficient number of patients to collect a critical mass of samples. Moreover, smaller drug companies often don't have the resources to find patients with a particular disease to contribute blood and tissue samples.

In 2005, the Multiple Myeloma Research Consortium was founded by Kathy Giusti, who suffers from the disease, an incurable and rare cancer of the blood. The Consortium started its own Multiple Myeloma biospecimen bank at a cost of two million to three million dollars, helped in part by a grant from the Denver-based Pioneer Fund.

Biospecimen banks have been started by a host of groups, including the

Accelerated Cure Project for Multiple Sclerosis, Cure Autism Now, the Joubert Syndrome Foundation and the Inflammatory Breast Cancer Research Foundation, using their extensive patient databases. To establish such banks, patients usually have to work through foundations, such as the Lance Armstrong Foundation, which has awarded grants to establish a tissue bank for testicular-cancer research.

Throughout 2007, a host of new computer-based technologies such as blogs, podcasts and virtual community software like that offered on SecondLife.com were enabling patients and caregivers to exchange information and advice about diseases, join a support group and generally accelerate the achievement of superlongevity. The American Cancer Society and the Centers for Disease Control and Prevention (CDC) are now using the Second Life website described in Chapter Five as a way to disseminate information about nutrition, as well as disease prevention, treatment and diagnosis. The American Cancer Society also plans to introduce a "Health Reminder Assistant" that will send health information via phone, instant messaging and email, as well as an interactive "Great American Health Suite" that will zero-in on cancer prevention. The CDC has used the Second Life Web site to hold virtual health fairs on subjects like flu pandemics and their prevention and control.

Patients and interested members of the public have created many health-related websites. Powerful examples are sites such as DailyStrength.com and Grouploop.org, which have become settings in which people with specific diseases can network, commiserate and search for cures. Grouploop.org is operated by The Wellness Community, a nonprofit group that offers education and support to cancer patients and families. The group claims that more than 15 percent of the approximately fifty thousand teen cancer survivors in the U.S. as well as teens from nine other countries including Israel and Japan use the website. This password protected site serves as a place where teens can connect at any time to post or read messages or participate in weekly scheduled support groups led by a professional. The site's search engine enables users to find other teens suffering from cancer based on such criteria as location, age and severity of condition. One eighteen year old suffering from non-Hodgkin's lymphoma drew emotional sustenance from the experiences of those she met on Grouploop.org. The teen said, "I was pleasantly surprised that it wasn't too downhearted and pessimistic—we are allowed to have fun and even joke about things, like the special treatment you get when you have cancer." The teens also discuss issues critical to their mental health, like the impact of cancer on their sense of identity and their fears about the future. This website also provides the teens a forum to exchange information on various treatments and possible cures for their ailments.

The public's search for information about diseases and their cures will only be enhanced by the appearance of science related websites throughout 2007. The Medical Blog Network (healthvoices.com) hosts blogs which link consumers and medical professionals. Organizedwisdom.com lets users network with each other to share advice and experiences regarding diseases, medications, and health procedures. In an effort to link parents to the best recommended sites and professionally reviewed medical information, Tufts University has built a Child and Family Webguide (Cfw.tufts.edu). Healia.com is a new health search engine that ranks article content on quality and relevancy. There are support and medical information groups devoted to a variety of specific diseases, including Wellnesscommunity.org (cancer) and Breastcancer.org.[162]

These examples cover a wide range of activities aimed at ultimately discovering cures for disease. Remember, in the future, it will be incumbent on all of us to become part of the global scientific enterprise to achieve superlongevity. It will be important for each of us to share with the larger community, probably through Internet groups, what we learn about the relative effectiveness of any new novel techniques and procedures we are sampling in our efforts to rejuvenate our bodies, stave off the aging process, and cure our diseases.

Let's not assume that the latest elixir or nanotechnological treatment will be universally distributed or even available to the general population, as flu vaccines are before and during flu season. It is more likely that breakthroughs supporting the Superlongevity Revolution will be achieved in a more serendipitous manner—a lone scientist will discover how to use stem cells to cure Alzheimer's, an engineer inadvertently will happen upon a breakthrough in nanotechnology, or some non-scientists will find and produce the next Lorenzo's Oil. Fortunately, technology is making it possible to research our own diseases and investigate how to extend our lives.

I believe that same technology will enable us to go to the next stage of scientific analysis, to make it possible for everyone to become a scientist. Just ask the victims of disease and their loved ones who are enlisting in the growing army of amateur disease-sleuths.

It is not impossible for a non-scientist to scale the lofty heights of scientific discovery. So-called amateurs have routinely made solid fundamental contributions to many fields. Ben Franklin was an unschooled but well-read curiosity seeker whose inventions include bifocal lenses, furnace stoves, lightning rods and the odometer. And, oh yes, electricity! The Wright brothers, both high school dropouts, taught themselves the principles of aerodynamics out of journals and books before they embarked on inventing the airplane.

An equally dedicated person today can advance the cause of superlongevity with a computer and access to the knowledge networks existing in cyberspace.

Become An Advocate For Superlongevity

We looked at the emergence of what I labeled the Superlongevity Lobby, groups and people who are actually organizing, lobbying, writing letters and setting up websites for the express purpose of moving the Superlongevity Revolution along.

Many of these groups promote involving the public becoming active advocates for the idea of superlongevity, legislation supporting anti-aging research, and a myriad of other concerns related to radically extending the human life span. For instance, as we saw with the Alliance for Aging Research's innovative "Advocacy Toolkit" makes the political action process accessible to even the political novice.

AARP, which is the acronym for the *American Association of Retired People*, is busily engaged in political action on a wide variety of issues. With a membership of thirty-five million people, AARP's opinion counts. It has taken strong public stands on improving health care coverage for workers and non-workers alike, strengthening the social security system, and broadening the reach of Medicare. AARP is also working within particular localities to ensure that communities respond to the needs of their rapidly growing older populations.

This dynamic organization not only targets its activism toward government. Since AARP can serve as a quasi-buying service for its members through senior discount programs for products and service, the organization can pressure companies and whole fields to become more responsive to the needs of fifty+ consumers. Nations such as Japan, who are slightly ahead of the United States on the aging demographic curve, provide AARP with a way to learn how to deal with work and retirement issues.

AARP's online "Legislative Action Center" will identify for you key upcoming legislation in the battle over aging and superlongevity research, tell you who your elected officials are, even how to contact the media to express your opinion on such issues. And of course, AARP will educate you on the issues and explain why you should agree with their positions.[163]

We usually associate political action on aging issues as the province of organizations like AARP whose membership tends toward the more senior end of the life cycle. However, other organizations with members of all ages, such as the Immortality Institute and the Longevity Meme, will become major combatants in the struggle to accelerate the pace at which new anti-aging technologies and pharmaceutical products are researched, developed, and introduced as consumer products.

By early 2007, the various groups and individuals forming the immortality lobby showed signs that they might combine into a viable organizational force. One organization, "The Coalition to Extend Life" (C.E.L.), was formed for the express purpose of building a "national movement" in support of what they broadly label "immortality research" and to actively pressure Congress, governmental agencies, and the Administration to create and support a "Manhattan Project" whose sole aim is to cure what they label "the terminal disease of aging."

Their first job is to gather one million signatures of American voters who support this goal on a pro-immortality petition and present this document to those with governmental power. The actual petition is short and to the point. It calls for the creation of a National Institute for Immortality that would serve as a funding conduit for research in the area of superlongevity. The petition also exhorts Congress to enact laws providing tax breaks and grants for universities and companies working on projects related to life extension.

On their website, C.E.L. explains why political activism is necessary for the achievement of superlongevity. Although science is bringing us to the threshold of immortality, C.E.L states, the real battle to reach that goal will be fought at the ballot box and in political forums. This organization recognizes that many groups and factions will oppose indefinite life extension for various economic and ideological reasons—they cite the battle over stem cell research funding as an example. Politicians will make decisions based on what they perceive to be the "national consensus" on the question of the morality of life extension research.

But how do those in power determine what the "national consensus" is on the issues? Polls? E-mails? Lobbying groups? The answer is: all of the above. The Coalition believes that the majority of Americans support indefinite life extension, as long as that long life is lived as a healthy vibrant individual. However, C.E.L. believes that because the pro-superlongevity majority is not well-organized, opponents of all political and ideological stripes will be able to "hijack public opinion" and persuade elected officials to outlaw life-extension research. Therefore, the Coalition proposes to provide the pro-life extension majority with an organization that can make its voice heard.

To build this national movement, the Coalition hopes to educate the American public about immortality and life-extension, as well as contact and support candidates for political office who will promote immortality and "oppose those (officials) who will not." They are trying to recruit volunteers to work in their communities to collect signatures for the petition-drive, engage politicians in discussions on life-extension research and legislation, and solicit contributions for the organization's war-chest.[164]

All organizations involved in the fight for immortality such as C.E.L. must recognize that cultural battles in the U.S., Europe, and most of the industrialized world are also fought in the media, including television and radio talk shows, newspaper op-eds and "letters to the editor", as well as on school boards and university curriculum committees. Blogs and websites are not enough. They must focus on those agenda-setting targets if they hope to win the debate over superlongevity. And these organizations must understand the nature of the forces amassed to undermine the superlongevity revolution, which I will discuss at length in the next chapter.

As more and more people become aware that science is making discoveries that could help extend their lives by decades, and possibly even rejuvenate them physically and mentally, I believe they will become increasingly vocal in demanding that products and technologies based on such discoveries be made available. In fact, the young and generally less-senior cohorts possibly have a greater stake in this matter. After all, they are more likely than their elders to be alive when the lion's share of anti-aging technologies such as nanotechnology becomes realities.

WHAT BUSINESSES AND ORGANIZATIONS SHOULD DO

Not only will individuals have to change their behaviors to prosper in the Superlongevity Era, but companies and organizations of all types will have to adjust and prepare for the demographic and cultural changes brought on by the Superlongevity Revolution. Most of all organizations must recognize the emerging career-recareering pattern of their employees especially those in areas we have delved into throughout this book, and determine how they will structure their human resources policies to reflect this new pattern as the lifespan grows to one hundred and beyond.

The imminent mass retirement of the Baby Boomer generation in the United States and elsewhere will give corporations and other organizations a taste of the potential impact of impending changes in the career lifecycle on employment, recruitment, retention and retirement.

Develop a Broad Mission Statement Regarding Employees' Careers

First and foremost companies must decide not so much on a policy but a philosophy regarding employee longevity. Does the company want individuals to remain in the company for their entire careers, for a shorter period, or for just several projects? Should businesses seeking long term relationships with employees consider developing and investing in programs specifically designed to maintain them, such as a job sabbatical or formal mentor program?

Companies must make sure that their employment strategies reflect a new demographic reality. Company executives might think they do not want employees to remain in the company for their entire careers, given that such careers might stretch for more than seventy or eighty years. On the other hand, businesses must also determine whether they can function properly without the services of many of these workers they intend to surplus.

The recent human resources and manpower problems General Motors has encountered portends trouble ahead for companies that do not develop strategies for dealing with the new work life cycle.

General Motors employs well over one 100,000 workers, mostly unionized, who were owed very generous pensions with health benefits when they retire. The company's financial status has been tenuous, to say the least. Bleeding millions of dollars in losses, GM's credit rating was slipping deeply into speculative-grade territory, making it more difficult for the company to finance operations. Searching for a way to bolster its credit rating and stock price and get operations out of the red, the company decided to offer 113,000 hourly-wage workers a package of $35,000 to $140,000 in lump-sum payments to leave the company. Workers with 27 years or more at GM would receive full retiree benefits, while workers with less seniority could keep their accumulated pensions.

Hoping that 30,000 workers would take the package by 2008, GM was more than mildly surprised when 4,600 employees accepted buyouts and about 30,400 chose to retire, decisions they evidently made within days of GM's buyout announcement. It seemed as though many workers GM always considered extremely loyal were nearly tripping over each other to get to the exit door.

Although the company is putting a bright smile on this mass exodus of what is largely Baby Boomers, GM now has a new set of problems. For one, some plants may be left short-handed. At a GM metal-stamping plant in West Mifflin, Pennsylvania, roughly half of the UAW workers, 241 out of 520, accepted packages to leave, including cash buyouts. GM officials said it will use temporary employees as necessary, but the workers eligible for the package are those with the most experience and skills, such as tool-and-die makers, and thus most difficult to replace with temps.

Worse, GM will be supporting these departing workers for the rest of their lives, a period which for many will be much longer than the GM pension plan's actuaries are calculating. Assuming that many of these new pensioners started their GM careers in their late teens or twenties, a sizeable portion could be starting life on the GM dole at fifty or younger.[165]

Considering the future pension costs and the loss of skills, not to mention the cost of replacing these workers and their skills, some are wondering whether this buyout makes financial sense.

The lesson is clear. In an era when people will enjoy radically extended life spans and a concomitant protracted period in which they career and re-career, companies must clearly think through their employee recruitment and retention philosophy. Perhaps companies should work closely with all employees on personal career development plans, to determine who they might want to retain, and who wants to remain, for what could be an extraordinarily long time.

Companies Must Maintain Their Knowledge Base

If employees in this new era will be as mobile as I expect, changing not only jobs but embarking on whole new careers periodically, employers unable to hold workers will have to find ways to retain their knowledge and skill.

Knowledge-retention programs that companies are establishing today will serve as models for the future. The Raytheon Corporation, the giant aerospace firm with 80,000 employees, has a large group of aging Boomers who might retire in the near future and a very large younger group. The company realizes how important it is to find ways for the older cohorts to transfer their knowledge about company practices, problem solving techniques, and innovation to this younger group. Raytheon has developed a method called Catalyst Engagement in which key seasoned employees and relative company "newbies" are placed on the same projects and work teams in the hope that the wisdom of the elders will be absorbed by the junior employees.

In the Superlongevity era, companies might find it necessary to capture the skills and knowledge of senior employees who have already departed in order to take career hiatuses, pursue further schooling or re-career. Confronting this problem, Allegheny Ludlum, the specialty materials manufacturer, is tapping the wisdom of a cadre of retired employees, who have agreed to work flexible schedules as trainers and coaches for managers and technicians at all levels of the company. They coach their junior employees in such areas as engineering, technical, sales, and other categories. Other companies, including Federal Express, United States Steel, and Timken Steel, are also tapping their ex-employees as a knowledge base.

The mentor programs which we described earlier as a way to anchor older and younger workers and to provide a range of career guidance services can also serve as convenient vehicles for knowledge capture. I have worked with several companies in establishing mentor programs and have seen the power of such relationships in bringing the younger managers up to speed. One company entitled The Loyalty Factor, a Portsmouth, New Hampshire-based training and consulting firm, helps companies set up mentor programs that pair retiring boomers with echo boomers in learning-based teams. According to company officials, the object of these programs is for retiring managers to grow tomorrow's leaders through mentoring.

An IBM consulting arm, the IBM Institute for Business Value, is on the forefront of this training on HR trends. It works with client companies, helping them capture the knowledge and skills of senior employees and disseminating that knowledge to large numbers of workers. An associate partner, Eric Lesser states that, "Most companies don't have a sense for where they are at risk in terms of critical knowledge going out the door."[166]

Institute Formal Mentor Programs
Formal mentor programs have existed in business in one form or another for

at least the last twenty years. These programs, which link senior members of an organization with a junior employee, are established to achieve a myriad of goals. Companies hope such programs will help in the personal or professional development of managers, sharpen employee skills, and possibly lead to the eventual advancement of women and minorities, many of whom historically have had problems developing such relationships with white male senior executives. Other mentor programs have been created as a component of company leadership development programs.

Some of the more prominent companies to establish such programs are Douglas Aircraft Company, Coca Cola, General, Hoechst Celanese, Chubb & Son, the United States Postal Service, JFK Health Services, Inc., Nabisco, Champion Corporation, NYNEX, Pitney Bowes and Procter & Gamble. Various branches of the military are utilizing such programs to develop talented recruits into officers. DuPont Corporation has by far one of the most sophisticated and elaborate formal mentor programs in the United States. The mentoring concept has taken root in many of the company's divisions, including Agricultural Products, Automotive Products, Facilities Services, Haskell Laboratory, and the Polyester Films and Polyester Resins units.

As the Superlongevity Revolution continues, companies could well look to formal mentoring programs to help them adapt to the changes in the career lifecycle that are bound to occur. Research has shown that mentor programs have profound effect on workers' feeling toward the company and their role in it. For the younger worker, selection as a protégé into such a program signals that the company sees them as a valued employee that it wants to nurture for leadership roles in the company. Also, as the protégé's relationship with the mentor evolves, this younger employee learns from the mentor more about the organization, its culture and importantly, its politics, information that can only help the protégé move on the fast track. And the more the protégé succeeds in the company, the more he is likely to remain a loyal employee.

Will participation in the program reduce the likelihood that the employee sometime later may leave the company to re-career or take a career hiatus? Given the fact that we will all be confronting living into our mid-one hundreds the answer probably is no. However, such a program will help the company develop their employees' skills and organizational savvy much more quickly than if no mentor program exists. Also the program could very well increase the number of years the person eventually stays with the company. A person who was well mentored might wait until fifty or sixty to re-career rather than leaving at age forty.

The managers, senior scientists or administrators asked to serve as mentors in such a program will also be more likely to remain and contribute their knowledge. This is because when company executives request that a senior manager serve as a mentor in a formal program, they are signaling to that manager that the company values the person's knowledge, skill, wisdom and just plain understanding of "the way we do things around here," the organization's culture. Equally important is the second message conveyed, that the company sees this senior employee as a valuable part of the company's future. Since this program will continue for years, the company is saying, and we need you to help us develop this organization's talent as we grow.

Mentor programs have emerged as a powerful organizational tool just at the right time, given their potential to help organizations cope with the prickly human resources issue being created by demographic the Superlongevity Revolution.[167]

Health Coverage in the Superlongevity Era

In the Superlongevity Era, the scientific marvels that emerge from the laboratories will be daunting. At first, they might also be expensive. Some assume that for this reason companies will just abandon covering their employees' health, and force them to either finance their coverage themselves or turn to government assistance. After all, is it not true that more and more Americans are losing their health coverage?

Let us discuss for a moment the myth and reality of health insurance coverage in America. For political reasons or perhaps just out of ignorance, politicians and pundits repeatedly mouth the mantra that 40 percent of Americans do not have health care coverage." That figure is a very poor interpretation of the fact that 60 percent of Americans are covered by employer-provided insurance. What they do not tell you is that government covers more people—one in four Americans have government-provided health insurance, such as Medicare, Medicaid, Veterans benefits, and the like. According to the Census Bureau, the percentage of Americans without coverage has inched up, to 15.7 percent, not 40 percent. That number is not a cause for jubilation, but neither is it as dire as the statistics being bandied about in the media.[168]

Benefits such as health care usually are part of an overall package, which also includes wages and perks, designed to attract the best workers to a company.

A company that decides to trim that overall package by scrimping on salaries or benefits risks losing the competitive advantage in the labor market. It is hard to imagine a company successfully attracting newly minted Harvard MBAs, top engineers, valued IT personnel and top-tier academics to organizations that fail to provide health insurance to their employees. Barring a major recession, at least for the next few decades workers will have an advantage in the labor market. Boomer retirements from their companies will create huge numbers of job openings that must be filled by a smaller cohort of workers. Health care will be a major attractor in the battle for talented personnel.

Rather than contemplating dropping health coverage in this climate, companies should adopt a completely different approach, one geared to the medical realities of the Superlongevity Era.

For one thing they should become what I call "health care sleuths." By this I mean that companies should literally hunt for the best health insurance coverage for their employees at the best price. While many companies do this as a matter of practice, defining "best" in the Superlongevity Era will be more difficult. New medical developments can occur almost anywhere in the world at any time, and are usually not particularly well-publicized. Individuals are becoming aware that they have may gain important information about a new procedure, therapy or drug from friends or in an Internet chat room as well as or even easier than from their doctor. Companies must devise quick ways to get access to that same type of information.

They must also aggressively pressure their health care providers to similarly take on this "health sleuth" mentality and scour the globe for innovative treatments for particular illnesses. The provider might discover that a treatment exists in another country not available locally. Or the treatment might be available locally, but the health care provider will not cover it simply because the therapy is too costly. In either case, the company should consider suggesting to the health care provider that it cover the treatment in question if the employee would take the "medical tourism" route—go to another country that will do the procedure for a fraction of the price charged by home-grown doctors.

Health insurers should also be monitoring the covered doctors and medical practices to make certain these physicians are staying current on medical breakthroughs and the availability of cutting edge scientific technologies. While physician training has always been an important staple of quality medical care, in this new era, in which breakthroughs in stem cell research and possibly nanotechnology might bring us to the doors of immortality, it will be incumbent on doctors to receive almost daily and weekly updates on medical developments.

Employers should also realize that their employees are deluged with stories in the mainstream media about new medical breakthroughs. This barrage of information, like advertising, creates a hunger for access to new therapies and cures for whatever maladies they have. So employees will petition their companies to pressure providers to expand coverage to include these new therapies.

As the Superlongevity Revolution generates more powerful therapies and pharmaceuticals that can extend our life and turn us into "ultra-humans," employees will exert even greater pressure on their employers and providers for access to and coverage of the medical miracles cascading from the labs. As a result we can expect greater tension between employee, employer and health care provider. It is not hard to imagine employees demanding that they be covered for rejuvenation therapies, cellular regeneration technologies, artificial retinas, smart drugs and a host of other products in the ever-expanding medical goodie bag.

To minimize health care costs, employers should help their employees in disease prevention as well as finding cures. Today's wellness programs within companies serve such a purpose, encouraging employees to diet, exercise, reduce stress and quit smoking. However, employers must realize that the very definition of "prevention" will be broadened considerably. What is genetic engineering of offspring to eliminate the genes for specific disease if not the ultimate in "prevention"? Cellular regeneration and/or other rejuvenation technologies are "preventing" old age and its concomitant infirmities. Employers and the health care provider must realize that the very concept of prevention can easily be expanded to such esoteric, and potentially costly, therapies to preempt disease.

In the Superlongevity Era organizations of all types will be confronted by other issues. The overall health of company retirement plans will certainly be a problem. General Motors and other companies are complaining about their "legacy" costs, the price they are paying for agreeing to pay out lifetime benefits to people whose post-employment lifetimes might stretch for many decades. There is little doubt that the company pension concept will eventually evolve into the portable retirement fund, such as the 401k, which allows workers to receive pension contributions from several employers over time but take their pension package with them to every new job. This type of pension plan wisely anticipated the radically extended life spans we will see as the twenty-first century unfolds.

Companies might want to invest some of that money they would have placed in conventional pension plans into job sabbatical funds and other programs geared toward retaining valuable employees.

SCHOOLS: PREPARING THE YOUNG FOR SUPERLONGEVITY

All generations should be made aware of the fact that the Superlongevity Revolution is upon us, and that they will be experiencing lifestyles quite different than those of previous generations. In fact, the case could be made that the age group that should be targeted most for this consciousness raising are those at the beginning of life, children and teenagers.

That brings us to the role of schools in the emerging Superlongevity Era. As we discussed earlier, universities will play a major role in the schooling and re-tooling of the workforce as people pursue careers and then re-career. And elementary, middle and high schools need to teach students the fundamentals they will require to succeed in their jobs and careers.

In addition, I envision these schools, and perhaps even at the freshman level in universities, offering preparation for a society in which people will live to very high ages.

The model that I have developed for this type of education is what I label Superlongevity Training®. This type of educational program could be tailored to its audience, either as a semester long college course, a week-long course in grade schools, and even as a one or two day training course for adults. I envision the younger students taking initial training at ten - twelve years of age, and again in the junior or senior year of high school.

This training should cover a number of issues, including:

The Coming Demographic Changes This part of the module should deal with the dramatic increase in the life span throughout the twentieth century, as well as the projections by demographers, futurists and others for the radical extension of the lifespan over the next several decades.

The Science Making Extended Life Possible This section would deal with all of the current and projected breakthroughs that will make super-longevity possible, including nanotechnology, stem cell research, caloric restriction and a host of other medical miracles.

How Superlongevity Will Change Family Life. Here the training will look at such issues as the impact of superlongevity on marriage, childrearing and the emergence of the multigenerational family.

Being Responsible For Your Health. In this area the students will be presented with another emphasized in this book. Ultimately, it is individuals who are responsible for their own health, regardless of what miracles science and medicine bring forth. The training focuses on how to become proficient in researching health issues and gathering information on the latest developments in science and medicine that can help you extend your life.

The Changing Career Lifecycle. This module examines the changing nature of careers. As we have discussed, the new career model will include at least two careers, interrupted by a number of events including sabbaticals, hiatuses, and re-training. Here we'll discuss what we now call "retirement" might disappear as people confront the possibility of living for 150 years or more.

Their training should include hands-on materials that help students envision their professional and personal lives through this very long life span. We always ask students "what do you want to be when you grow up?" This exercise would take the whole process a step further, and have them envision multiple careers, education, family, job sabbaticals and career hiatuses. The student will be guided through that intricate process of scenario building, and learn how to take into account "wildcard" events, those life occurrences which can upend the best-laid plans.

Especially in the case of a Superlongevity Training course aimed at younger groups, supplemental materials such as videos and even video games should be used to illustrate the way our lifestyle is and will be changing. These videos should show people working and thriving at ever more senior ages. Students would certainly find stimulating artists current renditions of the enhanced "ultra-human" we have described herein.

THE MEDIA'S ROLE IN THE SUPERLONGEVITY REVOLUTION

The media will have a number of roles to play in smoothing the adjustment to the very long life spans people will enjoy in the Superlongevity Era. For instance, movies and other media have the ability to present the public with films and television programs that deal with issues such as rejuvenation and the radically extended life span. By their very nature such works will be in the realm of fantasy, or as I like to refer to them, alternate reality scenarios.

In 1985, *Cocoon* was only the second film Ron Howard had directed. It opened with little fanfare. It was reasoned that people didn't want to see a movie about physically old people suddenly dealing with the dilemma of rejuvenation. Fortunately, a great many people did. The movie was a box office success, and received more acclaim when one of its performers, veteran actor Don Ameche, won the Best Supporting Actor Oscar. Other cinema mainstays including Wilford Brimley, Hume Cronyn, Jack Guilford and Jessica Tandy were also featured. In fact, most of the cast were seniors.

Part science-fiction tale, part warm-hearted fable, *Cocoon* tells the story of three senior citizens who periodically slip out of their retirement home to enjoy a swim in the large pool nestled in an abandoned estate next door. Suddenly, these three seniors start to feel decidedly younger. (The scene in which Ameche break dances is a cinema classic.) As it turns out, this pool is filled with pods, alien cocoons, which are being stored there by the Antareans, extra-terrestrials in human form led by Walter (Brian Dennehy). He explains to the seniors that the seniors' newfound youth and vigor comes from the cocoons every time they swim in the pool. The aliens are pretty "humane" in their outlook. They permit the men as well as other residents of the retirement community who learn about the pool's magic powers, to continue to swim in the pool.

The movie deals with several philosophic and social issues related to the subject of rejuvenation, matters that society as a whole and each of us as individuals will ultimately have to consider as the Superlongevity Revolution spreads.

For instance, one of the seniors, Bernie, has no interest in prolonging life any longer than necessary, echoing the feeling of some today that rejuvenation and life extension are a violation of natural law. He forbids his dying wife Rosie from sampling the pool's powers, and she dies. Realizing now that he wishes his wife were still alive, he takes his wife to the pool, which by then unfortunately has been drained of its life-giving qualities due to its overuse by the retirement home residents.

Cocoon's concept of a "window of opportunity" for using or applying technologies that lead to rejuvenation reflects some of the dilemmas we will face in the Superlongevity Era. For instance, the decision to genetically engineer our children for certain traits—hair color, intelligence, height, athleticism—will have to be made before the child is born. If a couple takes the moral stance that genetic engineering is wrong or unnatural, they have to realize that they and the child will live with that decision for the rest of time. Certain technologies might emerge that can stop the aging process, but cannot rejuvenate the individual. Hence, the decision to undergo that particular therapy will have to be made sooner than later if you want to spend your superlong life as a twenty-seven year old and not a fifty-five year old.

At the end of Cocoon, the aliens offer the seniors the opportunity to leave Earth with them and gain eternal life on the aliens' planet, or remain on Earth with the comfort of family and friends, but sooner or later die. To the audience's surprise, the movie did not choose the Hollywood-style sentimental ending — the finale shows a boat-load of seniors being transported upwards into a departing Antarean spaceship for the unknown planet and immortality. The explanation for their choice could not be clearer than when one of the characters played by Brimley, told his disbelieving grandson: "When we get where we're going, we'll never be sick, we won't get any older and we won't ever die."

Twenty years later, the work is not rerun often on television, and is at the back of the bin in most video stores, if they carry it at all. That is a shame, considering that the movie was one of the few popular films that offered the public a positive image of physical rejuvenation.

In many ways, our species is about to venture into a region as alien and novel as the Antarean's, the new world of superlongevity and immortality. We will leave behind our convenient concepts of limited life spans, an expected rhythm of our life cycle, and many of the comforting and tradition images of old and young. Our traditional concepts of work, childrearing, retirement, and intergenerational relationships will be upended. Philosophical and religious beliefs might be challenged by the notion of life without end.

Movies and films, I believe, should move beyond the realm of fantasy and fairy tale, they need to start to deal with the possibilities of living to a very great age in more realistic plot contexts. It would be wonderful to see a human drama series that explores a world a few decades from now in which families and individuals deal with superlongevity and rejuvenation becoming a reality. Such a series would offer the public a view of an emerging future as it were about life in the Superlongevity Era.

An animated sitcom called "Futurama," which ran from 1999-2003 and will return in 2008, played with the concept of rejuvenation and superlongevity. Professor Hubert J. Farnsworth, a.k.a. the Professor, is somewhere in his 160's — although he hardly looks physically young, however, he is sexually active. There is no reason that a sitcom could not be successfully launched which similarly explored all of the human foibles that I am sure super-longevity and rejuvenation might uncover. The media should deal more realistically with current age and aging issues as well. While CNN and other cable channels are beginning to explore later life career changes in spot features, it would be instructive for the public to see more programs featuring true stories about people who at later ages are embarking on new careers, engaging in sports, learning how to play an instrument. Such a program would provide the public a vision of the opportunities presented by living a very long life. At some point the media should also help dispel the image of the average older person as poor and dependent. After all, the reality is that the most important positions in the world CEOs, Presidents, baseball owners, boards of directors, Supreme Court judges, are largely filled by people in their sixties, seventies and eighties. For the most part these jobs require wisdom, perspective, and in many cases "wealth" go to the old, not the young.

One of the obstacles in presenting a vision of emerging lifestyle issues in the Superlongevity Era is the media's habit of presenting the future in an overly pessimistic light. Until the early 1970s one could find a smattering of movies that reflected an optimistic view of the future. Although intense and at times bewildering, Kubrick's masterful *2001: A Space Odyssey* spoke of a future in which humankind would be exploring the cosmos and colonizing planets. The only "bad guy" in the future was the stubborn computer HAL, mankind had seemingly joined forces to conquer space. Even the comical animated series *The Jetsons* presented a benign view of centuries to come—to this day at least one member of an audience will at some point ask me "Where's my flying car," referring to the transportation of choice in the Jetsons' world. The original *Star Trek* showed us a future in which the human species was doing quite well and even got along with its alien neighbors, for the most part.

Since the 1970s, movies have increasingly portrayed the future as saturated with violence (*Bladerunner, The Fifth Dimension*), overpopulated (*Soylent Green*) and generally run by the malevolent side of HAL's family (*The Matrix series*). More often than not, democracy and liberty have eroded considerably (Spielberg's *Minority Report*), and genetic engineering is being used to create a social class system made up of supermen and worker drones (*Gattica*).

2007 saw no abatement of fear mongering regarding the potential misuses of genetic science. Best selling author Michael Crichton brought out another hit novel, simply entitled *Next,* in which he explored the darkest sides of the genetic engineering revolution. The message of *Next* is clear: everything that can go wrong in the world of genetic science invariably does.[169]

In the book, hospitals, even the most respectable and prestigious teaching and research hospitals, routinely pilfer the tissues and DNA of select patients in order to sell these rare medical properties for commercial use, sometimes for billions of dollars.

The author introduces us to an orangutan genetically engineered to speak German and French. Amazingly, this advanced primate does not just mimic words as a parrot or cockatiel might, but rather it uses specific words and sentences to express desires, displeasure and opinions on a variety of subjects. Crichton does not seem bothered by the fact that engineering such a creature would be a medical impossibility given what we know about primate brain structure. This is only the first of many transgenic pets on the horizon, including giant cockroaches and permanent puppies.

One character we meet is the CEO of a genetic research company who is seeking to divorce his flagrantly unfaithful wife. In order to get custody of their children, he concocts an ingenious scheme to establish his wife's genetic predisposition to bipolar illness, Alzheimer's disease and Huntington's chorea, which would make her unfit to be a mother. As the CEO of a company at the forefront of genetic testing, he is prepared to fake the lab results to get his way. This CEO is only one of many greedy out-of-control geneticists in the book, who are prodded on by a gaggle of rapacious patent and trial lawyers.

To reinforce his message about the dangers of genetic research, Mr. Crichton includes in the book realistic looking "news blurbs," each set off from the novel's text on its own page in grayish newspaper type. One long "news item" purports to be a recounting of a lecture by a "noted scientist" in which he demonstrates how the entire field of stem cell research is a premeditated fraud perpetrated on the public by researchers and scientists hungry for lucrative grants for their labs and companies. "It is unclear," this scientist states, "whether the stem cell dream…will come true." Stem cell based cures, he says, are more than a half-century away.

I have to wonder whether the average reader realizes that this "news item," along with most of the others punctuating the text, have been created by Mr. Crichton. I am also curious to know why the author's entire approach to *Next's* subject matter so sharply diverges from the method he used in his previous novel, *State of Fear*, a critique of the global warming hypothesis and its proponents. In that book he diligently documented every claim and scientific statement with footnote after footnote citing real-world peer-reviewed journals and articles. Ironically, the anti-scientific elites and literary establishment who viciously attacked *State of Fear* for daring to question the validity of the global warming theory are now embracing the shoddily documented book *Next*.

People in the media, including movie producers and best-selling novelists, should be concerned that on some level their products become a powerful teaching tool for the public at large. Since many people only peripherally follow developments and events in science and technology, they digest works like *Next* and *Gattica* not merely as science fiction but as representations of valid scientific fact. Many people will learn much of what they will ever know about genetics as a field and a scientific business from Crichton's book. And they will have their attitudes about genetics, superlongevity, and life extension in general shaped by the vision of the future presented in the mass media. Let us hope that the media presents a "fair and balanced" view of the possibilities and potential of life extension and rejuvenation as well as other marvels.

NEW VALUES FOR A NEW AGE

We have looked at how individuals, corporations, our educational institutions and the media must adjust to the realities of the new demographic phenomenon I call the Superlongevity Revolution. However, in the end, it is our values that must change to ease our transition to life in the *Ageless Nation*. Society and all its members must transform centuries-old attitudes toward age, aging and the life cycle itself.

As we've discussed, we must also change our expectations about the sequence at which certain life events happen. After all, it is going to be difficult to hold on to these cherished images of an ordered sequence of life when people will be having children at one hundred and re-careering at eighty.

Learning To Value the Very Long Life

The great American humorist Mark Twain once said that there are three stages of life—childhood, adulthood and "My goodness, you haven't changed a bit." Mr. Twain's clever comment refers to the common belief that people experience physical and mental decline at the end of their lives. This stereotype is ingrained in our culture and shared by most of us, consciously or not.

There will be a very intriguing period of adjustment in which our image of the physical state of people at very great ages becomes increasingly challenged by the new reality of people at those ages looking and functioning like persons decades younger. Like most stereotypes, these outdated images will fade slowly.

One way to begin shedding those images now is for us to study and learn from the experiences of those individuals who have lived long and productive lives with little decline in their intellectual and physical capacities.

I first became familiar with the stories of P.G. Wodehouse several decades ago when I began to read his delightful and extremely well-written tales of life among the members of what can only be labeled the idle "lower"-upper classes. The two characters that Wodehouse created and for which he will always be remembered are Bertie Wooster, ne'er-do-well but lovable scion of the upper classes, and his butler Jeeves, who continually bails out Wooster from a myriad of often self-imposed predicaments.

I knew that Wodehouse had written these stories over a protracted period of years, but I had no idea how long his writing career lasted. Wodehouse was born in the 1880s, went to a British prep school, became a writer in the early 1900s, and over the next few decades wrote for British and then American theatre, mostly Broadway, and even briefly became a scriptwriter in Hollywood in the 1930s. I recently read a new biography of Wodehouse, and was stunned to discover that around age sixty he was faced with a traumatic life change that became a six-year adventure.

At that point in 1940 Wodehouse was living as an expatriate in France. Suddenly he found himself on the wrong side of the Nazi front lines as Germany invaded and occupied France. The Nazi high command moved most of the ex-pats into work camps, even though these were non-combatants who should have been sent home as the war unfolded. After a year interned in this camp, the Nazi high command refused to release Wodehouse, even though he was a non-combatant. Throughout the war they moved him to various locations in Germany and France. He continued to write his lighthearted stories despite his imprisonment, and even managed to get manuscripts to publishers. The Nazis did not release him until the end of the war in 1946. After the war Wodehouse moved to Long Island, New York and continued following his disciplined writing schedule for nearly thirty years.[170]

What I find amazing about the Wodehouse story is his ability throughout an experience that mentally demoralized many of those imprisoned with him to retain his focus on the "big picture," his literary output. (He is considered by many to be one of the finest writers in twentieth century English-language literature.) Wodehouse was just then embarking on a brand new adventure at sixty, a point in life that many in our society consider the "retirement age." The fact that P.G. Wodehouse never considered sixty years of age, or any age, for that matter, anything more than a number is the positive mental attitude that enabled him to continue his literary production until his death at age ninety. [171]

P. G. Wodehouse, Jacques Barzun and many others have demonstrated to us that as long as you are productive, chronological age is irrelevant. Let us hope most of us learn how to make productive use of life spans of 140 years and more in much the same way as Wodehouse and other have done in their much shorter lives of only ninety years of age or so. To do so, each of us will have to change our attitudes about what we can accomplish at later stages of life. Without such a change in attitude across our society, all the medical miracles in the world will not be worth much.

Perhaps the aforementioned Superlongevity Training can be fashioned to include a module which teaches the value of the very long life. I could not imagine a better introduction for such a lecture than a recounting of the life of P.G. Wodehouse.

Constructive Engagement Must Replace "Checking Out"

Recently I saw an interview with television pioneer Art Linkletter. At one time, he had television shows on NBC, CBS and ABC simultaneously, including "People Are Funny" and ``Kids Say the Darndest Things," which was also the title of one of his many best selling books. In the six weeks previous to the interview, Art Linkletter had sailed on the Queen Mary 2, made two business trips to Washington, D.C. and then traveled to Rome for a cruise through the Mediterranean. He made speeches everywhere he went, just a few of the sixty or more speeches Linkletter makes every year.

In the interview, I watched Linkletter share his views on society and today's television programs. It was also a vehicle to promote his twenty-eighth book, entitled *How to Make the Rest of Your Life the Best of Your Life*, a topic about which Mr. Linkletter is a leading expert. After all, he is ninety-four years of age. He has been married to the same woman for seventy of those years.

Why does he maintain such a hectic schedule? Linkletter's reply tells us much about the importance of staying mentally, physically, and organically connected to the world at older ages. "It's my life," Linkletter say referring to his speeches and writing. "I don't know what the hell I would do without it." He mentioned, by the way, that he does not play golf.[172]

Linkletter exhibits a frame of mind which unfortunately too many people gradually abandon as they advance through life.

As troubling it is to admit, at a certain point in their lives many people "check out." No, I am not here referring to their deaths, but a negative mindset.

By "checking out", I mean that a person has reached that mental stage in which they no longer consider the world in which they live relevant to them or their lives. Similarly, the person does not consider himself to be especially part of or important to the day-to-day running of society.

In truth people can reach this point at any age, though many people begin "checking out" at the latter stages of their careers or when they retire. They stop staying current with news events, culture and sports, gradually reduce their friendship networks and stop making new acquaintances altogether.

On the other hand, many people, Art Linkletter being one of them, never allow themselves to get to that point. They exhibit what I label "Constructive Engagement" in life—even if they have retired. They never see the world as irrelevant to them, and continue to involve themselves by shaping or changing some aspects of the world. In their communities they might be on their condo governing boards or county school boards. They might write "letters to the editor" on community, state or even national affairs, or call talk shows to argue with the host on some issue. Some might choose to devote themselves to their families, mentoring and guiding the younger children in the family. They might volunteer for a literacy program or a soup kitchen.

And many continue to work in one capacity or another, in their jobs, new careers, or as consultants. P.G. Wodehouse, whom we discussed earlier, never checked out from life—his whole life was spent contributing to our culture in his books, stories, and plays. Jacque Barzun retired from academia, but he continues to write books and essays, as well as give speeches, that profoundly affect intellectual discourse and people's view of history.

Part of the reason some people check out from life is the very limited time we think we will spend on this planet. Until recently, a person worked until he was sixty-five, and knew that death was imminent. As the perceived end point appears on their mental horizon, some feel that there is less need to worry about the state of a world that they will be leaving very soon.

But superlongevity will change our relationship to time itself. First, as the Superlongevity Revolution progresses people will live longer and longer periods. Second, since they will be living in an era in which new breakthroughs continually extend that life expectancy, they will have very little idea if and when they are going to die.

Under such conditions, by necessity we will stay constructively engaged. We will career and re-career for as long as we live, and take advantage of job sabbaticals or career hiatuses. More importantly, we better stay actively involved in our world in order to try to influence and shape it as best we can. After all, we will be here for quite some time.

In the *Ageless Nation*, if people do temporarily disengage themselves from the day to day affairs of their world, perhaps on a job sabbatical or career hiatus, they will most likely do this not to "check out" but to rethink their lives, their world, and their life options. They will do this to recharge, and to refresh. They will be in better mind and spirit to constructively engage the world and make it a better place.

As much as our institutions and each of us try to prepare for life in the *Ageless Nation*, let us remember that our path to the Superlongevity Era will take many serendipitous twists and turns. The best advice for getting along in the coming years might be to "expect the unexpected."

chapter nine

Will the Superlongevity Revolution Ever Happen?

Assuming that science and technology continue the magnificent progress made over the last several decades, there would seem to be few obstacles preventing the *Ageless Nation* from emerging and flourishing.

I believe that scientific and medical research is well on its way to bringing us to the threshold of superlongevity much faster than anyone popularly imagined. And that was before several mini-scientific revolutions occurred, including the decoding of the Human Genome and the series of laboratory successes in stem cell research.

As I pointed out in my earlier book, *Seizing the Future*, however, human history is filled with examples of social, economic and political forces inhibiting or attempting to halt technological and scientific development. Probably the most famous of such instances was that of the Luddites, a social movement of English workers in the early 1800s who protested the introduction of textile machines they felt would eliminate their jobs. The Luddites' solution was to destroy such machines in several towns. They became so powerful that they often fought pitched battles with the British Army. The movement was eventually put down violently and its leaders were deported, most to Australia.

However, the name stuck. The term "Luddite," is often appended to anyone opposed to technological change of any type, for any reason.

As the development of technological innovations has accelerated, so has the resistance, organized or otherwise, to their introduction. In years past, many towns and rural areas, as well as the horse and buggy industry, opposed the widespread adoption of the automobile. Many of the personal media gadgets we take for granted, including television, radio, and phonograph, were viewed by some as threatening the sanctity of the home, a threat to parental authority, and a general invasion of privacy.

Today, nearly every technological innovation has its critics, some of whom are sufficiently organized to prevent widespread implementation of the given inventions. Environmentalist groups have successfully blocked the building of nuclear power plants and the drilling of offshore oil in the United States, while political and business groups have stymied the growth of high-speed rail systems throughout America. There is an organized international movement that is preventing the exporting of genetically modified foods from the United States to Europe and elsewhere.

In earlier pages, we've seen that the emerging Superlongevity Revolution and its enabling technologies have not escaped the notice of a broad range of government, religious, and environmental groups. The opposition that is voiced usually falls into a few distinct categories. There are those who for whatever religious, philosophical, economic or environmental reasons categorically oppose radical life extension as well as the enhancement of the human being, what I referred to as the ultra-human phenomenon. Then there are those who seemingly have no problem with superlongevity, but might find morally objectionable or even repugnant some of the methods used to eradicate disease and increase life expectancy, such as embryonic stem cell research or human cloning.

In this chapter we will look at whether such opposition might prevent or postpone the day when superlongevity and even near-immortality become reality.

COULD SUPERLONGEVITY BE LEGISLATED OUT OF EXISTENCE?

Members of the pro-superlongevity group are always amazed that some people adamantly oppose any radical extension of the human life span. However, their amazement quickly turns to anxiety when they discover that many of these critics are in positions of power that enable them to influence legislation that severely limits research and implementation of new technologies that are key to the Superlongevity Revolution.

The President's Council on Bioethics is one of those powerful groups that supporters of superlongevity fear could sabotage efforts to radically extend the human life span. In 2001, President Bush created the Council to provide an "adequate moral and ethical lens through which to view particular developments in their proper scope and depth." Part of its stated mission is, "Advising the President on ethical issues related to advances in biomedical science and technology." The Council was to deal with the ethics of two technologies that were quickly maturing, stem cell science and cloning. However, the Council was empowered to deal with the full spectrum of biotechnological output.

Many proponents of superlongevity were already hostile to the Council because of the context in which it was created. In August 2001, under pressure from members of Congress and religious groups, President Bush stated that he would severely restrict Federal funding for embryonic stem cell research to a few dozen lines of such stem cells in existence at that date. (Many of the approved lines later proved to be contaminated, and some contained genetic mutations, making them unsuitable for research.) President Bush announced in the same speech that he would create a President's Council "to monitor stem cell research" and perform other activities.[173]

The Council has come under suspicion mainly because of the statements and ideological background of some members. Of all the members of the Council, however, Leon Kass, the first chairman of the Council who guided the production and overall direction of a major report on the ethics of biotechnology, and Francis Fukuyama, author of the anti-biotech screed *Our Posthuman Future: Consequences of the Biotechnology Revolution*, have been particularly scrutinized.

In the ensuing years Bush used this Council as a source of guidance on the development of his administration's overall scientific policy regarding biotechnology and stem cell science. The pronouncements, findings, and conclusions emerging from this Council could influence and shape legislation and Presidential executive orders emitted from the Bush White House.

Given the importance of these matters, it is not surprising that the Council membership that was finally assembled read like a veritable "who's who" of the scientific, legal and academic fields. Among this body there are few intellectual lightweights. The group's Chair Leon Kass is a professor at University of Chicago and a leading expert in bioethics. Many of Kass's books deal with issues such as the "perfecting of the human being" and the ethics of cloning. Francis Fukuyama is a Professor of International Political Economy at Johns Hopkins University. He also wrote the famous book *The End of History and the Last Man*.

On the Council were also Charles Krauthammer, noted syndicated columnist and medical doctor, as well as William F. May, Ph.D. from the Department of Religious Studies, University of Virginia. Other ethicists included Gilbert C. Meilaender, Professor of Christian Ethics at Valparaiso University Rebecca S. Dresser, J.D., M.S. and Daniel Noyes, the Kirby Professor of Law and Professor of Ethics in Medicine at Washington University, St. Louis. The sciences were also well represented by among others Elizabeth H. Blackburn, Ph.D., a professor in the Department of Biochemistry and Biophysics at the University of California at San Francisco and Donald W. Seldin Distinguished Chairperson in Internal Medicine at the University of Texas Southwestern Medical School.

Now let's look at the positives of the major report produced by this group. *Beyond Therapy: Biotechnology And The Pursuit Of Happiness*, is a well-researched and thoughtful work which covers the full gamut of issues that new biotechnologies present to our society. The report also provides a thorough review of the state of scientific achievement in the area of life span extension and human enhancement.

The report is broken into six major sections. The first section, "Biotechnology And The Pursuit Of Happiness," discusses a range of philosophical issues, such as the role of biotechnology in the fulfillment of our "Dreams of Perfection and Happiness," and also "The Primacy of Human Aspirations."

Then the report tackles the germane issues in biotechnology. The second section, "Better Children," deals with the issue we encountered earlier, designer children. It deals with the technical aspects and ethical considerations of prenatal diagnosis and screening, genetic engineering of desired traits, and selecting embryos for desired traits. The report considers how such technologies would affect equality, families and society. The Council members seem concerned about what types of traits people will select for if given powers to genetically engineer their offspring. The Council looked at issues related to using psychotropic drugs and stimulants to modify the behavior of children, and expressed concerns about the criteria used to classify children as Attention Deficit Disorder (ADD).

The next section, "Superior Performance," deals with various performance enhancing drugs such as steroids and human growth hormone. The Council puzzled over such issues as "superior performance" and why we demand physical perfection in our athletes. In this section the members asked questions about the meaning of competition and the fairness of utilizing body enhancement drugs.

The fourth section is the one attracting the most attention and criticism from the superlongevity lobby. It is entitled "Ageless Bodies," and deals with the issue of superlongevity and immortality. It describes the various methods and scientific technology for possibly achieving these lofty goals, including caloric restriction, genetic manipulations, prevention of oxidative damage, and telomere research.

In this chapter's conclusion, the Council expresses strong misgivings about radically extending the human life span. One quote states: "Yet if there is merit in the suggestion that too long a life, with its end out of sight and mind, might diminish its worth, one might wonder whether we have already gone too far in increasing longevity." The report follows this with a mystifying statement: "If so, one might further suggest that we should, if we could, roll back at least some of the increases made in the average human lifespan over the past century." The report then poses the question of whether there is an "optimal human lifespan and an ideal contour of a human life?"

Let us turn to criticisms. Although the report immediately states that no one on the commission wishes for the human life span to be shortened or that anything be done to prevent the achievement of superlongevity, the report's writers reintroduce the "problem" of enhanced life spans a few pages later. If we pursue "indefinite prolongation and ageless bodies for ourselves" the Council on Bioethics asks, "Will we improve the parts and heighten the present, but only at the cost of losing the coherence of an ordered and integrated whole?"

At points the report seems to be suggesting that the current life span is somehow more "human" than the very long lives science might bequeath to the human race. The Council poses the question: "Might we be cheating ourselves by departing from the contour and constraint of natural life (our frailty and finitude), which serve as a lens for a larger vision that might give all of life coherence and sustaining significance?"

In *Seizing The Future*, I asserted that opponents of superlongevity would argue that "all things have a natural, predetermined span of existence that humanity will violate by tampering with rudimentary processes such as cellular and atomic behavior." Reading Council statements revealing their fears that in extending life we might lose "the coherence of an ordered and integrated whole," I experienced, as Yogi Berra would say, "déjà vu all over again."[174]

While no one is suggesting that drugs and biotechnology will solve all human dilemmas, the Council seems to go a step further in its skepticism about human enhancement. It discusses the risk of attacking human limitation altogether, and warns against "seeking to produce a more-than-human being, one not only without illnesses, but also without foibles, fatigue, failures, or foolishness."

Very often in the report, regardless of the accolades bestowed upon science and scientists, the council uses terms like "a dangerous utopianism" and "dangerous temptations" when describing the biotechnological revolution. (The words "danger," "endanger" and "dangerous" appear fifty-one times in the 300 page report).[175]

Heightening suspicion of the intent and purpose of the President's Council on Bioethics was what seemed to be the mysterious reshuffling of the Council's membership. In March 2004, the White House removed from the ethics panel Elizabeth Blackburn, the University of California at San Francisco a professor of biochemistry, and William May the former bioethics professor at Southern Methodist University. Curiously, both had been outspoken supporters of embryonic stem-cell research, believing that such research could lead to valuable therapies for many diseases. The three new members replacing Blackburn and May had expressed opposition to embryonic stem-cell research, putting them in ideological harmony with the remaining members of the panel.

Many cried "foul" when this shift hit the news. Laurie Zoloth, director of bioethics at the center for genetic medicine at Northwestern University in Chicago, Illinois, and board member of the International Society for Stem Cell Research, was livid. "Elizabeth Blackburn is one of the most respected senior scientists who have looked carefully at this issue," Zoloth said, "and it would seem to be prudent to replace her with somebody who has that level of skill and experience in science," implying that the three people who replaced her did not have the same level of scientific knowledge. Bernie Siegel, director of the Genetics Policy Institute, was more blunt, stating that Blackburn "had the gumption to speak her mind," referring to her statement endorsing therapeutic cloning research in the Council's earlier report "Human Cloning and Human Dignity'."[176]

One can be vehemently opposed to embryonic stem cell research and at the same time be solidly in the pro-superlongevity and pro-immortality camp. In fact, there is growing evidence that adult stem cells will prove a valuable tool in the battle against a host of diseases, including Alzheimer's. President Bush says he enthusiastically supports science's quest for cures using adult stem cells. However, members of the "superlongevity lobby," many of whom already perceive Bush and his Council as inherently hostile to human life extension, had their perceptions reinforced when the President fired Council members who publicly called for more embryonic stem cell research.

Statements made by Leon Kass and other members of the Council after the report was published, also suggested that these people, who have the attention of the President, have grave misgivings regarding the entire human enhancement enterprise.

Leon Kass, who was the chairman of the Council from 2002 to 2005, and oversaw the publication of the 2003 report *Beyond Therapy*, has become a lightning rod for the suspicion that somehow superlongevity might be slowed by executive action or legislation. In 2004, Kass discussed his views on human life extension and other matters on SAGE Crossroads, a web-based video program that bills itself as "the premier online forum for emerging issues of human aging." The interview allowed visitors to watch, listen and interact with prominent experts in the field of aging via chat and e-mail technologies. The program's interviewer was Morton Kondracke, well-known American journalist and TV news personality regularly appearing on *The Beltway Boys* and *The McLaughlin Report*. He is also the editor of Capitol Hill's *Roll Call*.

During the interview, Dr. Kass made several comments which seemed to critics to be arguments against longer, healthier lives. One of his comments were viewed by many to suggest that having a limited life span helps us appreciate the time we have on this planet. "Time is a gift," Kass asserted. "But the perception of endless time or of time without bound in fact has the possibility of undermining the degree to which we take time seriously and make it count." This type of thinking has been with us since the beginning of, well, time. However, it is usually used to help people cope with the idea and reality of human mortality—the fact that we all will die gives urgency to all our activities. A common manifestation is the aphorism that was turned into a recent country music song, Tim McGraw's "Live Like You Were Dying." However, when this type of thinking is viewed more closely, to be justifying not pursuing the dream of superlongevity, red flags start to be raised.

Kass's defense of mortality continues. In *The Iliad* and *The Odyssey*, he says, human beings were defined as mortals. The immortals, Zeus and the other gods, in spite of their agelessness and their beauty, lived shallow and frivolous lives. "Precisely because they know that their time is limited, and that they go around only once," Dr. Kass, states, mortal humans "are inclined to make time matter and to aspire to something great for them." This leads Kass to ask "is there some connection between the limits that we face and the desire for greatness that comes from recognition that we are only here for a short time?" He suggests that if we extend the human life span so far that no one can realistically conceive of his or her own death, "we are not inclined to build cathedrals or write the B Minor Mass, or write Shakespeare's sonnets and things of that sort."

Kass warned that in our quest for immortality, "You might discover only too late that what you wanted was not exactly what you really needed or desired. What you wished for is not really what you wanted." Here he quotes as "proof" the Midas myth, the king famous for the deadly "Midas touch," which turned everything he came in contact with into gold. Later in the interview he labels those desiring superlongevity "utopians" that might turn our society into one like Huxley portrayed in his nightmarish *Brave New World*. Kass gives no reason why a society in which we eliminate disease and live to 140 years of ages in perfect health would thus become one in which there would be "No science. No art. No self- governance. No friendship. No love. No family."

I feel the contrary is true. Throughout this book, I have asserted my contention that the citizens of the *Ageless Nation* would be compelled to create a better world, because they will have to live in the future they are helping build. But Kass believes the opposite: "It is an exaggeration, but at least raises the question of whether those limits, which come with sorrow, whether those limits are somehow necessary for all the great human things."

At this point Kondracke directly asked Kass whether such views would incline him to try to influence the government to take a "go-slow" approach to funding anti-aging research programs. "You would let it go forward or you would encourage it?" the moderator asked. "You would increase funding for it? What would you do as to aging research?"

Kass, a self-described conservative, or rather neo-con, seemed to have problems explicitly stating that he favors government regulation on human behavior. Eventually he stated that he does favor "possibly government regulatory activities" in areas such as genetic engineering of children and other unspecified areas that "violate certain normal human taboos and boundaries." However, while Kass asserts that he believes in doing what we can to prevent degenerative disease, he seems to be dead-set against supporting research that extends the human life span:

"And we might try to hope to separate those interventions that deal with the degenerations that are not necessarily life prolonging. I mean, if one could do something about Alzheimer's, if one could do something about chronic arthritis, if one could do something about general muscular weakness and not, somehow, increase the life expectancy to 150 years, I would be delighted."

While many share this fear of removing the limits to human longevity, Kass held a position of authority and power to shape legislation in the field of bioethics and biotechnology, as does the President's Council on Bioethics as a whole. [177]

Another member of the Council has expressed a variety of fears and apprehensions about not only superlongevity but the entire "ultra-human" phenomenon. Francis Fukuyama articulated such fears in a roundtable discussion chaired by the editors of *Foreign Policy* magazine. The editors asked eight prominent policy intellectuals to answer the question: "What ideas, if embraced, would pose the greatest threat to the welfare of humanity?"

Fukuyama criticized the idea that we should "liberate the human race from its biological constraints." Why would Fukuyama find that so dangerous? For one thing, there is the problem of "equality" or the lack thereof if the ultra-human phenomenon takes hold. He worries that "If we start transforming ourselves into something superior, what rights will these enhanced creatures claim, and what rights will they possess when compared to those left behind?" In other words, we must all remain equally mediocre, lest the less-gifted, or the "less-transformed," are seen as, well, less-gifted. However, if smart-pills and other mental-enhancers are available to all, how does that threaten anyone? As futurist Ron Bailey, author of *Liberation Biology*, states: "Later in this century, when safe genetic engineering becomes possible, it will enable parents to give their children beneficial genes for improved health and intelligence that other children already get naturally." [178]

As we have seen over the last several decades, societies that strive for universal equality are in constant danger of achieving universal mediocrity. Does it not make sense that the more intelligent and physically adroit the citizens of a society are, the better the society will function?

Fukuyama suggests that we show some humility and not strive to expand ourselves beyond our human limits. "The environmental movement has taught us humility and respect for the integrity of nonhuman nature," he says, advising us that "we need a similar humility concerning our human nature." Fukuyama warns that if we do not develop this sense of humility, those who want to develop the ultra-human will "deface humanity with their genetic bulldozers and psychotropic shopping malls." [179]

The positions Fukuyama and Kass have taken while at the helm of shaping United States policy toward bioscience, seem to have caused some members of the "superlongevity lobby" to panic regarding the future of anti-aging funding in the United States. They appear to be taking little solace from the fact that in 2005, Edmund D. Pellegrino, M.D., Professor Emeritus of Medicine and Medical Ethics at the Center for Clinical Medical Ethics at Georgetown University Medical Center replaced Kass as new Council chairperson.

Pellegrino is quite clear about his attitude regarding the use of medicine to "enhance" the human condition. In an essay he wrote for the Center for Bioethics and Human Dignity, Pellegrino states his view that the role of medicine as "treating the sick." Physicians who use medicine for uses such as "enhancement of some bodily or mental trait, or some state of affairs they wish to perfect" are portrayed as having crossed some invisible "divide between treatment and enhancement." Moreover, Dr. Pellegrino seems uncomfortable with "the use of biotechnology to redesign human nature and thus to enhance the species in the future," and speaks disparagingly of "the adrenalin surge of seeing how far the human body and mind can be pushed."

Pellegrino admits that it will be difficult for physicians, regulatory agencies, and other authority figures to restrict the use of medicine and biotechnology in our search for human enhancement and superlongevity, especially because, "Satisfaction of personal desires, freedom of choice, and 'quality life' have, for many, become entitlements in a democratic society." However, many in the pro-longevity community feel that Pellegrino will use his powerful position as Council on Bioethics head to retard the research into and practical application of human enhancement science.[180]

One pro-superlongevity web-based organization, *The Longevity Meme*, is campaigning for the out-and-out abolition of the Council on Bioethics. It describes the Council as a "body expressly designed to produce the anti-research answers that a small set of politicians want to hear, irrespective of the science, the costs, the benefits...Stacked with members who are strongly opposed.....to embryonic stem cell research and therapeutic cloning, the Council has become a conduit for its members' and chair's 'anti-life-extension views'." The group encourages the public to write the President and all other elected officials and demand that the Council be shut down. The organization provides web links and instructions for reaching all relevant parties in the decision making process.

This campaign, which started in 2004, has yet to accomplish its goal. The Council continues to publish reports and publicize its view on science, and still has a profound impact on legislation.

On July 19, 2006, President Bush officially vetoed a bill supported by both houses of Congress called the "Stem Cell Research Enhancement Act of 2005," an attempt by Congress to get Bush to modify his blanket 2001 ban on Federal funding for embryonic stem cell research. The bill would have cleared such funding with very strict restriction. For instance, the stem cells would have to be "derived from human embryos that have been donated from in vitro fertilization clinics, were created for the purposes of fertility treatment, and were in excess of the clinical need of the individuals seeking such treatment." In other words, Federal financing would still be restricted to stem cell lines derived from embryos created for in vitro fertilization, which were slated to be discarded.[181]

President Bush said that he vetoed the bill because "This bill would support the taking of innocent human life in the hope of finding medical benefits for others." He felt that the bill crossed a "moral boundary that our decent society needs to respect."

Scientists were never prohibited by law from doing experiments with embryonic stem cells. However, they could not get Federal funding for such research, and thus had to use stem cell lines that had been derived either in other countries or with private funding in the United States. Bush's supporters point out that under his presidency the National Institutes of Health, while spending only thirty-eight million dollars in 2006 for human embryonic stem cell research, spent $571 million on other forms of stem cell research. Peer-reviewed scientific publications have documented the fact that seventy-two different diseases and conditions have been successfully treated via adult stem cells. Also, significant results have been produced in animal research using adult and cord-blood stem cells applied to diabetes, spinal-cord injuries, and Parkinson's disease.

Explaining his veto, President Bush emphasized the efficacy of adult stem cells by having on stage with him four people who were currently being successfully treated with therapies derived from adult stem cells.

Politics can and will continue to have a momentous impact on the shape and direction of scientific research. And the people who sit in positions of "expert power" can buttress any position, pro or con and thereby shape legislation and executive decisions.

During the early days of the Bill Clinton regime, the promoters of Hillary Clinton's health care system, popularly labeled "Hillarycare," voiced concern that "very old people" might endanger the viability of our health care systems and other social programs. On more than one occasion I heard members of her panel use terms like the "appropriate" or "optimal" human life span. I always wondered what age they had in minds as "appropriate." Eighty-five? Ninety? And I was never sure how the panel would deal with those who violated the "optimal maximum age" law? Would the government cut off all social benefits, including access to Medicare?

While a Presidential-level body, as well as the government itself, may adopt stances antagonistic to goals such as the achievement of superlongevity and the enhancement of the human race, these bodies can delay but not prevent progress in these areas.

In my earlier books *Seizing The Future* and *The Future Factor*, I described the wide spectrum of groups and people – governments, environmentalist organizations and even the UK's Prince Charles – who actively campaigned against a panoply of scientific and technological breakthroughs critical to human progress, such as genetically modified crops, nuclear power and cloning. Yet most of these technologies are being developed and utilized in various parts of the world.

In fact, it is becoming ever more difficult to squelch the development and proliferation of technologies, including those that enhance human beings and extend lives. News of novel technological breakthroughs rapidly spreads quickly across the globe via satellite television and the internet. These same media inform the public about the benefits of the technology, and where they can obtain it. Americans will travel to other countries to avail themselves of the benefits of stem cell and other therapies possibly banned in the United States in order to cure serious illnesses.

Information about denied funding on new technologies also spreads the internationalization of the news. For instance, using new embryonic stem cell lines, biologists in some countries have no such restrictions. The knowledge necessary to someday use such stem cell research to cure a host of diseases is readily available to scientists in all countries. Hence, the international research effort continues even if some of its elements are banned in particular regions and countries.

The pro-superlongevity groups and organizations seem to overlook their own power to shape public opinion on the subjects of human enhancement and the radically extended life span. In the 1990s there were few groups of individuals taking hard line pro-immortality and pro-enhancement positions in the media or in print. Now dozens of small groups have sprung up, calling themselves everything from "transhumanists" to "immortalists." They are seeking out media outlets and newspaper journalists to get their views heard. These groups simply refuse to go away and concede defeat to bioethics councils, governmental or private, that would squelch the human drive to perfection and live healthy, vibrant lives for as long as possible.

One problem I feel these champions of superlongevity will encounter is the difficulty of distinguishing friend from foe—they will be surprised at who turns out to be their most vocal critics. In the process some will learn painful lessons about the growing "battle for the future." In *The Future Factor* and elsewhere I have warned that ultimately those campaigning for what I labeled "hyperprogress" would discover themselves to be at fundamental odds with the "deep ecologist" wing of the environment movement. This antagonism might surprise some transhumanists. After all, aren't we all trying to improve the planet as we improve the species?

I believe they will discover that deep ecologists do no want growing population of eternally youthful immortals. In fact, zero-population growth has become the mantra of most environmentalist groups. The achievement of a true Superlongevity Revolution, even if people severely restrict their childbearing, is bound to lead to a growth of the total number of people on the planet. From the deep ecologist point of view, every additional person further drains the scarce and limited resources of "mother earth." However, in some corners of the blogosphere the deep ecologist view point is already being questioned. On the Betterhumans.com website, one blogger wrote an article entitled "Hey, Deep Ecologists: The Planet Is Not Your Nature Preserve," criticizing the anti-progress and anti-human tendencies of radical environmentalists.

In fact, those favoring superlongevity may find friends in some unlikely places. One organization is FasterCures: the Center for Accelerating Medical Solutions. The founder is one-time corporate bad guy and now acclaimed philanthropist Michael Milken, who lists among his other initiatives the

Prostate Cancer Foundation, the Milken Family Foundation and the Milken Institute, an economic think tank. FasterCures attempts to "accelerate the process of discovery and clinical development of new therapies for the treatment of deadly and debilitating diseases." They work with researchers, governments, foundations, and other groups to try to get new drugs on the market and new therapies of all types to the patients who need them. The foundation's "acceleration agenda" strives to increase patient participation in clinical trials, improve the approval process for new drugs, promote a medical records and biospecimen database for researchers, as well as promote the translation of basic research findings into therapeutic breakthroughs. [182]

All of the energy devoted to hastening the progress of the Superlongevity Revolution is laudable. However, my feeling is that regardless of the machinations of governments and the efforts of social movements and philanthropists to sway the course of history, the public will ultimately determine the future of the Superlongevity Revolution. The question is whether the people themselves really want to live exceedingly long lives.

HOW WILL THE PUBLIC REACT TO THE SUPERLONGEVITY REVOLUTION?

Gauging public reaction to the superlongevity concept, I have described in this book is problematic, since many of the questions and issues raised by living to 140 years of age are rarely probed in conventional opinion polls. However, several recent polls and my own as well as others' past research do give us glimpses of how the public views the aging process.

Over the years at seminars, conferences, training sessions, during media appearances, and with my own students I have had the opportunity to observe the public's reaction to the concept of superlongevity. In the process I have discovered some interesting information about the conditions which might influence people's attitude toward superlongevity.

I begin my probe by asking my audiences whether they would desire to live to 150 years of age. Many people initially respond with a great deal of apprehension—they envision themselves hobbling along at this great age, suffering from every malady known to humankind, but somehow magically, and sadistically I might add, kept alive by science.

Then I phrase the question with another condition. I ask the audience how they would feel about living to 150 years old, in a healthy and vibrant body of a twenty-five or thirty year old. Suddenly, most members of the audience change their tune entirely. If they could live to that great age with no loss of energy, with no fear of cancer, Alzheimer's disease, or diabetes, with the ability to earn a living and enjoy travel and leisure with their families, they are all for superlongevity.

Conventional polling agencies have not surveyed the general population on the same issues. However, the public is regularly grilled by pollsters about attitudes toward the aging process, retirement, and related issues. Such polls show that average individuals give a great deal of thought to their own life prospects as they proceed through the latter parts of the life cycle. From their responses to several polls, which shed light on public perspectives on aging and age-related issues, we can at least begin to judge how the public will react to an ever expanding life span, what I have labeled superlongevity.

In early 2006, *Parade Magazine* and Research!America, the nonprofit organization that promotes medical research, polled a cross-section of 1,000 Americans on their attitudes about aging and longevity, and published articles describing and analyzing the concerns of Americans regarding aging and its effects on health and their lives in general. In 2006 USA Today and ABC News teamed up to quiz the United States public about their views on various issues related to the aging process. Earlier, in 2001, the Alliance for Aging Research commissioned a national opinion survey of 1,000 adults which provided a snapshot of attitudes toward aging and aging research in America. In June 2001, a web-based version of that same survey was launched online, and subscribers to their webzine were invited via email to participate. In 2005, the Nottingham University Business School's Centre for Risk & Insurance Studies conducted a public opinion survey of 3,966 adults aged over sixteen years across Great Britain dealing with various aspects of public perceptions of mortality and life expectancy.[183]

Desired and Expected Life Spans

Polls indicate that the public generally endorses the idea of living long and healthy lives. In the Alliance for Aging Research two out of three Americans (63 percent) polled want to live to one hundred. Parade/Research!America asked people, "If you had your choice, how long would you like to live? That is, until what age?" A full one quarter of the population wants to live past ninety-five, another 32 percent wants to live past eighty-five, and most of the others want to continue on into their late seventies or eighties. On average people desired to live to the ripe old age of eighty-eight. (One curious outcome was the not-insignificant percentage, 14 percent, that had no idea how long they wanted to live. I would guess that these folks simply have not pondered the question, assuming they had little control over the answer.)

The respondents' expectations about how long they will live are a bit lower than they would like. When asked "If you had to guess, how long do you think you will live? That is, until what age?" only 10 percent expected to live to ninety-five or greater, as opposed to the considerably larger 26 percent that want to live that long. About the same percent expect to live past eighty-five, and we have about the same number of respondents claiming that have little idea how long they will live. Respondents in the survey expected on average to live about eighty-two years old, at least six fewer years than they hoped. Ironically, the eighty-two age number is only slightly higher than the actual average life expectancy age as measured by the United States census, in the high seventies.

I see in these numbers a solid endorsement by the public of the concept of superlongevity. I also believe that respondents would choose to live to much greater ages if they were certain that they would live to those ages in a vibrant healthy state with few infirmities that would limit their professional and personal activities.

Health Concerns

One USATODAY poll asked the respondents "How convinced are you about the following issues as you get older? Is that something that worries you a great deal, somewhat, not so much, or not at all?"

The poll found that 92 percent of respondents are at least somewhat concerned about one or more of ten items listed in the survey. As measured in this poll, three out of four people said they are most concerned about losing their health. About the same number of people were very or somewhat concerned about the ability to take care of themselves and "losing mental abilities" as they aged, reflecting further insecurity about the impact of aging on physical and intellectual capacity.

Response to one item on the survey demonstrates the critical importance people place on the automobile in our society. A solid 60 percent of the respondents feared losing the capacity to drive a car as they grew older, a clear indication that they associate the ability to drive with physical independence and strength. We live in a society in which it is difficult to function without regular access to dependable transportation, which in most people's eyes is the automobile first and foremost.

More than half the respondents were somewhat worried about "running out of money," being a burden on their families, and winding up in a nursing home as they grew older.

For all the media hype about how important image and appearance are in our society, it is interesting to note that personal vanity has little role to play in the list of concerns. Only 22 percent of those polled were even somewhat concerned about losing their looks as they aged, especially when placed within the context of health and personal independence issues.

Ironically, the survey found that people over age 65 are less worried than younger people about the aging process. An average of results for the ten items listed found 45 percent of older people expressing concern, compared with 57 percent of those under sixty-five. This finding could be explained by the simple fact that for the most part our fears about aging are largely overblown, probably fueled not by reality but by media images of infirmity and illness among the aged.

However, a *Parade* poll found that most people believe that individuals can control to a point the aging process through personal action. And a clear 83 percent claim that they are taking action to stay healthy as they age, though such actions vary. More than half of Americans (56 percent) engage in physical activity to stay healthy as they grow older, while 26 percent put at the top of their list "watching what they eat."

Responses indicate that Americans realize, however, that there is just so much we as individuals can do to forestall aging. Science must also contribute to the Superlongevity Revolution.

Support for Research

The public overwhelmingly supports research that will bring us better health in older years. Importantly, it splits from the views expressed by many members of the Bioethics Committee on several issues related to the use of medical research to extend life.

Parade/Research America poll asked the public, "How important do you think it is to invest in research to prevent, treat and cure diseases and disabilities that primarily affect older Americans." A whopping 65 percent said "very important" and most of the rest answered "somewhat important." A miniscule 3 percent claimed that spending money on age-related diseases was not a high-priority item.

The Alliance for Aging Research survey uncovered a certain sense of urgency about accelerating medical research. Clearly two-thirds of the respondents believe that unless we find cures for major diseases affecting people in old age, the United States will not have enough hospitals, doctors, and equipment to care for the aging baby boom generation. The Parade/Research America poll revealed that Americans feel that this will be money well spent.

The question of who should foot the bill for all this research is a matter of contention. To the Parade survey question, "Would you be willing to pay $1 per week in taxes if you were certain that the money would be spent on research to prevent, treat and cure diseases and disabilities that primarily affect older Americans, or not?" 64 percent responded no, 31 percent said yes. The Alliance for Aging Research found that 80 percent of their respondents wanted the Federal government to increase its level of support for anti-aging scientific research.

The public expects a big payoff for all this investment in medical research. When asked whether they think certain medical breakthroughs will occur within the next twenty years, 65 percent responded that they thought we would have a cure for diabetes, and a clear majority expected there to be cures for heart disease, Alzheimer's disease and Parkinson's disease. Surprisingly, almost half, 48 percent, expected there to be a cure for cancer and AIDS by 2026.

The Alliance for Aging Research poll indicated that people would prefer as little interference from government as possible in the scientific research process. 61 percent of respondents believe that scientists should be free to explore new areas of medical research with a minimum of federal regulation. About the same percent are in favor of government-supported embryonic stem cell research, putting them at odds with the Bush administration, the Presidential Council on Bioethics, and prominent religious leaders.

One of the more important findings for public adaptation to the Superlongevity Revolution comes from the Parade/Research American survey. To the question "How valuable do you think it is for scientists to do research specifically designed to lengthen life?" 42 percent of the respondents answered "very important" and 43 percent answered "somewhat important," with 14 percent stating "not important."

True, something short of one half of the population surveyed would enthusiastically support superlongevity-focused research, a figure which is significantly below the 65 percent or so that would unabashedly spend money for disease-prevention. The good news is that even tepid support for spending on life extension research in and of itself implies an endorsement of the concept, and certainly the public does not oppose using medical technology for purposes that are, to quote the Council on Bioethics, "Beyond Therapy."

What Does "Being Young" Mean Anyway

The Parade/Research!America poll asked very interesting questions that explored the meaning of concepts like "young" and "old." They asked the respondents "What one thing, more than any other, makes you think of a person as being 'young'?" Fifty percent of all respondents said that the one characteristic that differentiated "young" from "old" is *active/energetic/busy*. *Appearance* was a far distance second, named by only 13 percent, about the same number who mentioned a completely non-physical attribute, *positive attitude*. Only 3 percent of the entire sample said that they would consider a person "old" based on his physical age alone.

The surveyors then asked the question from a slightly different point of view. What one thing, more than any other, makes you think of a person as being "old"? Forty-five percent said that a person's physical and mental limitations would most influence their perception that that person is old. Appearance was mentioned by about one out of ten respondents. Again, the actual age of the person seems not an important factor in shaping others' view of them as "old."

At this time, we have little data measuring people's attitudes regarding the ultra-human phenomenon, the use of medical technologies to enhance human physical performance and mental skills. However, we can infer from the above responses that if we were able to use pharmaceuticals and other technologies to increase a senior's activity and energy levels to those of a younger person, friends and family would consider this person young, even if he or she were eighty or ninety years old. If science does unlock the secrets of true physical rejuvenation, the very concept of "old" would eventually disappear from the culture completely.

What can we deduce from the results of these studies about the receptivity of the public to the idea of living a very long life? For one thing, people have no problem with getting chronologically older. However, they are anxious about getting "old," which they define by a host of problems and limitations they associate with aging.

I have found in my own research that one of the reasons people state they would not want to live to extended ages is that they believe to do so would cause them to be alive in an "impaired state" of one form or another. We can surmise, however, that given the ability to avoid the rash of infirmities associated with aging, most people would have few qualms about dramatically extending their life spans.

Importantly, the public sees a clear connection between scientific research and the achievement of a healthy superlongevity. They support the idea that government, industry, and the public must do what it has to in order to not only cure disease but also extend the human life span. And they believe there should be limits on just how far federal agencies should go in limiting regulation of the scientific research process.

PHYSICIAN-ASSISTED SUICIDE IN AN AGE OF ETERNAL LIFE

One of the areas we have looked at is the role of government as a player in the Superlongevity Revolution. We have asked the whether the government is a help or hindrance to the progress of the achievement of the radically extended life span. In the United States the debate largely has centered on the ways and means of accomplishing this goal, and the speed at which we should enter the next stage of the Superlongevity Revolution.

In general, the focus of the debate is on life and how to improve it. It is about positive results by the best means.

There are, however, some developments that seem to be running in a direction counter to our movement into the Superlongevity Era. The most flagrant violation of the emerging zeitgeist of this new age is the growing practice of physician-assisted suicide in Scandinavian countries and one U.S. state, Oregon. I believe these programs will find themselves in the center of the debate over superlongevity and eventually near-immortality.

One of the major anomalies in the current social climate is that the clarion call for the legalization of doctor-assisted suicide is occurring just as modern medicine is enabling us to cure more and more diseases and dramatically extend life.

Direct euthanasia, involving a clinician giving a lethal drug by injection when the patient is not capable of doing so, is legal only in Belgium, Colombia, the Netherlands, Japan and Oregon. In the United States, the Oregon law was tested at the Supreme Court level. While some thought the Court decision somehow "legalized" euthanasia, the judges ruled narrowly on the right of the Federal Government to intrude on certain state medical practices.

In 2006 California some legislators were hoping it would become the second state to legalize physician-assisted suicide. The bill, which would have put into effect a program patterned after Oregon's "Death with Dignity" law, was defeated in committee by one vote. The State Senator who cast the deciding vote, Senate Judiciary Committee chairperson Democrat Joseph Dunn, said that his "nay" vote came as a result of his concern that financial concerns by patients and the health care industry could drive legalized physician assisted suicide in the future. He seemed to be suggesting that people would be led to their decision to commit suicide by pressure coming from cost-conscious and cost-cutting health insurance providers, or perhaps from family members not wanting to deal with the emotional and financial burden associated with caring for a physically-impaired loved one.

Almost the same week in mid-2006 that the California bill was killed, the doctors at the British Medical Association conference held in Belfast voted, by a 65 percent to 35 percent margin, to fight any attempts to legalize euthanasia and physician-assisted dying. By this vote they significantly changed their stance from only a year before, when they voted to adopt a neutral position, neither opposing nor supporting assisted dying. What changed was a campaign by anti-euthanasia grass-roots doctors to get the issue debated again and clearly voted down. The reasons were quite clear. According to Dr. Peter Saunders, there is growing awareness among doctors that a bill permitting euthanasia would put pressure on vulnerable patients to "request an early death because of the financial and emotional burden they feel it puts on other people." A 1994 House of Lords Select Committee Report on euthanasia echoed similar sentiments, stating that it would be "virtually impossible to ensure that all acts of euthanasia were truly voluntary and that any liberalization of the law in the UK could not be abused." [184]

The experience of the Netherlands doctor-assisted euthanasia program gives second thoughts on whether such fears are ungrounded. It is very likely that some disturbing aspects of the Dutch physician-assisted program prompted Joseph Dunn and the U.K doctors to experience fearful visions of patient abuse if such a program was enacted in the United States and the United Kingdom.

The Netherlands was one of the first countries to legalize euthanasia. The Dutch program, like Belgium's, permits a physician to end a patient's life, provided that the patient requests it, that he or she is mentally sound at the time and that a second medical professional confirms the terminal diagnosis.

Examining how such programs truly operate brings up further questions. According to the only complete report on euthanasia practices from the Dutch government, of the 130,000 Dutch citizens who died in 1990, some 11,800 were helped to die by their doctors. While some of these deaths would fall into the classic "die with dignity" model, the government reports that over half of that 11,800 were killed by their doctors without their consent.

This ruthless attitude toward the old and infirm has not gone unnoticed by some of its potential victims. Many old people now fear Dutch hospitals. A recent survey revealed that more than 10 percent of senior citizens polled feared being killed by their doctors without their consent. According to news reports one Dutch senior-citizens group printed up wallet cards that tell doctors that cardholders oppose euthanasia.

How did such a medical culture develop? As the cost of socialized medicine in the Netherlands grew, doctors were lectured at conferences and training programs about the climbing cost of care. Many hospitals began posting signs reminding doctors (and patients, we can assume) how much old-age treatments cost taxpayers. The result was a growing social pressure from doctors and others, says Arno Heltzel, a spokesman for the Catholic Union of the Elderly, the largest Dutch senior-citizen group. He describes a ghastly relationship developing between the elderly and their doctors, hospitals and even friends. "Old people have to excuse themselves for living. When they say that all of their friends are dead, people say `maybe it is time for you to go too' rather than `you need to find new friends'." In the Netherlands, polls have found that as many as 92 percent support euthanasia.[185]

As Dutch euthanasia became more commonplace, so did the fulfillment of some of the more horrific predictions about its consequences. We now have evidence that some of the terminally ill are, or feel pressured to die just a little bit sooner so that their hospital beds might be freed up or their organs made more readily available for transplant. [186]

Since the implementation of legalized physician-assisted suicide programs in the Netherlands, the target population has expanded dramatically to include disabled infants. Disbelief greeted the British medical journal Lancet's 1997 study which claimed that some 8 percent of all infants who die in the Netherlands are killed by their doctors. In 2004, this study's findings were confirmed. Groningen Academic proposed guidelines for mercy killings of terminally ill newborns and made a startling revelation: the hospital has already begun carrying out such procedures, which include administering a lethal dose of sedatives.

The main Dutch doctors' association KNMG has been urging the Health Ministry to create an independent board to review euthanasia cases for terminally ill people "with no free will," including children, the severely mentally retarded and people left in an irreversible coma after an accident. The fact that people have been known to emerge from such comas physically and mentally intact doesn't seem to faze the Dutch physicians. After all, a cost-benefit analysis would probably reveal that it would cost the state too much to keep that person alive in the hope that the individual would someday emerge from that comatose state.

While most countries look at the Dutch program with skepticism, if not out and out distaste, this does not mean that some form of program could not be structured in such a way that the mass of the population would find it ethically bearable. The program pioneered in Switzerland might provide a model for a more palatable form of legalized suicide. The Swiss law on suicide states that although a doctor cannot be directly complicit in a person's suicide, he may provide a lethal dose of drugs to a terminally ill person, as long as the physician is convinced that the patient has no chance of recovery and is mentally and physically capable of making the decision to die. The law's key provision, and its major loophole, is the provision that the patient must administer the drug him- or herself.

So while Swiss law forbids Dutch-style euthanasia, in which a doctor administers the drugs to end a patient's life, it establishes the conditions for legalized suicide by simply taking the doctor out of the direct act of euthanasia.

Switzerland has become a Mecca for those seeking to end their lives. A controversial Zurich-based organization known as Dignitas now serves as a "euthanasia agent," offering assisted suicide to people suffering from incurable conditions. Dignitas rents an apartment in the city where clients self-administer a fatal dose of barbiturates and slowly fade away while listening to their favorite music. Ludwig Minelli, a Swiss lawyer who is the head of a euthanasia group that runs assisted suicide centers says 573 people from all over the world have died at Dignitas centers. Critics of this program refer to the growing number of non-Swiss taking advantage of this program as "death tourists," terminally ill people who come to Zurich to take their own lives. It is rumored that Minelli plans to create a chain of such centers across Europe.

In Switzerland, a group called Exit last year helped 120 patients commit suicide. Now there are questions about how many of these people were really incurably ill; a Basel University study pointed to one elderly man Exit said had terminal lung cancer, but the coroner reported as having suffered from bronchitis.[187]

If euthanasia ever became institutionalized in the United States, doctors would have another powerful tool to coax patients to make the decision to end it all: the legal restrictions on the prescribing of pain medication, especially opiates, even to the severely ill. According to Andrew Lasher, a palliative care physician at California Pacific Medical Center in San Francisco, many of his colleagues believe that physician-assisted suicide is often unnecessary. With proper care from physicians trained specifically to ease pain and bring comfort at this complicated moment, many who may seek to end their lives would actually choose to live. The only reason they are even considering terminating their lives is they wish to avoid a life of unbearable pain.

I believe there are a host of reasons for actively opposing any such euthanasia program, aside from the obvious ethical questions over the sanctity of life and potential abuse by practitioners and health insurers.

Although presented as a "humane practice," physician-assisted suicide ultimately undermines our attempts to cure diseases and improve the human condition. If we can work on cures for the diseases ailing such people, instead of euthanizing them, we will be closer to discovering what works, thereby helping multitudes of people with the same malady. Society cures diseases when confronted with the sheer horror of the impact of the disease on individuals and populations. We discovered the remedies for small pox, polio, and a host of other diseases because these illnesses were a visible plague on society. But euthanasia makes diseases invisible, and as we all know, out of sight, out of mind. We are not just sequestering the ill in hospitals; we are eliminating them from the rolls of the living. By doing so, we minimize the emotional pain our society feels over the impact of these diseases on those afflicted with them.

Our emotional pain viewing the impact of such diseases motivates us to continue searching for a cure. For instance, if we had decided to euthanize everyone who tested positive for HIV in the 1980s, we wouldn't have made advancements to find a cure. Today's various drug cocktails helping AIDS sufferers live long and productive lives would never have been discovered.

I think physician-assisted suicide provides society an easy way out of the dilemma of human disease and death. Our job is not to kill the afflicted. Our duty is to cure them!

A century from now, I feel historians and sociologists will be baffled by one of the great historical conundrums of the modern age. Why, they will ask, was there a proliferation of suicide programs just when we were so close to curing every major disease?

I predict twenty-second century philosophers will be stunned that even the average observer, let alone high-powered policy planners and medical experts, living circa 2010, could not foresee that the medical breakthroughs of the first decade of the twenty-first century would quickly cure every malady known to man, making these "death with dignity" programs superfluous. They will ask why people didn't "connect the dots" back then. Looking back they will wonder because it should have been obvious that stem cell science was going to cure everything from Alzheimer's disease to the crippling effects of spinal cord injury. And soon thereafter biotechnology would essentially eliminate cancer, while nanotechnology and cloning were opening the doors for organ and tissue regeneration. They will also ask why when science was so close to eliminating the very diseases that were making peoples' lives so miserable that they elected to have the state kill them with lethal doses of drugs.

These twenty-second century pundits will no doubt exclaim as they reflect on our era much like Shakespeare did, "What fools these mortals be."

That's why I believe rather than considering how to enact "death with dignity" laws, we should be exerting all our energy on how we can comfortably maintain humans' lives until we find a cure for these diseases.

SUPERLONGEVITY WILL HAPPEN

The obstacles to the emergence of the Superlongevity Revolution do not lie in our scientific acumen or our technological prowess. There is no doubt that our science will eventually bestow upon us a modern Fountain of Youth—that eventuality is closer than we think. No, the impediments to superlongevity, if there be any, will lie not in our science but in our institutions, and perhaps even in ourselves. Culture will be the final arbiter of the success of this venture.

Most ardent supporters of superlongevity, and the achievement of the ultra-human phenomenon, assume that the mass of the public wants to live forever, or to extremely high ages. On one survey only 7 percent asserted that they "wish to be immortal."

Without the inside information on the scientific and medical horizon the public is not able to assess the future of human life from the same perspective or with the same knowledge base as futurists are. One recent survey asked respondents whether they agreed or disagreed with the statement *"Some people say that within the next century, advances in medical research will increase human life expectancy to 120 years."* While 47 percent thought such a feat was possible, the same number thought that extending human life to the 120 year level was an unachievable goal.

As we have seen in this book, the Superlongevity Revolution is a process, not an event. We will have time to adjust—it is not an earth-shattering occurrence as much as a gradual societal shift to longer life spans. We are not asking the public to accept superlongevity as a concept. The public is asked to adjust to a world in which they will enjoy better health, longer lives and a more enhanced physical status, through pharmaceuticals and cellular engineering.

Most current combatants in the "immortality wars" assume that this issue will be settled by some major debate that occurs on national television sometime in the next decade or so. To the contrary, in the end, the Superlongevity Revolution will be a long term process in which we will experiment with not only scientific technologies to extend the lifespan but also new cultural and social institutions and as well as variations of existing ones as we adjust to the ever- expanding life span.

chapter ten

The Prospect of Immortality

In this book, we have come face to face with the implications of living for-ever. Since time immemorial humankind has hoped to discover the means to achieve immortality. 2600 B.C., the Babylonians, in their epic poem "Gilgamesh," voiced their desire to achieve eternal life. During the Crusades, various groups searched in vain for The Holy Grail, supposedly the chalice that Christ drank from at the Last Supper, in the belief that this vessel's mystical powers could bestow immortality on whoever drinks from it or is even in its presence. Schoolchildren know the story of Ponce de Leon's lifelong search for the Fountain of Youth in America.

Could our search for immortality finally be over? Many specialists studying the biology of aging believe that we have reached a critical turning point in our attack on aging. As we progressively master arcane medical techniques such as nanotechnology and learn how to manipulate our genetic structure, we will not only radically extend the biological human life span but draw ever closer to attaining near-immortality. Death will no longer be our species' inevitable destiny. By as early as 2100, many observers believe, it is distinctly possible that we will be on the threshold of what C.S. Lewis labeled "disabling death."

As we've learned the scientific challenges to achieving near-immortality will be daunting enough. But the real test for the *Ageless Nation* and its citizens will be figuring out how to adapt to the social, cultural, and psychological disruptions that near-immortality will doubtlessly cause. We saw in earlier sections how the "mere" extension of life to one hundred, 125 and beyond will have a tremendous impact on society. A world in which people expect to live on indefinitely will be so unlike our own as to be almost unrecognizable. As we discussed, in that world, each of us will be forced to re-examine our centuries-long assumptions about humankind, religion, and our place in the universe.

There are good reasons why I have appended the qualifier "near" to the word "immortality". It is logically impossible to live "forever," since technically the concept "forever" refers to a point in time we by definition can never reach. More importantly, even if every breakthrough and scientific wonder is available to every human being, people will still die. There will be no way to revive or reconstitute a person who is unfortunate enough to be incinerated in an airplane or space craft whose remains are strewn across the cosmos. People trapped in burning buildings or drowned at sea will die (assuming we have not yet genetically engineered them with fire resistant skin and lungs that can breathe underwater.) And alas, even in this brave new future, certain persons will elect to take matters into their own hands and end their lives, probably for problems that five years later they would have totally forgotten about or solved. In the age of immortality suicide will be the ultimate tragedy.

For the vast majority, though, life in the *Ageless Nation* will be exceedingly good. Let us take another look at that new world.

BUILDING THE ROAD FROM HERE TO ETERNITY

Death is such a constant in the scheme of human existence that rarely has our species even seriously asked whether this dreaded curse could be overcome. Immortality was a subject discussed in religion, philosophy and perhaps literature classes. Only in the last decade or two could you seriously broach the subject of near-immortality in a biology, genetics or physics lecture.

This change has come about because the breakthroughs in medical and scientific fields that we have been discussing throughout this book, including genetics, nanotechnology, and pharmaceuticals, are not only making us healthier, they are contributing to radically extended lives.

Chances are we will not achieve near-immortality by eliminating diseases alone. As gerontologists point out, you could solve all the major age-related diseases, and you'd still add only about fifteen or twenty years to our current eighty year average life span. To achieve immortality we will have to conquer the physical processes inherent in aging itself. Now let's turn to some ways that we might begin to achieve the seemingly miraculous dream of living our lives without a discernible termination point.

While some consider these schemes to achieve immortality implausible or unworkable, others are convinced that with the right funding and a little luck such ideas will become reality.

Making SENS of Immortality

The advantages of approaching a subject or a field of study with a fresh mind, or even with what some might consider a naïve point of view, are illustrated by Aubrey de Grey, of whom we've spoken before. De Grey is not the only person to suggest that immortality will be achieved via genetic and cellular manipulation and transformation—he is just the most famous. He is a tireless promoter of theories on how our species could achieve eternal life. He is convinced that he has formulated the theoretical means by which human beings might live thousands of years—indefinitely, in fact.

De Grey has never worked in a biology lab. In fact, his day job at Cambridge University is as the computer specialist in a genetics project—he manages a database on fruit flies, a staple of genetics research. However, de Grey has become a major force in the anti-aging professional world.

De Grey, forty one, lives in Cambridge with his wife, an American geneticist nineteen years his senior. Meeting her turned out to be extremely fortuitous for de Grey. For as far back as he can remember de Grey had always been convinced that aging is "something we need to fix." After his marriage, he taught himself and mastered the subjects of biology and genetics. He eventually acquired his doctorate in biology, but via an unusual Cambridge shortcut. Without registering for one graduate course in biology, de Grey submitted a book he had written on mitochondria, the power plants of cells, to the Cambridge biology department. The book was accepted and his doctorate was granted!

He has described his theories in scientific literature, publishing numerous articles in an impressive array of journals, including *Trends in Biotechnology* and *Annals of the New York Academy of Sciences*, as well as contributing commentary and letters to other publications like *Science* and *Biogerontology*. He has become a globe-trotting evangelizer for his views at gerontology conferences, as well as an editor of what some describe as a "fringy" quarterly journal, *Rejuvenation Research*. He makes his views known in every medium available to him, including *Popular Science* and *Technology*

Review. De Grey even sponsored his own international symposium on anti-aging. Journalists love to interview him since he is charismatic, articulate, energized, evangelical, and most of all, understandable.

Throughout his studies he has been obsessed with the one simple notion that death is a solvable problem. He is also convinced that he is the person who can achieve this lofty goal.

As de Grey perused scientific literature, he was struck by the fact that in spite of the remarkable molecular and cellular discoveries of recent decades, science had made little progress in solving the problem of death. He began to feel that the simple reason was the reward structure for academic scientists. If you were a young scientist trying to achieve academic success, namely tenure and promotion, choosing a goal like "finding the solution to death" could easily lead to an academic dead-end. According to de Grey, "High-risk fields are not the most conducive to getting promoted quickly." No academic has directly tried to solve the "problem" of death, at least not in the way de Grey thinks it should be solved.

De Grey does not think that the answer to our being able to live thousands of years lies in just one aspect of the aging process such as "free radicals," the unstable and troublemaking molecular by-products of metabolism. Rather, de Grey looks at aging as a group of interdependent processes, which he labels "The Seven Deadly Sins of Aging." These sins are based on cellular and molecular causes for human physical decline and ultimately death. He proposes multiple paths to repair these cells, a scheme he calls SENS or Strategies for Engineered Negligible Senescence.

The deadly sins that de Grey describes mostly involve what happens to our cells over time, and how he proposes to rectify these "sins." One is cell loss. Many of our organs, including our liver, kidneys and other organs suffer cell loss, which might impair their functioning. De Grey believes that we could engineer embryonic stem cells to create healthy new versions of every type of body cell, and get them into the body. Great idea, but the problem is that we have not yet developed the mechanism to deliver the various cell types to all the right places.

The next problem is the havoc caused by old cells that linger rather than self-destruct. According to Judith Campisi of Lawrence Berkeley National Laboratory, such cells are deadly—scientists think that they induce neighboring cells to become cancerous. De Grey proposes merely getting rid of these cells by inserting what he labels "suicide" genes that make the cells self-destruct. Or perhaps methods could be developed by which the body's immune system could fight these "senescent" genes.

When will we see these wonders available to the public? De Grey believes that these objectives might be achieved within as short a period as twenty-five years. Others are not so sure.

Many scientists consider some of de Grey's methods for solving cellular problems not so much creative as bizarre. For instance, his solution to deadly sin number seven, mutations of the DNA in the cell nucleus that contribute to cancer, is quite unusual. In this "Rube Goldberg"-style model, we would first extract cells from the patient, switch off their ability to produce telomerase, the enzyme that facilitates cell division, and modify them to tolerate toxic chemotherapy. Then a medical team would return those cells to the patient, who can now be given chemo to kill off any growing cancer cells. According to this Cambridge wiz, after periodic cell "reseedings," the cells will lose their susceptibility to cancer.[188]

In *EMBO* (European Molecular Biology Organization) *Reports*, an article signed by twenty-eight well-respected scientists severely criticized the science underlying de Grey's plan for perpetual life. The writers claimed that he was over-promising and over-simplifying others' work. Moreover, the signatories feared that his hyping of his solutions would erode the credibility that their fields, including genetic science and gerontology, have managed to achieve. They wrote that "to explain to a layman why de Grey's program falls into the realm of fantasy rather than science requires time ... " One of the signatories of the article, Steven Austad of the University of Texas Health Science Center at San Antonio, debated de Grey's ideas during a meeting of The American Association for the Advancement of Science in front to hundreds of science writers and educators.

Criticisms do not bother de Grey—in fact this prophet of immortality invites them. There is $20,000 on the table for anyone who can debunk his work. In July 2005, *Technology Review*, an MIT publication, announced a prize for any molecular biologist working in the field of aging that could successfully show that de Grey's prescription for defeating aging, SENS, is "so wrong that it is unworthy of learned debate." The magazine pledged to pay $10000 to the authors of a winning submission. De Grey's own organization devoted to promoting anti-aging science, The Methuselah Foundation, added an additional $10,000 to the award for anyone who meets the requirements of the challenge.

A year later, in June 2006, the magazine revealed that it would award part of the $20,000 to a team of scientists who took up the challenge. The winning team included Preston W. Estep III, Ph.D., President and CEO, Longevity Inc.; Matt Kaeberlein, Ph.D. in the Department of Pathology, University of Washington; Pankaj Kapahi, Ph.D., at the Buck Institute for Age Research, and several other experts in genome sciences, biochemistry, and molecular medicine. The judges stated that while the team did not demonstrate that "SENS is unworthy of discussion" they concluded that in their rebuttal to the criticism "the proponents of SENS have not made a compelling case for it."

The team had savagely criticized de Grey's concepts, labeling them "pseudoscience," a term usually appended to astrology, numerology, and a host of crackpot theories. Estep went through de Grey's solutions to the "seven deadly sins" and vigorously critiqued each one. They concluded that "SENS is based on the scientifically unsupported speculations of Aubrey de Grey, which are camouflaged by the legitimate science of others."

Yet, the contest judges felt that the team did not conclusively disprove de Grey's theories, possibly because the science to do so does not even exist at this time. The judges therefore awarded Estep and his team only half the prize-money.[189]

Mr. de Grey and other anti-aging proponents engage in such "public relations" strategies to raise public awareness of how close science is to reversing or stalling the aging process. Publicity leads to public awareness which can easily translate into public support for funding the basic research. Ultimately the taxpayers, governments and foundations will play key roles in determining how much monetary support goes to the research needed to radically extend human life.

The movement to extend life needs not only publicity but dramatic successes both inside and outside the laboratory to garner public support. According to de Grey one such eye-popping feat would be the radical extension of a two-year-old mouse to age five—such a mouse would ordinarily live to three. In a 2004 article on aging for the *Annals of the New York Academy of Sciences*, de Grey and seven other scientists wrote that, "We contend that the impact on public opinion and (inevitably) public policy of unambiguous aging-reversal in mice would be so great that whatever work remained necessary at that time to achieve adequate somatic gene therapy would be hugely accelerated."

Citizens of the *Ageless Nation* would start to make life choices based on the probability that they, too, will reach a proportional number of years. The writers contended that we would no longer tolerate death by diseases such as influenza, TB, AIDS, and other deadly killers, when under ordinary circumstances a person should live to 200 or 300. The public would clamor for eradication of such diseases and insist on massive funding of scientific research to obliterate them. [190]

Though Aubrey de Grey has many critics, I feel he certainly is a valuable catalyst, a creative outsider pushing the envelope of scientific thought on the prospects of superlongevity and immortality and how to achieve it. The fact that so many professional geneticists and biologists have desired to write and research with him stands as proof enough that they think he is on to something.

His weakness, I believe, is not on the scientific end, but the fact that his idea of immortality is bereft of any broader concept of the destiny and purpose of the human species. An interviewer asked de Grey why he was working so hard to create the science that would enable people to live 5000 years or more. By comparison to the breakthrough-level thought he expresses in regard to his scientific work, his response sounded clichéd. He claims that we must do so in order to "give future generations the choice. People are entitled, have a human right, to live as long as they can." The answer, while politically correct, hardly sounds like anything that would rally the public to the cause of superlongevity.

My own feeling is that we will be driven to radically extend the life span by our innate need to achieve mastery over and perfect the physical world, on earth as well as throughout the universe. My "Expansionary Theory of Human Development" describes this concept in full and suggests that this drive to perfect the universe is in fact humankind's destiny. Superlongevity is a critical part of this vision. Our extremely long lives will enable each of us to improve our skills, gather more knowledge, and acquire wisdom, all necessary tools in our quest to make this world a better place. One great tragedy of human existence is that some people become feeble and eventually die just when the world is starting to make sense to them and they are finally learning how to navigate their way through life and enhance the world around them. The Superlongevity Revolution would radically change all that—as people get older, they will possess the health and vigor of a physically young person, which would enable them to use that acquired skill and wisdom to an extent never before seen in human history.

That is the kind of vision that will spur our society to pursue the science of near-immortality until it is mastered. The human being is not an empty vessel that simply wants to exist forever. Existence must have meaning, and the quest for immortality, eternal existence, must be driven by a transcendent sense of our species' special role in the cosmos.

Another of de Grey's conclusions is troubling, and I believe will be proved erroneous. He has often stated that as we increase the human lifespan, individuals will be less desirous of procreating, in many cases because of a fear of overpopulating the planet. In several speeches de Grey has asserted that if forced to make a choice, the great majority of people would choose life extension over having children and the usual norms of family life. This being so, he says, far fewer children would be born.

Also, I disagree with de Grey's contention that "the imperative to reproduce is not actually so deep seated as psychologists would have us believe." In one interview he stated that "a large part of it (the desire to reproduce) may simply be indoctrination....I'm not in favor of giving young girls dolls to play with, because it may perpetuate the urge to motherhood." We will reproduce, because no matter how intelligent and masterful we become in this new era, our species' progress requires new individuals with fresh perspectives, visions, and skills, not to mention enthusiasm about a world which from their perspective is brand new and ready to be remolded to their preferences.

I am surprised that de Grey, who has the imagination to envision a world in which people will extend their lives into the millennia, would adopt the zero-growth concept of overpopulation (which we looked at in Chapter Nine). In my opinion the fear of overpopulation, of outstripping our food and energy resources, would be the very rationale people would use to prevent de Grey and others from even attempting to double or triple the current lifespan, let alone extend it into infinity. In addition, I see population expansion as not only a basic good, but as a necessity if we are to extend the human species throughout the solar system and into the cosmos—colonization of space would eventually require our numbers to grow into the trillions.

The "Build-A-Transhuman" Approach to Immortality

Mr. de Grey is not the only person designing blueprints for our immortal future. The *transhumanist* approach, as represented by the works of Ray Kurzweil, is perhaps an even more radical design for achieving this earth-shattering goal.

Kurzweil is an accomplished inventor, scientist, futurist and entrepreneur. Well-known for the musical instruments he has invented, including the famous electronic keyboard bearing his name on the front, Kurzweil has become famous for books such as *The Age of the Smart Machine, The Age of the Spiritual Machine,* and most recently *The Singularity Is Near: When Humans Transcend Biology.*

In *The Singularity is Near,* Kurzweil draws a blueprint for immortality that radically departs from the standard methodology for achieving this goal. De Grey and most other "immortalists" envision us gaining extremely long life by some biological manipulation of the human body. Kurzweil agrees with Hans Moravec of Carnegie Mellon University's Robotics Institute who claims that no matter how successfully we improve our DNA-based biology, a human that is solely biological will never compare to the kind of "being" that we will be able to engineer once we fully understand life's fundamental operating principles. Moravec states that we will always be "second-class robots."

This statement may seem a bit bizarre until one learns the context of Kurzweil's future scenario. Kurzweil sees us moving toward the "singularity" which he refers to in his book's title. According to the inventor, the singularity is a future period in which our "brain power is combined with the computer power in order to think, reason, communicate, and create in ways it can scarcely even contemplate today." He sees the merger of man and machine, which would be occurring at the same time as an explosion in machine intelligence and rapid innovation in gene research and nanotechnology. In Kurzweil's world there would be no distinction between the biological and the mechanical.

He does not deny the enormous power of the ability of drugs and genetics to extend human life and eradicate disease. Kurzweil agrees with de Grey and others that genetic and molecular science will extend biology and correct its obvious flaws (such as our vulnerability to disease). By the year 2020, the genetic revolution will have its full impact on society. Accelerating progress in biotechnology will enable us to reprogram our genes and metabolic processes to help us in fields such as genomics, to influence our genes, gene therapy, and rational drug design, in which we will formulate drugs that target precise changes in disease and aging processes. This genetic revolution will also enable us to therapeutically clone rejuvenated cells, tissues, and organs.

The Nanotechnology Revolution will also help us extend our lives, and will start to have its full impact by the mid-to-late 2020s. Kurzweil asserts that the revolution in nanotechnology will allow us to not only treat disease, but will enable us to redesign and rebuild our bodies and brains. As I mentioned earlier in our exploration of the Ultra-human phenomenon, Kurzweil envisions nanotechnology becoming a vehicle to enhance the operation of the human brain. By 2030 he predicts that we will augment our one hundred trillion very slow interneuron connections with high-speed virtual connections via nanorobotics, which will open the door to the creation of a kind of super-brain with enhanced memories and superior thinking capacity. The technology will also provide wireless communication from one brain to another, ushering in an era of human telepathy.

It is the next part of Kurzweil's vision that delights his fans but frightens and mystifies most everyone else. Kurzweil states that the revolution in artificial intelligence capacity of our computers will spark a change in the very nature of the human being. The so-called strong artificial intelligence revolution will lead to the creation of computer thinking ability that exceeds the cognitive powers of humans. From Kurzweil's perspective, "we are very close to the day when fully biological humans (as we now know them) cease to be the dominant intelligence on the planet." By the end of the twenty-first century, he contends, computational or mechanical intelligence will have become many trillions times more powerful than human brain power.

The next stage of human existence, according to Kurzweil, would be some as yet defined form of merger between human and machine, in which the human species incorporates machine intelligence into his body, or, as is more likely, the human merges into some global computer net. Even when Kurzweil is at his most specific about the shape and form of the future human, he still leaves the reader with questions. To wit: "The merger of these two worlds of intelligence is not merely a merger of biological and mechanical thinking mediums," but is also, Kurzweil says, a merger of "method and organizational thinking" that he claims will change us in an unimaginable way.[191]

Many critics wonder why we cannot be fully functional autonomous beings, fitted with bodies that will live forever, and just use our highly intelligent computers in the way we do now. Why the need to "merge" with an AI system? Kurzweil replies that even with our nanotechnologically enhanced brains, we can never achieve the status of "superintelligence" that he thinks our computer systems will attain. Furthermore, Kurzweil is convinced that "despite the wonderful future potential of medicine, real human longevity will only be attained when we move away from our biological bodies entirely." He predicts that we will move into a "software-based existence," in which we will gain the capacity to back ourselves up, which means storing "the key patterns underlying our knowledge, skills, and personality in a digital setting." For Kurzweil, then, living forever means achieving a virtual immortality.[192]

Some critics say Kurzweil's predictions are based on unjustifiable leaps from current technology. One technology writer for the *Wall Street Journal* made an excellent point about putting too much stock in the power and "intelligence" of the computer, which is key to Kurzweil's vision. Kurzweil claims that "artificial intelligence will be based, at least in part, on a human-made version of a fully functional human brain." According to Kurzweil, computers will think, feel, make decisions and ultimately have consciousness. But the writer, Lee Gomes, reminds us that we have heard before about just how advanced these machines would become. Thirty years ago it was thought these machines would by now be like HAL in the movie *2001: A Space Odyssey*.

For the machine to achieve human-like status, Gomes says, we must reverse-engineer the brain. For that to work, we must discover the brain's most basic secrets, including such knotty ones as consciousness. Then, we have to duplicate, not just simulate or model, the brain inside a computer. He reminds us that we can also simulate the weather inside a computer, but it will never create rain in our backyards. [193]

Will Immortality Really Occur?

No one knows for sure if the human species will achieve immortality via schemes fashioned along the lines of Kurzweil and de Grey. What we do know is that it is a good bet that if the rapid progress being made in a diverse number of scientific fields continues, we will radically extend the human lifespan to hundreds of years.

Our understanding of human biology is accelerating. Every day, it seems, we hear of another discovery about the relationships of some gene to a particular disease, or hear about some drug that has conquered but another malady. And our enhanced understanding of human physiology and genetics will soon be aided by nanoscale medical tools and nanotechnology itself. At that point, we will not be adding just years or decades, but possibly centuries to our lives. Since aging is largely the result of accumulated cellular damage and the concomitant biological processes which evolved to deal with them, when we learn to repair cellular damage and eventually elimi-nate it totally, we might then consider the possibility of the elimination of death. Although nanomedical life extension is not yet possible, over the last decade we have been able to develop a blueprint for how it might work. And we are getting closer to mastering the basic science underlying nanotechnol-ogy.

Let us not underestimate the power of the consumer as a force in our drive to achieve superlongevity and ultimately immortality. The more people demand products and services that increase the lifespan, the more producers, pharmaceutical and biotech companies, will be willing to pour billions of dol-lars on research to make that possible. The Superlongevity Industry is full of companies waiting to meet the needs of Baby Boomers, Generations X and Y, and all others that want safe, long-lasting miracle drugs that will add years to their lives and life to those years.

One conclusion that I have come to after reviewing the literature on life extension and superlongevity is to be neither overly dismissive nor too accepting of claims and counterclaims emanating from experts and their crit-ics. Both de Grey and Kurzweil come across as true believers with "science on their side" with a host of champions and corporate backers betting that their vision is correct. Both defy all critics and are willing to take on anyone when it comes to defending their visions. At the same time, both these thinkers' views of the road to immortality and the future of humanity are not only dif-ferent but are mutually exclusive. There is no room in de Grey's world for a "human-machine" merge, and Kurzweil thinks that all biological solutions to human mortality, no matter how sophisticated, are not enough.

The value of their thinking, I believe, is that they are willing to push the conceptual envelope to get members of the intelligentsia thinking and talking about the possibility and impact of near-immortality and superlongevity. It is only in this way that we can move policy planners, business and government leaders and the general public to begin to prepare for a future which is by its very nature totally unlike anything we have experienced in human history.

THE IMPACT OF IMMORTALITY

Many other writers and thinkers are beginning to seriously turn their thoughts to the question of the long term impact of superlongevity and immortality. The number of thoughtful books on this topic is proof that this is an issue which policy makers and others must begin to deal with. Among the writers who have weighed in on the subject, one, Joel Garreau, in his book *Radical Evolution*, explored a variety of scenarios resulting from radically extended lifespans. Other works include Ramesh Naam's *More Than Human: Embracing the Promise of Biological Enhancement* and an intriguing compendium entitled *The Scientific Conquest Of Death*.

This last work brings together in one volume a large group of writers and researchers who evidently spend most of their time pondering issues related to the subject. Ray Kurzweil, Marvin Minsky of MIT, and Nick Bostrom, British Academy Research Fellow at Oxford University offer essays on nanomedicine, the "war on aging," and the ethical and sociological issues related to immortality. The titles are intriguing, and indicate some of the "impact" questions that citizens of *The Ageless Nation* will have to deal with, such as "Superlongevity Without Overpopulation," "Time Consciousness in a Very Long Life," and "Upsetting the Natural Order." (I am very familiar with the last of these—I regularly receive e-mails wondering if we are somehow tampering with nature, playing God, or otherwise upsetting the cosmos when we extend human life beyond its "natural" limits.) One essay specifically examined the theological issues emerging from man's conquest of death. [194]

Again, let me repeat, in my opinion, that the achievement of immortality will affect every aspect of our lives, including our perceptions of time, our relationship with our families and friends, the way we view ourselves as individuals and as a species, and our religious and moral beliefs.

We have explored the impact of superlongevity, extending our lives into the one hundred to 150 year range. Now let's briefly explore some of the more intriguing possibilities of life in a world in which death has, for the most part, been exiled from human experience.

How Immortality Is Attained Will Determine Its Impact

Most of those people writing and theorizing about immortality treat this phenomenon as an "event." As de Grey portrays it, we will pick up the paper one day and read about a breakthrough experiment that suddenly bestows eternal life on all of humanity (like his lab mouse experiment I just described). According to this scenario, this is humanity's "eureka moment"—from that day forward, we and everyone we know will experience a "consciousness change" that immediately transforms the way we view ourselves and our place in the cosmos.

But as we've learned in the *Ageless Nation*, immortality and super-longevity are not so much events as processes. When we speak of achieving immortality, or even superlongevity, it is important to recognize that people will not just wake up one morning and discover that the average life span is 200 years, 300 years, or several centuries long. Regardless of the technological advances making extended and even infinite life possible, at first people will go through their lives as they ordinarily had. They will turn fifty and start to re-career, take a hiatus, and start another career. They turn seventy, and due to one or another of the anti-aging therapies we have discussed—nanotechnology, telomere lengthening, CR—they realize that even though they are getting chronologically older, they are remaining physically young. They get to one hundred, and they are still not physically aging. Science is placing on the table an increasing number of tools to help them never age. This process continues, and they realize that they can continue working, change careers, and pursue personal development and growth opportunities. At time goes on, they realize that their friends are also alive. Even though theorists speak about immortality and radically extended life in abstract terms, we must keep in mind that we as individuals and a society will experience and adjust to these changes over time.

It will be interesting how society changes as the realization suddenly wafts through the cultural ethos that people are not going to die. James Cascio, author of *Toxic Memes*, envisions four different "immortality" scenarios, each with slightly different impact.

His first scenario, which he labels the "Magic Pill," is most appealing. You would simply take an anti-aging pill that would rejuvenate you. As he says, "the physical toll of the years slips away, and you spend the centuries in your healthy twenty something body." Unfortunately, what we know of the evolving scientific roads to immortality suggests that this scenario is the least likely.

The next scenario labeled "Dorian Gray," after Oscar Wilde's title character might be the most likely to occur. Here, aging is not so much reversed as radically decelerated, and not by one specific therapy but by a full-pronged multi-technology driven set of medical treatments. People would get older, but incremental improvements in medicine and biotechnology would prevent them from becoming infirm. Old age would not mean poor health.

Society would possess a strong sense of the aging process, in contrast to the rejuvenated society which either temporarily or permanently turns old bodies into young ones.

Another scenario, called "Immortal Kids," while not completely out of the question, is quite troubling from a sociological perspective. Here, one could easily achieve a radical life span. However, the treatment for such can only be performed in the early days after conception or in a test tube. Because the modification would have been made in your genetic structure during gestation, once you are born your fate is sealed. Certainly, anyone alive now, reading this book, would be unable to get such treatment. But all children born from that point on would potentially be immortal.

The moral burden placed on parents would be enormous. If this scenario becomes a reality, expect a major national debate on the issue. Do not be surprised if the decision to genetically bestow superlongevity on the child is taken out of the parents' hands, as is the case with vaccination against certain diseases. The state will reason that it is actually erring on the side of caution to provide a treatment that will be impossible to pursue once the individual is born. Parents who want an exemption from this obligation will have to apply for such, and the acceptable reasons for this exemption, perhaps on religious grounds, would be specified by law.

In the last scenario, "Holy Fire" longevity, a person with an older body would undergo a series of biotechnological and nanotechnological treatments that in effect "resets" that the person to his healthy, twenty five year old body. The person would then begin to age again, and a half-century later would undergo this process once again. The interesting aspect of this scenario is that people would experience age, and we would see the "aged" amongst us. But our perspective toward them would be entirely different. Today, we see people who need all varieties of remedies for their situations, but because we know that the remedies are available, we just assume we are seeing the person on a "bad day." I see many people who need a haircut, or whose arm or leg is in a cast, or are sneezing incessantly from that day's excessive pollen. I trust they will get their hair restyled, the leg will heal, and either the pollen will abate or they will find just the right antihistamine. In this last scenario, we will view aging as a temporary condition we endure in between our "youth treatments." Aging, then, would be a condition which we manage, like diabetes or migraine headaches.

My feeling is that this process, however welcome, would take a bit of getting used to. I would probably find it rather dissociating to undergo that first nanotechnological transformation from my sixty year old self to a twenty-five year old "me." After all, even if I do not like the sixty year old reflection in the mirror every day, I at least know who I am. But who is this twenty-five year old rascal I see preening and posing in the mirror? And right in front of me, no less. However, considering the benefits of rejuvenation, I will suffer through and adjust to any residual alienation I feel toward my perfected self. In any event, I am certain that by the third time around I will have adjusted to this radical rejuvenation of my corporeal being.

A Social Class Structure Based on "Life Choices" Will Evolve
The greatest dividing line in the new society will not be rich and poor, old and young, man and woman. These will pale by comparison to the ultimate source of division between people, the choices that people make regarding superlongevity and immortality.

At least three different social categories will be derived from their "immortality status." The first group, call them the *mortals*, would be those who for whatever reason have made the choice (or had the choice made for them) to do nothing to radically extend their lives. They will avoid death and disease as we do today—vaccines, good hygiene, exercise, and a healthy diet. But for whatever reason they do not turn to cell rejuvenation, CR-based "youth pills," and nanotechnology-based cellular manipulations to ensure a life lasting centuries. They will die at the ripe old age of 90 or so, and toward the end possibly suffer the infirmity of age that we witness today. The second group, the *extended lifers*, would avail themselves of some technology that will radically extend their lives, say to 140-160 years, through CR-based pharmaceuticals that will also keep them physically young. Like the mice in current CR experiments, they will die in relatively young and fit bodies. The third group, the *immortalists*, will tamper with their genes and cellular structure, and will take any other steps necessary to extend their lives into the centuries.

Each group will have a different mindset. The first two are more alike, in the sense that they both have chosen to die at some point. They will differ in that the first group will experience more of the vicissitudes of what will be sentimentally referred to as "old age." The last group, staking a claim on eternity, will be the oddity, staking a claim on eternal life. How will they differ? Think about your work experience. How do you as a full time employee view the "temps," the summer help, and the interns who periodically appear in your organization to fill roles? Regardless of how much you personally liked them or how efficiently they performed their jobs, you and the permanent staff always perceive them as temporary. Their transient relationship to the organization shapes your view of them—the fact that they are just "passing through" means they cannot possibly possess the same stake in the organization's future as you have, nor are they as committed as you to the company's ultimate success.

Is this a fair assessment of these workers? After all, are they not putting in a full day's work and performing their tasks competently? Unfortunately, the answer to these questions is of little consequence. The full time permanent employees like you will instinctively question the temporary workers' commitment to the organization's well-being. Moreover, we do not involve the temporaries in any of our long-term projects, in the company's strategic planning activities, nor do we promote them into positions of authority.

In much the same way, the *immortalist* will view with a certain amount of distance, detachment, and even a vague suspicion anyone choosing not to commit themselves to a long life. If I know that 300 years from now I will be living with the consequences of my present actions and those of my nation's leaders, I will take very seriously every aspect of my world, such as the nation's economy (including the long-term national debt) and the planet's physical environment. And I will always wonder whether the "temps" really care as much as I do what happens after they depart from this physical world.

My guess is that the vast majority of people will choose the second or third options, assuming they are aware of and can afford the medical technologies making superlongevity possible. The world for which policy planners, business leaders and individuals should be preparing is one in which employees, citizens, friends, and family members will be living for a very, very long time.

Immortality as the Great Equalizer

Much has been made of the social and economic impact of medical technology. Critics have suggested that these technologies will be so expensive and scarce that only the rich will be able to pay the asking price of immortality. Will the richer countries have more access to these technologies? Will this be the source of friction between the social classes, with the poor watching as the rich becoming almost a separate species of immortal ultra-humans?

This criticism crops up in every discussion at every conference dealing with life extension. I think that these fears are overblown, if not groundless. Critics have thought that every major technology would become the plaything of the rich and the mega-corporations. In the 1880s and 1890s most automobiles were "horseless carriages" that only the wealthy could afford. Then Henry Ford began mass-marketing the Model T, and suddenly millions of members of the middle-class were driving cars. Only large corporations and universities had access to computers until Apple did what experts thought impossible, invent a "personal computer" that everyone could buy. Technology, especially in the computer and communications area, usually becomes cheaper—a decade ago who could imagine the average-income family owning a "home theatre." Certainly the movie industry didn't. Everyone can go to Europe now, everyone can travel at 80 mph, and everyone can protect themselves with a Taser.

Unless the system is somehow spiked (out of fears of overpopulation, perhaps?) we should all enjoy nearly complete access to the impending cornucopia of life-extending science technology. Moreover, once rich, middle class and poor will have such an equal chance of living for two or three centuries or more, there will evolve an even greater loosening of the restrictions of social and economic class. And in a very unexpected way.

What is the basis of inequality between the rich and poor? A person born into wealth is not just materially richer than someone born into the middle class — the opportunities for succeeding on his own are more plentiful. He can go to better schools (between 10 percent and 20 percent of admissions into Ivy League colleges go to children of alumni), and develop a strong social/business network, both through his school experience and his family's connections. People from humbler backgrounds can certainly reach high levels of success in America like Bill Gates and Warren Buffet have. However, most of the non-rich are hampered in their activities because they are trying to succeed within limited time frames in careers that stretch perhaps thirty to forty years after they finish their education. The non-rich have fairly limited periods to close the wealth gap between themselves and the rich.

And this is why superlongevity will become the great equalizer. Give an ambitious individual a century or two to make his fortune, and he will suddenly have the time (and the ultra-human strength, energy, and intelligence) to establish his connections, develop his big idea, and build his empire. Eventually, because of the gift of time, both rich and poor will realize that current equalities are at best only temporary. In the course of their very long lifetimes, the rich person and the poor might even exchange places. This possibility alone damp-ens the likelihood that a person's superior position will impress or intimidate the less fortunate, who now have decades and centuries ahead of them to make their fortunes.

Are People More or Less Likely to Have Children?

Many observers prognosticate that as our life spans become longer, we will choose to have fewer or no children. This belief is predicated on a few assump-tions. The first is that the drastic reduction in the death rates will lead to over-population unless people forego having more children. The second rationale is that since the current population will be physically young, there will be no need to bring into the world a new cadre of strong and healthy people to fill society's needs.

The perception that the Superlongevity Revolution will lead to overpop-ulation has been around for decades. As the Superlongevity Revolution has accelerated, environmentalists, academics, media pundits and some demogra-phers have been making the argument that as we extend the human life span, we are risking "overpopulating" the planet.

Certainly the Superlongevity Revolution will lead to an increase in the size of our population. By definition the death rate will plummet, especially if people live to ages predicted in this book. If people continue to have children at even a normal replacement rate, about 2.1 births per female in the population, the number of people in a country, or on the planet, will naturally increase.

The critics reason that as we increase our numbers, we will start to "over-populate" the planet—there will be too many people for the available resource base. Sensing this, they say, the members of the society will start to limit the number of children they have.

This prediction might make sense, if it was not based on one fallacious notion. The belief that a growing population will automatically lead to a scarcity of food, oil, water, etc., is fatally flawed, as I will explain.

For centuries assorted commentators have been warning us of the dan-gers of overpopulation. In 1798 English economist and demographer Thomas Malthus published his famous book *Essay on the Principle of Population* in which he presented a simple and pessimistic argument: "Human population," he wrote, "grows exponentially, like compound interest in a bank account, but farm output rises at a slower, arithmetic rate; the result, human population will inevitably and repeatedly outstrip its food supply." The idea that population will always outrun the supply of resources, and that therefore we must severely restrict population growth, has become known as *Malthusianism*.[195]

While various versions of this doom and gloom scenario have periodically emerged and become fashionable over the last two centuries, it really gained traction in the 1960s and 1970s, around the time the global population first breached the three billion person mark. Academics and government planners sounded the alarm and revived the old Malthusian argument: Our rapidly expanding population would soon exhaust all resources, including our food, water, oil, wood, even our air. In 1972 the Club of Rome published its notoriously inaccurate *Limits to Growth* tome, using a then-exotic computer forecasting technology to predict the state of the world in twenty years. The Club's study convinced the intelligentsia that at those current rates of population growth we would run out of oil by 1992, with shortages of other commodities, including food, sure to follow. Paul Ehrlich's book *The Population Bomb* scientifically calculated that our expanding population would usher in a genuine age of scarcity. Erhlich's future was indeed frightening. The skyrocketing price of natural resources such as oil would lead to a global recession. Worse, famines of "unbelievable proportions" occurring no later than 1975 would lead to "hundreds of millions of people starving to death" in the 1970s and 1980s.[196]

"Solutions" to our "population problem" proliferated. The prevailing mantra throughout Western society became "zero-population growth, or "zpg"—have as few children as you can, and if you cannot control your primal reproductive urges, try to keep your fertility output to one and no more than two children. Organizations such as Planned Parenthood, The Population Council, as well as various U.N agencies flooded developing countries such as India as well as the whole of Africa with anti-population propaganda along with birth control devices and drugs. Paul Ehrlich latched onto the popular phrase and started his own anti-growth organization, called Zero-Population Growth, Inc., which eventually grew to 70,000 members. (In 2002 they changed their name to The Population Connection.)

For the most part the anti-population forces failed in their attempt to squelch population growth. World population grew from 3.4 billion in 1970 to 6.5 billion today. The highest growth occurred in China and India. China's population grew from 829 million in 1970 to its current 2006 level of 1.3 billion, even though China's Communist rulers had in place a draconian "one child" policy. India's population grew from a little more than half a billion in 1970 to over one billion by 2001.[197]

In spite of the dire predictions that high population growth would lead to poverty and scarcity, both these countries, with their large and expanding populations, are poised to dominate the globe's economy well into the twenty-first century!

China, one billion people strong, is gaining the attention and investment interest of governments and businesses throughout the developed world. As China began to open its markets to Western businesses throughout the 1990s, U.S. and European companies literally fell all over each other petitioning the Chinese government for the right to build their phone networks, their electric power stations, and their high speed rail systems. Industry turned to China's huge supply of surplus labor for factory workers and technicians. As a result of the recent population surge, China has now become the world's second largest market for automobiles.

In many ways India is even more of a thriving success. The country's universities produce engineers and scientists by the truckload, and India's economy is improving so quickly that many Indian scientists who relocated to the U.S. in the 1980s and 1990s are returning to their country of origin to pursue their careers. Its economy is rapidly succeeding—as we entered 2007 India's industrial output grew at its fastest pace in a decade and the stock markets touched new peaks. India's index of industrial production broke an eleven year record, growing by 14.4 percent in November 2006.[198]

The additional people in India and China who our "family planning" gurus defined as part of the overpopulation problem are now the very individuals that today's multinational corporations deem "valuable customers" and see as an important source of workers for their labor pool.

The U.S. is also participating in the global population surge. In 2006, the U.S. population hit three hundred million, a one hundred million person spike in just forty years. U.S. Census Bureau analysts project a U.S. population of four hundred million within a scant few decades from now. Once America hit this most recent plateau, the media, intelligentsia and environmentalist establishment hit the panic buttons on their computers to fill cyberspace with blogs and op-eds decrying America's lurch into the new demographic abyss.

Their position was summed up succinctly in the subtitle of an Associated Press "news release" marking this new population milestone: "Environmentalists grapple with a nation addicted to more of everything." Dire predictions about America's future poured forth: we have "too many Americans" crowding our highways, classrooms, cities, suburbs, and country; depleting our natural resources; polluting the air with their SUVs and of course producing greenhouse gases that are causing global warming.[199]

You had to search deeply to discover any commentators or demographers stating the real truth: As it has in the cases of India and China, an expanding population will provide the U.S. with a powerful "tool" to maintain its position among the world's economic leaders well into the twenty-first century.

In fact, a *Business Week* prognosis of who will end up the winners and losers of the twenty-first century economy stressed the importance that large populations play in a country's fortunes. There is nothing magical here—these people are all potential producers and consumers. The figures show it. Currently the U.S. is producing 28 percent of all the world's goods and services as measured by gross domestic product (GDP). India produces 2 percent, China 4 percent. *Business Week* economists project that by 2050 the U.S. would still be producing its mighty share of the world's GDP, but now China would be producing 29 percent of the world's wealth while India would produce 17 percent.

These three countries, the U.S., China and India, all of whom have large and growing populations, would produce nearly three-quarters of the world's products and services![200]

While these countries' share of the world's GDP is increasing, that of Japan and the countries comprising the European Union (EU) is shrinking. Japan, which currently produces 16 percent of the world's goods and services, will become a minor player on the world stage, producing at most about 5 percent of the world's goods. The EU will see its economic impact weakening as its share of global economic activity shrinks from 29 percent to 15 percent. Sadly, the sun is setting on Europe's centuries-long global dominance.

To discover the reasons underlying this projected economic decline, Europe and Japan need look no further than their declining reproduction rate. A country needs a fertility rate of 2.1 per woman in order to replace itself. This means that each woman must reproduce an average of two children, one for herself and one for another man in the population. At Japan's current fertility rate of 1.3 children per woman its population will decline from the current 127.5 million people to an estimated 105 million people by 2050, a contraction that was already in progress by 2005. A look at their disheartening fertility rates tell exactly why European countries are in trouble.[201] Western European women were having an average of 2.4 children each in 1970. That figure has fallen below 1.4 by 2007. The fertility rate of Britain, Ireland, France and the Netherlands is a paltry 1.7, while that of Italy is a rock-bottom 1.29. Germany's is so low that by the end of the century its population is on schedule to shrink from its current 82 million to a frighteningly-low 24 million. Many new EU entrants from Central and Eastern Europe have even lower fertility rates. At this rate, the total population of current EU member countries will drop from 482 million people to 454 million people.[202]

There are many reasons growing populations like that of the U.S., China, and India can generate higher economic growth. For one thing, while it is true that larger populations in theory will use more oil, food, and other resources than smaller ones, such societies quickly adjust by developing the means to extend those resources and more importantly find substitutes for them.

China and India are putting this principle to work. As the two countries put a strain on the world's oil reserves due to their growing populations' petroleum consumption, they are also at the forefront of nuclear power plant construction. The U.S. and Japanese car companies that supply the car-oriented American population are developing gas-electric hybrids that get 60 miles per gallon as well as autos that run on hydrogen.

Their actions are illustrating a principle stated succinctly by Julian Simon, one of the late twentieth century's major defenders of population growth. Simon admitted that more people, and increased income, lead to scarcity of some resources with concomitant higher prices, but only in the short run. "The higher prices present opportunity, and prompt inventors and entrepreneurs to search for solutions." He adds that "in a free society, solutions are eventually found." A truly free society does not legislate alternatives such as nuclear power out of existence.

Simon also stated that "in the long run the new developments leave us better off than if the problems had not arisen." In other words, a country enjoys a higher standard of living per capita with its larger population than it did when its numbers were small. Simon reminded us that thanks to our free market capitalist system, the history of America is one of leaving the storehouse for every successive generation more endowed with wealth, knowledge and natural resources.[203]

In *Seizing The Future* I described how larger populations can help a society thrive. I said that "each member of a society either contributes, or has the potential to contribute, more to the system than he or she consumes." In other words, every new person born into a society is potentially a "value-added" component of our society. Not only will the brainpower of each new person enhance the human condition, but more than a few of the next generation will create the inventions and innovations that will improve the lives of all. An extreme example would be the contributions made by Einstein, Tesla, or Edison, whose inventions led to global productivity that far exceeded any part of the economic pie that they individually "consumed." That is the principle behind every successful organization—the sum is greater than its individual parts.

In the first decade of the twenty-first century the world's population is approaching seven billion people, but the predicted scarcities are not occurring. Indeed, many economists and scientists have calculated that even at the present state of scientific knowledge we could easily support a population many times our present level. New technologies, such as nanotechnology and bio-genetic engineering of crops, will virtually eliminate scarcity as we know it. So to limit our childbearing as the Superlongevity Revolution progresses would be needless and even foolish.

Another criticism of superlongevity in relationship to the population issue is that radical life extension will by its very nature lead to an "aging" population. I mentioned earlier Fukayama's statement that such a society would look like a "giant nursing home." Critics fear that this "aging" population would bankrupt Social Security safety nets and pension funds, put a strain a public resources, and make a shambles of the health care system.

These fears are based on one basic misconception: the citizens of the *Ageless Nation* will not be *aging* so much as merely advancing chronologically. Many of the breakthroughs that will lead to the radically extended lifespan, including nanotechnology and stem cell science, will also be the very tools enabling people to achieve the "ultra-human" physical state. So these older people, vibrant and physically young, will not only be able to maintain their productivity but in many instances will employ the wisdom and knowledge borne of experience to actually outperform their younger counterparts. How much of a strain can people put on Social Security if they are contributing to this fund every paycheck at the same time they are "collecting?"

As I pointed out earlier, people who know that they will be alive two hundred years or more from now will by necessity labor to ensure that the future is a prosperous one. After all, odds are they will be living in "the future," no matter how distant it might seem.

For the reasons just stated, I believe that during the next phases of the Superlongevity Revolution overpopulation will not be a problem. And therefore people will not decide to reduce the number of children they have as they face the prospects of living a very long life.

Another supposed reason why superlongevity would lead to low childbirth is that since everyone alive would be physically young new generations would not be needed. We would already have the people on hand with the strength and mental acuity necessary to maintain a robust economy. So why bother procreating new generations of people?

Such arguments profoundly miss the point of what new people bring to society's table. Newborns, children and adolescents bring a quality to the world that no adult can possibly possess, namely their sense of mystery and their enthusiasm for the newness of life itself. In order to continue to create and progress, the human enterprise needs the freshness of the recently-born, the rebelliousness of youth, and the creativity and spark of people discovering life and its wonders for the first time.

Also, there is simply no reason to expect that superlongevity is going to change the joy and comfort people get from their children. People engage in childbearing and family formation to fulfill basic needs for intimacy and continuity. Not only will people not forego having children but they will do the opposite. The very fact that a husband and wife know that they will live very long lives will motivate them to build the multigenerational extended family that I described earlier.

Will People Get Tired Of Living?

This question comes up frequently. When confronted with the possibility of living for 150 years or more, people often respond that they might just get "tired" of living. When I probe to discover what they mean by "tired," I do not get the sense that people are so much worried about physical exhaustion as they are concerned that they might lose the will to live. They are afraid that after a few hundred years they will get bored.

The reality is that as people approach their deaths, they usually become obsessed with the idea that they are running out of time to accomplish whatever life goals they had set for themselves. In fact, next to the realization that they are leaving friends and family forever, people most regret the fact that they have missed out on so many experiences they had promised themselves they would someday enjoy. The countries and cities they wanted to visit but never did, the courses they wish they took, the films they never saw, and the plays and concerts they never attended, all begin to gnaw at them as they approach the endpoint of their physical time on Earth.

In the *Ageless Nation*, the desire to stay among the living will be stronger than ever. True, the vagaries of life can always make us feel desperate enough to want to end it all—financial ruin, divorce, family tragedies of one type or another. However, remember that as the Superlongevity Revolution unfolds some sources of personal despair will no longer be a normal part of life. The very technology that endows you with a radically extended life eliminates or reduces the likelihood that tragedies such as the death of loved ones, affliction with an incurable disease, or a permanent disability from an accident will be part of your life experience.

After living for a few centuries, some people might feel that they need a vacation from it all, not because they are filled with a feeling of desperation or hopelessness, but just because they need to recharge the mental and emotional batteries. We mentioned earlier that periodic career and work hiatuses should fulfill this need. Or if they truly want to get away from it all, they might opt for a six month vacation at a resort on the moon, Mars, or a space station.

Still there could be the unfortunate few whose sense of ennui is so overwhelming that none of the options we reviewed seem sufficient. Is it possible that society will legitimize the use of cryonics in such cases? Today some people have chosen to have their bodies frozen by companies such as Alcor right before they die in the hope that when a cure for what ails them is discovered they can be revived and made well. In the future, perhaps people tiring of life will choose to go into some state of suspended animation, freezing or otherwise, for a six to twelve month period. This hiatus from life would provide the person time to break the monotony, clear her mind or just take a "time out."

Immortality Will Change Our Perceptions of Ourselves As A Species
On a very subtle level near-immortality will transform our views about ourselves as a species, especially in terms of the human species' role in the cosmos. Up to

this point in human development we have perceived our status as merely "passing through." Countless literary works allude to our status as "temporary inhabitant," of this planet, this universe. The idea that the world goes on but each of us disappears is an extremely humbling concept, to say the least.

True, up to this point in history, any of us could attain a sense of immortality through our artistic creations, and more commonly through our families, a business or other organization we founded, even through our claim on a particular piece of land or property. Families in France and England derive a sense of continuity and immortality by the fact that they have laid claim to and own land, property, and castles for centuries.

Currently, regardless of how we attempt to extend ourselves through time, we can at best achieve a form of faux-immortality. Truthfully, although my ancestors lived on this land, quite frankly, they are long gone, as I will be in this mortal body. As Woody Allen once put it, "I don't want to achieve immortality through my work—I want to achieve it through not dying."

However, as the Superlongevity Revolution unfolds and we slowly realize that any one of us might be here for the foreseeable (as well as the far distant) future, our species' self-image and sense of self-importance will change. We are no longer tenants on the planet, temporary occupants of the cosmos. We, as a species and as individuals, are here to stay.

One cannot underestimate how such a concept will transform our perceptions of ourselves as a species. In my book *the Future Factor*, I stated that the human species was destined to play a definitive role in the cosmos, specifically to develop and enhance the planets and the universe and bring life and light to an otherwise dark and lifeless places. The progression from mortal to near-immortal would solidify our notion that we are somehow special, somehow unique as a species, and bring us closer to acknowledging and fulfilling our unique destiny.

Religion And Immortality: Dust Thou Art—But What About the Future?

Throughout history, religions have had eminent domain status over the concept of eternity and the afterlife. So what happens to the state of religion when modern science and technology turn us into immortal beings, when there is no "afterlife" after our lives?

In their speeches, articles, and blogs proponents of immortality exhibit a pronounced belief that achievement of eternal life in the here-and-now will prove the death knell of organized religion. One blogger sums up their attitude perfectly: "As the prospect of physical human immortality materializes, religion will logically dematerialize and a new state of thinking will start."

There is no doubt that the attainment of human immortality would have a profound impact on most religions. The concept of an afterlife is integral to the religious belief systems of Judaism, Islam, and Christianity. After death we meet our maker, and more importantly our lives are judged and we receive eternal reward or damnation based on the sum total of our behaviors. This eventuality becomes a powerful regulator of human behavior. Even if the law does not catch up to your crimes and misdemeanors during your lifetime, God will be waiting for you at the end.

In this book, we've looked at several scenarios of immortality. Still, most people will ask, what happens when people no longer die? Will God ever have the chance to weigh in on the morality or lack thereof of our actions and behavior on Earth?

I think that religion will probably adapt its belief structure and dogma to human superlongevity and immortality in much the same way it has adapted to the Darwinian theory of evolution and Galileo's proof of the non-centrality of earth in the universe. Religion might eventually respond that although we have conquered physical death, God still will determine when and how the universe will end. At that point, there will be a "Final Judgment" at which time all of us will be accountable for our sins. Such a statement, like many religious dicta, can be neither proved nor disproved.

The doctrines of some religions might be more amenable to, and less threatened by, humankind's attainment of physical immortality than one would think. While Heaven is thought of as wholly spiritual, the Bible states that at least three individuals, Christ, his mother Mary and Elijah, ascended to paradise in their physical bodies, and presumably could exist there in that state. Also, some Christian doctrine teaches that at the end of time humans' souls will be reunited with their bodies on a physical planet, presumably Earth. Seen in that light, the idea of human immortality is not totally at odds with Christian doctrine. I can imagine future theologians engaging in rich intellectual discussions that seek to reconcile our man-made immortal status with established religious dogma.

The religious instinct is extremely strong and well-rooted in human experience, not to mention the human psyche. To predict that scientific achievement alone will cause its demise is premature. I believe that religion will evolve, adapting its doctrines to the phenomenon of human immortality. Moreover, it will incorporate into its dogma our expanding comprehension of humankind's role and destiny in the cosmos.

Some will object to our commandeering the forces of nature to re-create ourselves as immortal beings. They will imagine that such an achievement will tempt us to believe that humankind has now attained an almost "God-like" status. Many proponents of human immortality, especially those scientists making extended life a reality, are sad to say already giving in to that temptation. One only has to look at the hubris exhibited by some members of the Artificial Intelligence community, who imagine they are re-inventing all the rules of nature in their efforts to create the "post-human" or "transhuman."

Others, however, will imagine they are doing God's work by reducing human suffering as they eliminate disease and conquer death.

Who Wants to Live Forever?

A few years ago, I was giving a talk on superlongevity to a small men's group run by a local religious organization. After listening to my description of the coming Superlongevity Revolution and how it might change society, someone stood up and asked the assembled congregation: "But who would want to live to 120?" No one seemed to desire to take on this combatant. After a few seconds, I replied, "Probably someone who is 119."

I was only half-joking. In spite of our doubts and qualms about how the radically extended life span will change our world, we ought to step back from the "issue" of immortality and just ask a very common-sense question: who in his right mind wishes to die? We may claim that we do not fear death, which is fine. But who at his or her deathbed would reject a reprieve that magically manifested itself, a postponement of death for a year, a month, even another hour? I daresay that all things being equal, every one of us would accept this offer. No one really wants to die.

So let us place the questions and doubts about extended life within the context of life's alternative. Pundits worry that immortality will bring with it a host of social problems as well as moral and religious dilemmas. I suggest that these will all seem trivial by comparison to the joy and exhilaration that we will all feel when we "wake up and smell the coffee" and realize that we will most likely never have to experience the termination of our physical life.

In a wonderful and amusing article appearing in the aforementioned compendium published in 2004 by the Immortality Institute, Nick Bostrom, Director of Oxford University's Future of Humanity Institute, listed reasons why we should want to live forever. From his perspective, and from that of all his compatriots who are rooting for a breakthrough in life extension research, "to question why it would be desirable to lead a longer and healthier life might seem banal." However, he prepared this list because there are a large number of people who seemingly cannot conceive of any reason to extend their lives beyond the currently seventy-five or eighty years.

One of the first reasons Bostrom offers is to, "Find out what the future will be like." The longer I live, the more curious I become about the shape of the future. As frightening as our current times are, mostly due to the specter of worldwide terrorism, our species future is fraught with opportunity. Our technological advances are not just making superlongevity possible. They are opening up a new world of experiences. I want to be around when nanotechnology literally eliminates the scarcity and hunger that has haunted our species since time immemorial. I want to live long enough to become a "space tourist" and spend a week in orbit around the earth or the Moon, or better yet walk on the surface of the moon.

Superlongevity, Bostrom states, will enable him to watch his grandchildren and great grandchildren grow up. And, I might add, you will have the pleasure of watching the fifth and sixth generations that come after you proceed through their lives. In an earlier chapter, we discussed the benefits of living in a multigenerational extended family. A corollary of that sentiment is another reason from his list: "There are people who love you and who need you." Moreover, we should be able to "spend more time with friends and loved ones without a time bomb ticking quietly inside you all the while."

And some people need you who do not even know you. Bostrom reminds us that extended life will afford you "time to help others." An earlier-discussed activity, volunteerism, meets that requirement.

Some items on Bostrom's list of reasons to live forever involve personal and intellectual growth. These include, "More time to figure out the meaning of life, if there is one," and, "Have a chance to really grow up and find out what kind of wisdom and maturity might be attainable by a healthy 800-year-old." I would not mind seeing how other thinkers are coming along on the wisdom front either. As I mentioned, I was extremely impressed by the sense of history and perspective that Jacques Barzun exhibited in his book "From

Dawn to Decadence." To think, he was only ninety-four at the time. I would like to read an updated version he might write at 140 or so. As Bostrom says, art and creativity are inexhaustible. He also thinks that extended live would provide him the opportunity to "Learn the answer to some of the great mysteries— How does the mind work? Is there extraterrestrial life?"

He also makes a sports reference: "Watch Tibet beat Brazil in the football world cup final." All kidding aside, there are generations of sports fans who have lived and died never seeing their favorite team win the Stanley Cup or baseball's World Series. The Boston Red Sox and the Chicago White Sox each went over eighty years without winning a World Series. (The other Chicago team, the Cubs, last won a championship when Roosevelt was United States president. That's Teddy, not FDR.) Paradoxically, each team broke the drought in successive years, 2004 and 2005. As a long suffering fan of football's New York Jets, I have been waiting since 1969 for them to win another Super Bowl. I can guarantee that many people would opt for superlongevity if only to wait for their team to win it all.

Bostrom also wants those many years to "Play, create, and make love, to explore exotic mental states" and, as any obvious technophile would, "Build and experience virtual realities."

He reminds us that "If you live, you can always change your mind about it later." But, as he says, "death is irreversible." This mirrors my feelings about the scenario which requires us to decide before our offspring are born whether or not to genetically program them for superlongevity. As he says, to choose mortality for your children is a decision that once made cannot be reversed. Bostrom agrees that it is better to err on the side of caution—choose life.

Bostrom, an obvious idealist, omits the more material benefits of living the very long life. The longer you live the wealthier you should become. And if you are not rich at seventy or eighty, superlongevity will give you the time to figure out how to make your fortune by age 150.

His final item, "Live happily ever after," seems to epitomize the goal of the list itself. Given enough time, each of us will decipher life's code and figure out how to achieve our goals. Then we will create a set of new ones. [204]

After all, how can one truly live "happily ever after" unless you live forever.

Certainly, people who suspect they will be around 300 years from now will be strongly motivated to create a healthy and prosperous future. They will feel obligated to participate in the political process so they can build a future in which they will want to live.

The conventional lifecycle, severely challenged in Stage II, will be totally upended in Stage III. In a world where people live for centuries in a state of youthful health, traditional notions of career, family life and marriage will be disarranged. Curiously, though, such a radical change could ultimately provide society remarkable stability. The fact that each of us will be living alongside multiple generations of our family might imbue everyone with a heightened sense of continuity.

THE VOYAGE TO FOREVER

So, let me ask you again the same question I posed at the very beginning of the book: how long do you want to live? I am certain that the question seems more realistic now than when you started reading this work. You are now aware that there is a very good chance in your lifetime we will have mastered the science to extend life to ages never before experienced by the human species.

In my opinion, many people reading this book will confront, perhaps for the first time, the real possibility of the realistics of superlongevity and they will learn they must soon make those decisions, for themselves and others, which this phenomenon will force upon them. For instance, the decision to genetically engineer one's children is fraught with risk; but so is the determination not to do so. And in many cases, we will not have much time to make such life shaping choices.

However, in spite of the problems that we might encounter along the way, I believe we will come to recognize that longer life and certainly near-immortality will open a pathway to a world infinitely richer and more desirable than any our species has ever imagined.

We are all about to join the greatest expedition in the history of the human species, as we embark on our journey to the farthest frontiers of time itself.

Welcome to the *Ageless Nation*!

Endnotes

1 Mark Roth. "Great Expectations for Longevity are Rooted in History, But How Old Can We Go?." *Pittsburgh Post-Gazette*, Sunday, July 18, 2004.

2 Associated Press. "British Couple Has Designer Baby." CBS News, June 19, 2003, http://www.cbsnews.com/stories/2003/06/19/tech/main509430.shtml.

3 Susan Karlin. "New Drugs Target Cancer." *Discover*, January 2005.

4 Jessa Forte Netting. "New Secrets Of the Genome Uncovered." *Discover*, January 2006.

5 Nicholas Bakalar. "Fetal Skin Grafts Mend Burns and Eliminate Need for Surgery." *Discover*, January 2006.

6 Jessa Forte Netting. "Nasal Spray Halts Alzheimer's in Mice." *Discover*, January 2006.

7 Rebecca Skloot. "Vaccine Protects Against Cervical Cancer." *Discover*, January 2006.

8 Jeff Tannenbaum. "Annual United States Cancer Deaths Fall for First Time in Seven Decades." *Bloomberg.com*, February 9, 2006. http://www.bloomberg.com/apps/news?pid=10000103&sid=aDJVJ6a2tZvM&refer=us.

9 Michelle Cottle. "Why I Dumped the Baby Doctor: Pediatricians Often Treat Parents Like Children. That's why I got a new one." *Time*, February 19, 2006.

10 http://www.bio.org/events/2006/agenda/

11 Dan Buettner. "The Secrets of Long Life." *National Geographic*, November 2005, Vol. 208 Issue 5, p. 2-27.

12 Associated Press. "Cuban Centenarians Reveal Longevity Secrets." February 10, 2005.

[13] Jennifer Barrett. "The Gurus' Guide To Daily Nutrition: Five experts talk about what they take and offer tips for getting the vitamins and nutrients you need." *Newsweek*, January 16, 2006. http://www.msnbc.msn.com/id/10753216/site/newsweek/

[14] Arlene Weintraub. "Selling The Promise Of Youth." *Business Week*, March 20, 2006.

[15] Lisa Richwine. "Stem Cells From Brains Help Rats Walk, study says." *Reuters News Service*, March 28, 2006.

[16] Christina Ficara. "KY University Successful in Stem-Cell Research." *All Headline News*, March 8, 2006. http://www.allheadlinenews.com/articles/7002713201

[17] Deborah Smith. "It's In The Bag, Say Stem Cell Scientists." *Sydney Morning Herald*, March 27, 2006, http://www.smh.com.au/articles/2006/03/26/1143330931500.html

[18] PRNewswire. "Moraga Biotechnology Corp. Discovers a Primitive Embryonic-like Stem Cell in Adult Tissues." March 20, 2006.

[19] Nature Biotechnology. "A new source of stem cells." Press Release January 2007. http://www.nature.com/nbt/press_release/nbt0107.html

[20] Karen Kaplan. "Amniotic stem cell find could overcome barriers to using embryos." *Los Angeles Times*, January 9, 2007.

[21] Catherine Clabby. "University breeds hope for those in need of organs." *Raleigh News & Observer*, December 24, 2006.

[22] "Collaboration Established Between Wake Forest University Health Sciences and Tengion to Advance Regenerative Medicine Research" January 09, 2006. http://www.globeinvestor.com/servlet/ArticleNews/print/PRNEWS/20060109/CLM049

[23] "Bladder Factory: Engineering organs From Scratch." *Red Herring*, editorial, July 24, 2006. http://www.redherring.com/article.aspx?a=17772

[24] Knowledge@Wharton. "Industry Leaders Debate Big Pharma R&D (Too Little Hope?) and Stem Cell Research (Too Much Hype?)." March 22, 2006, http://knowledge.wharton.upenn.edu/index.cfm?fa=viewArticle&id=1430

[25] Robert Langreth. "Cracking the Code." *Forbes Magazine*, November 2005.

[26] Bubenik G.A Gastrointestinal Melatonin: Localization, Function, and Clinical Relevance Digestive Diseases and Sciences, Volume 47, Number 10, October 2002, pp. 2336-2348(13)

[27] David Stipp. "Youthful Pursuit: Researchers Seek Key to Antiaging in Calorie Cutback" *Wall Street Journal*, October 30, 2006.

[28] Nicholas Wade. "Aging Drugs: Hardest Test Is Still Ahead." *New York Times*, November 7, 2006. pg. F.1

[29] Zachary Seward. "Quest for Youth Drives Craze For 'Wine' Pills; Consumers Flock to Resveratrol, Though Anti-Aging Properties Have Been Shown Only in Mice." *Wall Street Journal*, November 30, 2006. pg. D.1

[30] Glenn Harlan Reynolds. "Nanotechnology and Regulatory Policy: Three Futures." *Harvard Journal of Law & Technology*, Vol. 17 No. 1, Fall 2003.

[31] Mitzi Baker. "National Cancer Institute Funds New Nanotechnology Center." March 2, 2006. Stanford Comprehensive Research Center. http://cancer.stanford.edu/features/research_news/nanotechnology_center.html

[32] Robert A. Freitas Jr. *Nanomedicine, Volumes I (Basic Capabilities) and II (Biocompatibility)*. Landes Bioscience, 1999.

[33] Sander Olsen, "Interview with Robert Freitas." *Nanotech.biz*, November 2005, http://www.nanotech.biz/i.php?id=robertfreitas.

[34] Lisa Takeuchi Cullen. "Not Quite Ready to Retire: Done with the 9 to 5 but not prepared to hang it up? This work may be for you: the bridge job." *Time Magazine*, February 19, 2006. www.time.com/time/archive/preview/0,10987,1161224,00.html.

[35] Michael G. Zey. "Business Better Not Let Baby Boomers Get Away." *Newark Star-Ledger, San Diego News-Tribune*, Friday, August 26, 2005, *The Christian Science Monitor*, November 5, 2005.

[36] Shaheen Pasha. "Corporations Woo Baby Boomers: With more than 1 in 4 workers eyeing retirement, companies scramble to keep valued employees." *CNNMoney* September 30, 2005. http://money.cnn.com/2005/09/29/news/fortune500/babyboomers_companies/

[37] Merrill Lynch Press Release. "The New Retirement Survey" From Merrill Lynch Reveals How Baby Boomers Will Transform Retirement." February 22, 2005, http://www.ml.com/index.asp?id=7695_7696_8149_46028_46503_46635

[38] Tom Johnson. "Climbing High Utilities team with colleges to train replacements for aging work force" *Newark Star-Ledger*, January 08, 2007.

[39] Peter Coy. "Old. Smart. Productive." *Business Week*, June 2005.

[40] Sebastian Moffett. "Senior Moment: Fast-Aging Japan Keeps Its Elders On the Job Longer." *Wall Street Journal* (Eastern edition) pg. A.1, June 15, 2005.

[41] Erin White and Jeffrey A. Trachtenberg. "Sabbaticals: The Pause That Refreshes." *Wall Street Journal*. (Eastern edition) pg. B.1, August 2, 2005.

[42] Sharyn Salsberg Ezrin. "The Last, Best Perk?" *Canadian Business*, October 30, 1998.

[43] Erin White and Jeffrey A. Trachtenberg. "Sabbaticals: The Pause That Refreshes." *Wall Street Journal*. (Eastern edition) pg. B.1, August 2, 2005.

[44] Tracey Porpora. "Coldwell Banker Agents Hone Skills in Diverse Industries." *Newark Star-Ledger*, July 14, 2006.

[45] Erin White. "'I Quit! ... for a While.' More Executives Leave Jobs For a Year or Two to Unwind, Explore New Opportunities." *Wall Street Journal*, August 2, 2005.

[46] Amir Efrati. "eBay Sellers Reshape Garage-Sale Dynamic" *The Wall Street Journal*, April 21 2006.

[47] Jack Ewing. "eBay's Rhine Gold: Thousands of German startups are using the auction site to sell goods." *Wall Street Journal*, April 2006.

[48] Steve Stanek. "Cyberscholars Follow Their Own Schedule: On-the-run students go online for graduate classes." *Chicago Tribune*, September 19, 2004.

[49] http://nyuundergraduate.search4careercolleges.com/

[50] Mary Jane Maytum. "Virtual Degree is Now Reality." *Business First: Louisville* August 06, 2004.

[51] Judy Goggin and Bernie Ronan. "Our Next Chapter: Community Colleges and the Aging Baby Boomers." League for Innovation in the Community College *Leadership Abstracts*, November 2004.
http://www.civicventures.org/publications/articles/community_colleges.cfm

[52] Sara Rimer. "As Centenarians Thrive, 'Old' Is Redefined." *The New York Times* June 22, 1998, p. A1.

[53] Henry Fountain. "For Centenarians, It All Begins at Birth." *The New York Times*, October 30, 2005. pg. 4.14.

[54] Ed Silverman. "Summer Jobs: Rock around the clock: For the Kootz, it's the Shore season with its nightly outdoor gigs that's most lucrative." *Newark Star-Ledger*, Sunday, July 23, 2006.

[55] "Starting Over." CBS Sunday Morning, May 28th, 2006.
http://www.cbsnews.com/stories/1998/07/09/sunday/main13562.shtml

[56] Bob Dart. "US Businesses Will Change With Aging Population." *Cox News Service*, March 12 2006.
http://www.coxwashington.com/reporters/content/reporters/stories/2006/03/12/BC _AGING10_COX.html

[57] Mary Beth Faller and John Stanley. "Quest for new experiences means variety of activities." AZCentral.com, Dec. 18, 2005 http://www.azcentral.com/specials/ special42/articles/1218boomer1218leisureamptravel.html

[58] www.elderhostel.com

[59] David Mannweiler. "Crystal ball sees space, RVs as the future of travel." *The Indianapolis Star/Gannett News Service*, February 22, 2006.

[60] Laura Koss-Feder. "Club Mad: Destination clubs are hot. But glitches leave some members hot under the collar." *Time Magazine*, March 26, 2006.

[61] Janice Hopkins Tanne. "Living on cruise ships is cost effective for elderly people." *British Medical Journal*, bmj.com, November 6, 2004.
http://www.bmj.com/cgi/content/full/329/7474/1065-b

[61] http://www.generalstudies.newschool.edu/irp/studygroups/study.htm

[63] Lesli Forbes. "Next Move? Many baby boomers say they plan to stay longer in the work force." *The State Journal* West Virginia Media, April 6, 2006.
http://www.statejournal.com/story.cfm?func=viewstory&storyid=9931

[64] http://www.timberland.com/timberlandserve/content.jsp?pageName= timberlandserve_engage_serv-a-palooza

[65] Kelly Greene. "Avoiding the Volunteer Trap: Too many retirees, when donating their time and energies, are falling into dead-end jobs." *Wall Street Journal*, April 24, 2006.

[66] http://www.nationalservice.gov/about/newsroom/releases_detail.asp?tbl_pr_id=251

[67] Jeffrey M. Schwartz, M.D. and Sharon Begley. *The Mind and The Brain: Neuroplasticity and the Power of Mental Force.* New York: Harper Collins Publishers, Inc., 2003.

[68] Jeffrey Kluger. "The Surprising Power of the Aging Brain:Scientists used to think intellectual power peaked at age 40. Now they know better." *Time Magazine.* January 13,2006. http://www.time.com/time/archive/preview/0,10987,1147163,00.html

[69] Sharon Begley. "Old Brains Don't Work That Badly After All, Especially Trained Ones." *Wall Street Journal.* March 3, 2006. pg. B.1

[70] Jeffery Kluger. "The Surprising Power of the Aging Brain." *Time.* Jan. 13, 2006. http://www.time.com/time/printout/0,8816,1147163,00.html

[71] Staying Sharp, a partnership between NRTA: AARP's Educator Community and the Dana Alliance for Brain Initiatives. "Engage Your Brain." AARP.com. http://www.aarp.org/health/brain/takingcontrol/engage_your_brain.html

[72] Walter S. Mossberg. "Survived the '60s? You May Want to Try This Nintendo Game." *Wall Street Journal*, March 23, 2006.

[73] Sharon Begley. "Scans of Monks' Brains Show Meditation Alters Structure, Functioning." *Wall Street Journal*, November 5, 2004.

[74] Lisa Takeuchi Cullen. "How to Get Smarter, One Breath at a Time: Scientists find that meditation not only reduces stress but also reshapes the brain." *Time Magazine*, January 10, 2006.

[75] Peter Smith. *Two of Us : The Story of a Father, a Son and the Beatles.* Houghton Mifflin, 2004.

[76] Jeffrey Zaslow. "Moving On: Mr. Moms Grow Up: A New Generation Of Granddads Is Helping Raise the Kids." *Wall Street Journal*, June 8, 2006. pg. D.1.

[77] Jeanette Borzo. "Sights and Sounds: It's easier and cheaper than ever to have video conversations online." *Wall Street Journal.* April 24, 2006.

[78] Grayling, Chris. "Conservatives Focus on High Speed Rail Options." December 28, 2006. http://www.conservatives.com/tile.do?def=news.story.page&obj_id=134268#

[79] Kansas City Star and wire service sources. "Swiss Pilot, Inventor Does Convincing 'Rocketeer' Impersonation." December 26, 2006. http://www.kansascity.com

[80] http://technocrat.net/d/2007/1/1/12805.

[81] Anne Tergesen. "Three Generations, One Roof." *Business Week*, October 31, 2005.

82 Anonymous. Growth Strategies. Santa Monica: Dec 2005., Iss. 984; pg. 2
    http://proquest.umi.com/pqdweb?did=948610451&sid=1&Fmt=3&cli
    entId=8606&RQT=309&VName=PQD

83 Ken Dychtwald. "Enrich Your Life with Closer Family Ties." Yahoo! Finance
    March 23, 2006. http://finance.yahoo.com/columnist/article/retirement/3006

84 Katrina McClintock. "Can You Ever Be Too Old To Have A Baby?" Aberdeen
    Evening Express, January 18, 2005.

85 Roger Gosden and Anthony Rutherford. "Delayed Childbearing." British Medical
    Journal, December 2005. http://www.bmj.com/cgi/content/full/311/7020/1585

86 P. Astolfi, L. Ulizzi and L.A. Zonta "Selective cost of delayed childbearing."
    Letters to the Editor, Human Reproduction, a European Society of Human
    Reproduction and Embryology Publication, February 1999.

87 Anne Marie Chaker. "Business Schools Target At-Home Moms; New Programs
    Help Women Return to the Workplace After Taking Years Off." Wall Street
    Journal, May 10, 2006.

88 Sue Shellenbarger. "Employers Step Up Efforts to Lure Stay-at-Home Mothers
    Back to Work." Wall Street Journal, February 9, 2006.

89 "Japan Becomes Parent-Friendly." Child Care Resource Center, Inc. Work and
    Family Resource Bulletin. April, 2006.
    http://www.ccrcinc.org/pdf/WFRB%20April%202006.pdf

90 Sue Shellenbarger. "Outsourcing Jobs to the Den: Call Centers Tap People Who
    Want to Work at Home." Wall Street Journal, January 12, 2006.

91 Gretchen Reynolds. "The Artificial Womb." Popular Science, 2006. Also see
    http://en.wikipedia.org/wiki/Artificial_womb for further discussion of womb
    technology.

92 Helen Pearson. "To Get Pregnant in Your Sixties." DISCOVER Vol. 26 January
    2005. Also, Misia Landau. "Ovaries Exhibit Ongoing Power to Produce Eggs."
    Focus,
    http://focus.hms.harvard.edu/2004/March19_2004/reproductive_biology.htm

93 Lindsey Tanner. "Boys May Be Entering Puberty Sooner." The Associated Press
    September 13, 2001. See also: Archives of Pediatrics & Adolescent Medicine:
    http://archpedi.ama-assn.org . And Michael Limoneck. "Teens Before Their
    Time." Time Magazine October 30, 2000.

94 Harbour Fraser Hodder. "The Future of Marriage: Changing demographics,
    economics, and laws alter the meaning of matrimony in America." Harvard
    Magazine, November/December 2004. www.harvardmagazine.com/on-
    line/110491.html

95 Dan Hurley. "Divorce Rate: It's Not as High as You Think." The New York Times,
    April 19, 2005.

[96] Thomas Hargrove. "Want to live longer? Get married: Death records in 2003 reveal wedlock benefits men, women of all races, socio-economic groups." *Scripps Howard News Service.* February 12, 2006. http://www.detnews.com/apps/pbcs.dll/article?AID=/20060212/OPINION01/602120311/one hundred8

[97] Sam Jaffe. "Giving Genetic Disease the Finger." *Wired News,* July 6, 2005. http://www.wired.com/news/medtech/0,1286,68019,00.html

[98] NBC WNDU. "New genetic therapies could help children with muscular dystrophy." April 7, 2006

[99] Dana Williams. "Mapping Genome." *Hornet News,* February 22, 2006

[100] The Associated Press. Researchers: Epilepsy Cause Identified." March 30, 2006.

[101] Robert Preidt. "Genes Help Predict Sickle Cell Stroke Risk 'It's a big improvement on current tests, researchers say'." *HealthDay News,* March 21, 2005.

[102] Mapping the Genome" Dana Williams Hornet News Editor February 22, 2006.

[103] Carol Midgley. "Embryos For Sale." *The Times (London),* Online, January 12, 2007. http://www.timesonline.co.uk/printFriendly/0,,1-7-2542397-100,00.html Tom Strode. "Texas 'baby supermarket' offers ready-made embryos." Jan 15, 2007 http://www.sbcbaptistpress.org/bpnews.asp?ID=24770 For additional information: http://www.theabrahamcenteroflife.com/

[104] Ramez Naam. "A Child Of Choice." From *More Than Human: Embracing the Promise of Biological Enhancement.* New York: Broadway, 2005.

[105] Eric G. Swedin. "Designing Babies: A Eugenics Race with China?" *Futurist* May-June 2006.

[106] In my book *The Future Factor,* I extend the Darwinian Theory into a new and fairly controversial area. I claim that while Darwin and others are that we are preprogrammed to select for the best genetic traits and tendencies in order to ensure the propagation and progress of the species, the very reason we do try to improve the species is for an even higher purpose. This purpose is to enhance and ensure the survival of the physical universe, a process I call "vitalization," the imbuing of the universe with life and growth. I propose that the appearance of humanity is actually conditioned by the universe itself, in order to ensure its survival from entropic forces such as the "big heat" or big chill billions of years into the future.

[107] Shaoni Bhattacharya. "Barbie-shaped women more fertile." *NewScientist.com,* May 2004.

[108] Bonnie Wu. "The biology of beauty; Physical appearance may be a window to genetic fitness." *South China Morning Post,* October 28, 2005.

[109] Don Babwin. "Man's face answers query: Kids or fling?" *The Washington Times* May 10, 2006. http://www.washtimes.com/national/20060510-123437-4680r.htm

[110] Thomas H. Maugh. "Artificial vision makes gains: Optimistic researchers poised for a breakthrough in field of restoring sight." *Toronto Star,* September 27, 2002.

[111] Kelly Young. "'Bionic eye' may help reverse blindness." *NewScientist.com News Service*, March 31, 2005. See also: Michael Stroph. "The Bionic Eye: We See the Future Better Than 20/20." *PopSci.com*, http://www.popsci.com/popsci/whatsnew/d56f0e0796b84010vgnvcm1000004eecbccdrcrd.html.

[112] Duncan Graham. "Cochlear implants open up a new world of hearing." Deaf Today.com from *The Jakarta Post*, June 14, 2006. http://www.deaftoday.com/v3/archives/2006/06/cochlear_implan_28.html

[113] Scott Allen. "Stereo sound: A growing number of deaf people are getting a second cochlear implant to improve hearing, but insurers say the long-term benefits are unclear." *Boston Globe* June 12, 2006.

[114] Dan Ferber. "Will Artificial Muscle Make You Stronger? *Popular Science*, July 2005.

[115] "Biotech Anti-Aging: 96% Using New Product with Synthetic Human Elastin Report More Youthful Appearance." *News Release Wire.com* May 9, 2006 http://www.expertclick.com/NewsReleaseWire/default.cfm?Action=ReleaseDetail&ID=12587

[116] Elizabeth Svoboda. "In 2021 You'll Grow a New Heart: Researchers are zeroing in on a long-sought goal of human healing: organs that can regenerate themselves from within." *Popular Science*, June 2006.

[117] http://www.osiristx.com/

[118] Siri Steiner. "Will We Merge With Machines?" *Popular Science*, August 2005.

[119] "Smart drugs for all in 20 years" From correspondents in London. *The Times of London*. June 5, 2006.

[120] The President's Council on Bioethics. "Beyond Therapy: Biotechnology and the Pursuit of Happiness." October, 2003 www.bioethics.gov

[121] James Vlaho. "Will Drugs Make Us Smarter and Happier?" *Popular Science*, August 2005.

[122] Joel Garreau. "Smart pills are on rise, is taking them wise? Number of healthy students using bootleg pills seems to be soaring." *The Washington Post* June 11, 2006.

[123] Ray Kurzweil. "Reinventing Humanity: The Future of Machine-Human Intelligence." *The Futurist*, March/April 2006, Vol. 40, Iss. 2, pg. 39.

[124] David Pescovitz. "Your Wits: Pampered, Sharp." *Popular Science*, July 2005.

[125] James Vlaho Popular Science: Will Drugs Make Us Smarter and Happier? July 2005.

[126] The President's Council on Bioethics. "Beyond Therapy: Biotechnology and the Pursuit of Happiness." October, 2003 www.bioethics.gov

[127] ""Michelle Tackla. "Cultural turn, turn, turn: During tumultuous '60s, cosmetic surgery evolves as stigma fades; techniques are refined." *Cosmetic Surgery Times*, January 1, 2004. And, Michelle Tackla. "Cultural shifts and rifts: Cosmetic surgery, breast augmentation comes of age." *Cosmetic Surgery Times.* November 1, 2003.
http://www.cosmeticsurgerytimes.com/cosmeticsurgerytimes/author/authorDetail.jsp?id=4609

[128] CNNMoney.com. "Biotechs reach all-time sales high in 2005 Biotechs revenue in 2005 exceeds $60 billion for the first time, says report." April 4, 2006.
money.cnn.com/2006/04/04/news/companies/biotechs/index.htm

[129] http://www.hoovers.com/offer/co/factsheet.xhtml?COID=10628&cm_ven=PAID&cm_cat=OVR&cm_pla=CO3&cm_ite=genentech

[130]Aaron Smith. "Big Pharma thinks small Merck, Pfizer among companies ramping up licensing deals with smaller biotechs to beef up pipelines." *CNNMoney.com*, March 23, 2006

[131] Aaron Smith. "Playing a drugmaker vs. a biotech: When biotech and Big Pharma lock horns in the next phase of a patent battle, will investors profit?" *CNNMoney.com*, June 27 2006.

[132] http://stemcells.nih.gov/info/basics/

[133] National Institute of Health News. "Neurons Grown from Embryonic Stem Cells Restore Function in Paralyzed Rats." June 20, 2006.
http://www.nih.gov/news/pr/jun2006/ninds-20.htm

[134] Aaron Smith. "Rats walk but money waits: Paralyzed rat treatment points up stem cell break-through, but sales remain elusive." *CNNMoney.com*, June 22, 2006.

[135] http://www.geron.com

[136] http://www.advancedcell.com

[137]PRNewsWire. "Leading Financial Service Discloses New Opportunities in Medical Research Industry in Upcoming Investment Conference Call" http://www.americancapitalist.net, June 28, 2006.
http://www.prnewswire.com/cgibin/stories.pl?ACCT=109&STORY=/www/story/06-28-2006/0004389003&EDATE=

[138]http://www.alcor.org/

[139] http://www.cryonics.org/

[140] Nicholas Von Hoffman. "Freezing Their Assets." *The Nation.*, February 14, 2006. http://www.thenation.com/doc/20060227/vonhoffman

[141] http://en.wikipedia.org/wiki/Category:Cryonically_preserved_people

[142] http://www.orbimed.com/portfolio.asp

[143] www.mpmcapital.com

[144] http://www.bio.org/events/2006/

[145] http://www.wellcome.ac.uk/node8000038.html

[146] http://www.nia.nih.gov

[147] www.beeson.org

[148] http://www.ellisonfoundation.org

[149] Andrew Pollack. "Fighting Diseases With Checkbooks." *New York Times*, July 8, 2006.

[150] http://www.agingresearch.org/advocacy/zones.html

[151] http://www.calorierestriction.org

[152] http://foresight.org/

[153] http://www.transhumanism.org/

[154] http://www.kurzweilai.net/

[155] http://www.sens.org

[156] Jonathan Clements. "The Secret to a Happier Retirement: Friends, Neighbors and a Fixed Annuity." *Wall Street Journal*. Jul 27, 2005. pg. D.1

[157] Jay Lindsay. "Inventor Sets His Sights On Immortality: Will Nanotechnology Spark Breakthrough In 20 Years?" The Associated Press. Feb. 12, 2005.

[158] Ray Kurzweil and Terry Grossman. *Fantastic Voyage*. New York: Plume, Reprint edition, 2005.

[159] Maoshing Ni. *Secrets of Longevity: Hundreds of Ways to Live to be 100*. Chronicle Books, 2006.

[160] Wendy Champagne. "Medical tourism is booming as governments battle to provide services." *Sydney Morning Herald*, June 1, 2006.

[161] Zey, Michael. Seizing the Future, 2nd Edition.

[162] Laura Landro. "Social Networking Comes to Health Care: Online Tools Give Patients. Better Access to Information And Help Build Communities." *Wall Street Journal*, December 27, 2006.

[163] http://www.capitolconnect.com/aarp/takeaction.aspx

[164] PRWEB. "Group Formed To Promote Immortality As A National Priority" http://www.prweb.com/releases/2006/8/prweb430361.htmity.
Further information about the group can be located on their website, www.coalitiontoextendlife.org

[165] Lee Hawkins Jr. "GM's Buyout Package Attracts 35,000 Workers; Response Lets Auto Maker Accelerate Job-Cut Target, Raise Cost-Savings Goal in Detroit and Kris Maher in Pittsburgh." *Wall Street Journal*, June 27, 2006. pg. A.3

[166] Paul Harris. "Beware of the Boomer Brain Drain!" *T + D. Training and Development*, January 2006.

[167] Michael Zey. *The Mentor Connection*. New Brunswick, NJ: Transaction Books, 2001.
Michael Zey. "Cybermentoring and Beyond." Published in the 2001 Proceedings of the Institute of Behavioral and Applied Management. The second reading describes the integration of a host of electronic communications devices into the mentoring process.

168 David Wessel. "How Will the United States Fill Its Benefits Gap?" *Wall Street Journal*, April 13, 2006. pg. A.2

169 Michael Crichton. *Next*. New York: Harper Collins Publishers, 2006.

170 Robert McCrum. *Wodehouse: A Life*. W. W. Norto, Paperback Reprint, 2005.

171 Robert McCrum. *Wodehouse: A Life*. W. W. Norto, Paperback Reprint, 2005.

172 Bob Thomas. "Art Linkletter Hitting Road To Promote Book On Making Most Of Old Age." Associated Press, July 17, 2006.

173 Maria Godoy and Joe Palca. "A Brief Timeline of the Stem-Cell Debate." *NPR*. May 3, 2006. http://www.npr.org/templates/story/story.php?storyId=5453492

174 Michael Zey. *Seizing the Future: The Dawn of the Macroindustrial Future*. Transaction Publishers, 2nd Edition, 1998.

175 The President's Council on Bioethics. "Beyond Therapy: Biotechnology and the Pursuit of Happiness." October, 2003 www.bioethics.gov

176 Kristen Philipkoski. "Bioethics Shuffle Ignites Outcry" *Wired News*, March, 02, 2004. http://www.wired.com/news/medtech/1,62494-0.html.

177 "Ageless Bodies and Happy Souls: The Future of Aging in a Biotech Era. An Interview with Leon Kass, MD, Chairman, President's Council on Bioethics." Interview by Mort Kondracke, April 12, 2004. http://www.sagecrossroads.net/Portals/0/transcript13.pdf

178 Ronald Bailey. "Liberation Biology: The Scientific And Moral Case For The Biotech Revolution." Prometheus Books, January 2005.

179 Ronald Bailey. "Transhumanism: The Most Dangerous Idea? Why striving to be more than human is human." *Reason Online*. August 25, 2004 http://www.reason.com/rb/rb082504.shtml

180 Pellegrino, Edmund D. "Biotechnology, Human Enhancement, and the Ends of Medicine." *Newsletter* of The Center for Bioethics and Human Dignity. November 30, 2004. http://www.cbhd.org/index.html

181 Stem Cell Research Enhancement Act of 2005 HR 810 http://www.thomas.gov/cgi-bin/query/D?c109:3:./temp/~c109X3JNkF::

182 http://www.fastercures.org/sec/bod

183 Results of these polls can be found at the following websites: http://www.researchamerica.org/polldata/ http://www.agingresearch.org/survey/pollsummary1.cfm http://abcnews.go.com/Health/PollVault/story?id=1232993

184 Lyndsay Moss. "Doctors vote to oppose euthanasia." *The Scotsman*, Friday June 30, 2006. http://news.scotsman.com/health.cfm?id=953212006

185 *"The Dutch Way of Death"* By Richard Miniter. *Wall Street Journal*. April 25, 2001. pg. A.20

186 "Going Dutch." *Wall Street Journal*, Editorial, October 6, 1999. pg. A.22

187 Steven Ertelt. "Switzerland Attorney: Euthanasia Group Has Arranged 573 Assisted Suicides." *LifeNews.com*. July 3, 2006.

[188] Joseph Hooper. "The Prophet of Immortality: Controversial theorist Aubrey de Grey insists that we are within reach of an engineered cure for aging. Are you prepared to live forever?" *Popular Science*, January 2005.

[189] www.technologyreview.com/sens/

[190] Aubrey de Grey, ed. *Strategies for Engineered Negligible Senescence: Why Genuine Control of Aging May Be Foreseeable*. New York: New York Academy of Sciences, 2004.

[191] Ray Kurzweil. "Reinventing Humanity: The Future of Machine-Human Intelligence." *The Futurist*. March/April 2006.

[192] Jay Lindsay. "Inventor sets his sights on immortality: Will nanotechnology spark breakthrough in 20 years?" *The Associated Press* Feb. 12, 2005.

[193] Lee Gomes. "Kurzweil's Human-Computer Merge More Hype Than Truth A Back-Cover Brush With a High-Tech Seer And Some of His Pals" *Wall Street Journal*. October 5, 2005. pg. B.1.

[194] Edited by Immortality Institute. *The Scientific Conquest of Death: Essays on Infinite Lifespans*. Libros En Red, 2004.

[195] Thomas Malthus. *Essay on the Principle of Population*. Oxford University Press, USA.

[196] Donella H. Meadows, Dennis L. Meadows, Jorgen Randers and William W. Behrens III. *The Limits to Growth*. New York: Universe Books, 1972.
Paul Ehrlich. *The Population Bomb*. New York: Ballantine Books, 1968.

[197] Various population estimates and historical data from The United Nations document "The World At Six Billion." 1999.
http://www.un.org/esa/population/publications/sixbillion/sixbilpart1.pdf.

[198] "Economy on roll as industrial growth, Sensex touch new high" *ZeeNews.com, India edition*. January 15, 2007.
http://www.zeenews.com/znnew/articles.asp?aid=347500&ssid=50&sid=BUS

[199] "U.S. Population Nearing 300 Million-Environmentalists Grapple With A Nation Addicted To More Of Everything." *The Associated Press*, Oct 16, 2006.

[200] "A New World Economy: The balance of power will shift to the East as China and India evolve." *Business Week*.

[201] "Japan Population Starts to Shrink." *BBC News*, December 22 2005.
http://news.bbc.co.uk/2/hi/asia-pacific/4552010.stm

[202] James Graff. "We Need More Babies!" *Time Magazine*. Sunday, Nov. 21, 2004.
http://www.time.com/time/magazine/article/0,9171,901041129-785317,00.html

[203] Julian Simon and Norman Myers. *Scarcity or Abundance: A Debate on the Environment*. W W Norton & Co. Inc., August 1994.

[204] Nick Bostrom. "The Scientific Conquest of Death "Who wants to live forever?" From: *The Scientific Conquest of Death: Essays on Infinite Lifespans*. Ed. By Immortality Institute. Libros En Red, 2004.

Index

<u>NOTES</u>

<u>NOTES</u>

NOTES

NOTES

<u>NOTES</u>

<u>NOTES</u>